T0304834

Orderly Britain

Orderly Britain

How Britain has resolved
everyday problems, from
dog fouling to double parking

Tim Newburn and Andrew Ward

ROBINSON

ROBINSON

First published in Great Britain in 2022 by Robinson

1 3 5 7 9 10 8 6 4 2

Copyright © Tim Newburn and Andrew Ward, 2022

The moral rights of the authors have been asserted.

A CIP catalogue record for this book
is available from the British Library.

ISBN: 978-1-47213-796-8

Typeset in Adobe Caslon by Hewer Text UK Ltd, Edinburgh
Printed and bound in Great Britain by Clays Ltd, Elcograf S.p.A.

Papers used by Robinson are from well-managed forests and other responsible sources.

Robinson
An imprint of
Little, Brown Book Group
Carmelite House
50 Victoria Embankment
London EC4Y 0DZ

An Hachette UK Company
www.hachette.co.uk

www.littlebrown.co.uk

In memory of Andy Ward, 1949–2022

Contents

Introduction

We British are, by and large, an orderly people. On one level that's no great claim to make. It is merely an observation that life on these islands is organised, generally predictable and largely co-operative, rather than chaotic and anarchic. It is orderly, in part, because we need to get along, but also because everyday life is heavily rule-governed. Some of these rules are formal – laws and other regulations – many are informal – the norms and expectations that surround much of what we do. What, we might ask, is peculiarly British about this? Are we distinctively orderly? In one important sense the answer has to be 'no'. We are similar to a range of other countries we might compare ourselves with – other European nations for example. They, too, are largely orderly – and rule-bound. But in another sense the answer is 'yes'. And the reason for that lies in the *ways* in which we are organised. The regularities of life in Britain differ in some ways – some significant, some subtle – from similar things in other countries. This, of course, is merely another way of saying that it is possible to see some cultural distinctiveness in the ways in which we go about things.

It is *the way in which we go about things*, and the ways in which these have changed, that is our concern here. Our focus is on the patterns of our everyday life, our practices and customs, and our recent history; Britain in the post-war era and some of the ways in which the organisation of daily life has altered. Undoubtedly the post-war period has been one of profound social change. After the privations of wartime, by the late fifties Prime Minister Harold Macmillan said many British people felt they had 'never had it so good'. The sixties were the time of the so-called 'permissive' era. As Philip Larkin wryly suggested, 'sexual intercourse began in nineteen sixty three ... between the end of the "Chatterley" ban and the Beatles' first LP'. The lights went out and rubbish remained uncollected in the seventies' three-day week, and the final decades of the century were dominated by Thatcherism and, subsequently, Tony Blair's 'third way'. We've seen entry into and departure from the European Union, the arrival of the internet and social media, and increasingly dramatic climate change. Arguably, we have also been witness to some potentially significant changes in our sensibilities. The feminist and anti-racist movements have sought to shift attitudes toward and the treatment of women and minorities, homosexuality has been decriminalised and gay marriage sanctioned. The most recent round of the annually conducted British Social Attitudes Survey suggested that we had continued to become more liberal where matters of law and conformity are concerned, but also more unequal with greater numbers feeling there was 'one law for the rich and another for the poor'.[1]

Not surprisingly profound change prompts debate about what it all means. Is it a sign of social improvement or decay, of moral progress or decline? Certainly we live in times in which there is no shortage of authors offering views on what we're like and where we're heading as a nation. If one can identity a general trend among these observers it is that a great many are unenthusiastic about various developments, arguing that things are getting worse in one way or another.[2] Whether they are right or wrong about our direction of travel, their diagnosis of what will sell a book is very likely correct. Psychologists have long identified what they call our 'negativity bias', in essence the finding that we tend to pay more attention to, and indeed learn more from, bad news than we do good. On a similar but wider canvas the evolutionary psychologist Steven Pinker has argued that despite the fact that our lives are getting progressively better, we have great trouble acknowledging it.[3] Our seeming predisposition to see the past favourably and to be concerned that we're now going to the dogs is sometimes referred to as 'declinism'. According to one historian, the questions 'what went wrong?' and 'who is to blame?', both of which are characteristic of declinism, have been staples of British conversation for the best part of a century and a half.[4] We love nothing better, it seems, than discussing our national decline.

All of which brings us back to British social order and how we perceive it and talk about it. Here, as elsewhere, declinism is not hard to find. The author Lynne Truss, for example, has dedicated a whole book to mourning 'the apparent collapse of civility in all areas of our dealings with strangers'.[5] Truss sees modern Britain as a place which has suffered a dramatic decline in deference, and in which a sense of rights (and possibly entitlements) has clearly trumped any notion of responsibilities. In this view Britain is a country where old-fashioned standards of politeness and manners have progressively fragmented, to be replaced by a confused and confusing new world characterised on the one hand by informality – where seemingly anything goes – and, on the other, by political correctness – producing a minefield where it's no longer possible to say anything without upsetting someone.

In a similar vein, the US-born author Bill Bryson observed a few years ago that 'Britain used to be a much more orderly and well-behaved society', but now, 'the British have become more greedy and selfish'.[6] Where, in his first bestselling book on Britain, *Notes from a Small Island*, published in the nineties, Bryson remarked on the 'deference and a quiet consideration for others' that was a 'fundamental part of British life', by the time of its follow-up twenty years later he now felt that 'lots of people are governed not so much by whether something is right or wrong as by whether they think anyone's watching'.[7] Increasingly of course, thanks to the ubiquity of closed-circuit television, it is perfectly possible that someone *is* actually watching. Indeed, far from witnessing the arrival of some increasingly laissez-faire reality in which standards have broken down, there are those who take the view that we're now far too minutely governed, subject to too much interference and micro-management by a nanny state. Certainly we're not short of advice about how to behave. One of the more obvious examples is the proliferation of signage, especially safety signage, that has now invaded many areas of our lives. So extreme has this intrusion become that one author has described it as the arrival of the 'busybody state', one 'defined by an attachment to bureaucratic procedures for their own sake: the rule for the sake of the rule, the form for the sake of a form. Its insignias are the official badge, the policy, the code and the procedure.' This, claims Josie Appleton, is a world of 'hyper-regulation', characterised by signs at the beach which say 'Beware: uneven surface' and where staircases are marked with 'Caution: trip hazard'.[8] In her and others' view we are becoming increasingly infantilised and restricted by interfering and meddling authorities seeking to monitor and manage our lives in ever-extended and fine-graded ways.

Whether one thinks things are getting better or worse, what is clear is that order – the nature of our social fabric – like all social phenomena, does not stand still. It has to be continually produced and reproduced. As we have noted, this involves formal mechanisms such as the law, the police, the justice system and so forth and, crucially, informal systems: primarily social rules, customs and expectations, and the day-to-day oversight of conduct brought about by human interaction. This is precisely the starting point of *Orderly Britain*. In what follows we will focus on a small number of largely mundane issues, matters that the French author Georges Perec referred to as the 'infra-ordinary' and the 'endotic' (as opposed to the extraordinary and the exotic)[9] – dog mess, smoking, drinking, queuing, public toilets, parking, and the pandemic – as a means of examining British social life and some of the ways in which the nature of the order and ordering of that social life has altered since the mid-twentieth century.

Having said that we are our interested in Britain's recent past we should acknowledge immediately that we are not attempting a fully fledged social history, or anything like it. Our gaze is not trained on the usual concerns of national politics, our changing economic fortunes, or our shifting make-up in terms of class, race or religion. Rather, we will look at our everyday routines, taking some unusual, or at least *less* usual subjects as the basis for an examination of our social order. Considering the quotidian and the mundane has the advantage of focusing on matters that involve all of us, more or less directly. By contrast, affairs of state and other matters of standard social histories, though they may have an important impact on us, generally do so only indirectly and often feel rather distant from us. Here, we will explore phenomena which are more or less on the margins of conventional social history and social science, but which form a part of many if not most people's regular routines and concerns. As such they are matters that help shape our lives and the ways we live them.

One of the ways in which we approach this is to think in terms of social routines. What are our habits and practices, or what William Graham Sumner called our 'folkways'?[10] Have these changed and, if so, how and why? We begin with dogs. The British have had a thing about pets for a long time and as anyone who has had one knows, they bring responsibilities. They need feeding, watering, some need grooming and, crucially, dogs need walking. Now, you may not necessarily think of it this way but dog walking is a socially structured, socially patterned activity. One study, for example, divided British dog walkers roughly into two groups: what it called *functional* dog walkers, who were doing it primarily as a matter of necessity, and *recreational* dog walkers for whom the walk was undertaken as a benefit to both pet and owner.[11] Clearly, most of us would recognise that taking a dog for a walk is one of the things that a 'responsible' owner would do. But, what else? The researchers found that having a dog in public was felt to imply a variety of other responsibilities such as keeping the dog safe and having consideration for others (avoiding confrontations with other dogs; keeping the dog on a lead where necessary). In short, they concluded that rather than dogs simply fitting in with owners' existing routines, in fact owners' 'plans and activities were altered and extended to incorporate the needs, preferences and pleasures of dogs'.[12]

It is not difficult to see therefore how something as mundane as dog walking is very much patterned and structured. It involves routines which, though practised in various ways, are bounded by sets of 'rules' – social expectations about how both pet and owner will conduct themselves. Again, in some cases these are formal – accompanied by threats of fines and so forth – but much more usually they are informal – they are generalised social expectations about, for example, what constitutes 'responsible' behaviour by dogs and humans. This leads us neatly to the particular feature of dog walking that we focus on in the book's first chapter: picking up after pets. This may seem both a commonplace and possibly unpleasant task, but it has social significance, not least that it is a relatively recent development. What we want to ask here is what this development tells us about ourselves and the nature of our daily lives. From dogs and their detritus we move to smoking and drinking. These are matters that have clearly been subject to substantial changes in behaviour in the post-war era, but in which directions and to what effect? Our practices and expectations have changed. The questions we will ask shortly are how did these things happen, and what does it say about us? We're not here to reach some overall judgement about whether things are getting better or worse. Things are rarely that simple. We simply hope to chart some of the changes we think are observable in post-war Britain and then you can make your mind up about what this says about us and the society we live in. No doubt you already have views about whether people in modern Britain are more or less orderly (more or less civil, freer or more restricted and so on).

Our focus then is on some of the cultural characteristics of the British, or what the renowned anthropologist Clifford Geertz referred to as a people's 'oddities'. A focus on such features Geertz thought was a potentially instructive way of learning more about a society,[13] and it is in this spirit that we take a few of Britain's everyday routines, looking at how they've changed in the post-war era, in the hope they might shed some novel light on old questions of what kind of society we are. At heart the general topic is far from a new concern. Writers since at least Thomas Hobbes in the seventeenth century have sought to understand what holds us together and enables an otherwise loose collection of individuals to function as a social group. In the nineteenth century, with industrialisation and urbanisation in full flow, analysing the construction of social order was one – indeed perhaps *the* – fundamental overriding concern of the social sciences. Here we examine the ordinary and everyday – picking up after pets, drinking, smoking, queuing and so forth – as a set of social routines, involving established practices, social expectations and more formalised regulations. Each of them has changed in some manner in the post-war period, offering us a vantage point from which to consider our recent history, our social practices and our social order.

We should note that our choice of subjects can also be seen through the lens of social problems. By 'problem', we are not implying some objective or measurable difficulty. As the American sociologist Joseph Gusfield observed many years ago, human problems don't spring up fully formed into our consciousness. Not all things we experience as painful become targets for action, nor do they necessarily hold the same meaning for everyone or at different times. When talking of social problems, therefore, we are referring to things that have become defined, socially, as matters that we have collectively begun to view as being in some way detrimental to our collective well-being. This process is by no means straightforward, and often involves struggle and conflict between different groups, these groups frequently making very contrasting claims or assertions.[14] Successfully defining some-thing as a social problem has very significant potential conse-quences, encouraging us to think about the 'problem' differently, to begin to respond to it in new ways, and to modify our behaviour for what is thought to be, or is argued to be, the communal good.

Considered in this way, 'social problems' from dog shit to double parking raise a host of interesting and potentially revealing questions. How do things become defined as a problem? When do these 'problems' generate political salience and become promi-nent? Who – which bodies and groups – are involved in more or less influential ways in the process by which they become identi-fied as problems? How are problems validated and what are the claims that underpin their emergence? Put simply, how do we justify their status as a problem? In one form or another, many of the subjects in this book have come to be seen as problems, or have come to be associated with problems, that are in need of tackling. We will look at what happened in each case and what it was about it, or perhaps matters linked to it, that provoked the reaction it did, and what the consequences were.

So, we've established that our subject-matter here is partly about some of the changing routines of life in post-war Britain and that many of the subjects, in differing ways, can also be viewed as involving something eventually thought of as a social problem. Problems imply the need for intervention and regula-tion and raise questions of freedom, restraint, constraint, control, civility and conformity. In consequence this book is also necessar-ily a study in social control. Now, in some respects 'social control' is a rather vague term. Used in its most straightforward way, it is a narrow or limited expression that refers to formal and coercive means such as the police, the courts and so forth. But it also has a wider meaning which refers to all those other, less formal means that help ensure predictability and stability in social life, not least the group norms and social expectations that guide our conduct. As we will see through our various illustrations here, in some respects it is often the case that it is the informal means of control that are dominant. This is not in any way to suggest that formal social control is unimportant. Rather, as long observed, it is more that the two often act in concert: the power of formal sanctions often relies on less formal underpinnings and, in turn, the boundaries that are regulated by informal controls are signalled and symbolised by more formal ones.[15] Consequently, in looking at how we use varying means to regulate social behaviour, and to manage and organise the pattern of our daily routines, further questions are raised about the balance between these different modes of control, and how particular strategies of control come into being in the form and at the time they do.

We began writing this book before the outbreak of COVID-19 and its profound consequences. This extraordinary pandemic continues to have a dramatic impact on everyday routines and practices, and it is impossible to ignore. In the context of the matters raised in this book we can see the pandemic as a massive social experiment in the disruption of the everyday. As such it offers a unique opportunity to explore further how and in what ways Britain has remained *orderly*. At the end of the book, having explored dog mess, drinking, smoking, queuing, toilets and parking, we finish by looking at the COVID-19 pandemic and how it played out in its first year or more. What was the impact on daily life, on our social expectations and social relations? Does it reinforce the lessons in the book or does it require us to modify our view of the nature of our social order? In many respects we think that when we reach the end of our journey post-war Britain will look both a more complex place and a more *ordered* one; one that has seen some very substantial changes in social practices, some significant changes in attitudes, all occurring within a web of rules, regulations and social expectations that in many ways are quite radically different from those that existed a half-century or more ago. As we've said, our first step on this journey is to consider how we manage the issue of dog shit. Naturally, we must tread carefully.

CHAPTER ONE

Dog Shit

What is it about dogs?

Crufts, styled as 'the world's largest dog show', has been running for well over a century, pets are listed as the main beneficiaries in approximately 1.5 million UK wills, and the five biggest animal charities have a joint income of over £300 million a year. Dogs are overwhelmingly viewed positively.[1] They are 'man's best friend', obedient companions who offer affection and attachment. Nevertheless, domestic dogs have always been a source of regulatory concern, from the threat of rabies in the nineteenth century and worries about the growing numbers of stray dogs on the streets, to more contemporary concerns with 'dangerous breeds' and 'status dogs'. In recent times their sheer number – estimated to be over twelve million or so in the UK[2] – has meant that increasing attention has focused on a particular canine-related concern: dog faeces.

The problem, succinctly captured by *The Times* in August 1976, is that dogs defecate 'with variable regard for human squeamishness'. Of course, for as long as there have been dogs, there's been dog shit. However, it is only in recent decades that dog fouling has become a recognised problem deemed worthy of significant social intervention. In short, something of a quiet social revolution has occurred in post-war Britain. In the space of a few decades we shifted from being a nation in which pet dogs were allowed to deposit all over our pavements, streets and parks, to one in which it was expected, nay required, that owners should pick up after their pets. For those concerned about the state of our streets and open spaces this is no doubt viewed as an entirely positive move. But for those who worry about increasing regulation it is a change that has come with a price: not least signs on every lamppost threatening those that don't comply. We may have long complained about dog mess, but only recently has it become a public policy issue. As a society we are now much more concerned with getting dog dirt out of sight, and there is an increasing supply of plastic bags, dog-waste bins, and poop-scoops to help us with the task, all accompanied by hard to miss reminders in the form of notices in our streets, parks, playgrounds and other public areas. A wide range of policies have been developed and issued by local and central government, and a host of sanctions are now in place for punishing miscreants (generally owners rather than dogs). So, let's examine how and why this happened.

Not so long ago you were considered a responsible dog owner if you guided your dog to the side of the road to do its business, assuming the rainwater would wash the mess away. In *My Dog Tulip*, the distinguished man of letters J. R. Ackerley wrote that he was averse to his dog using the gutter because he had heard stories of dogs being knocked over by cars. It was only under duress that Ackerley cleaned up any dog mess, such as when Tulip dumped a load on a greengrocer's shop doorstep and the staff chased after him, gave him newspapers and told him what to do.[3] Was Ackerley out of step with the times in not bothering to dispose of his dog's waste? The writer and comedian Alexei Sayle's Merseyside memories suggest almost certainly not. Reflecting on his Liverpool childhood in the first volume of his autobiography, *Thatcher Stole My Trousers*, Sayle remembered that among his then girlfriend Linda's particular gifts: 'She also didn't smell of dog shit which was an unusual attribute back then. In addition to her many qualities Linda had a secret skill which was that she had the ability never to step in canine excrement. At that time people's dogs defecated whenever they felt like and the streets were a constant assault course of dog poop. Most people stepped on some at least once a day.' Liverpool was typical. City streets across the nation were a far from pretty sight and experience in the fifties and sixties. How times have changed.

Dogs, licences and danger

To put the current situation in context it is helpful to look back to some earlier attempts at regulation and our history of managing pet dogs. Licensing was first introduced in the late eighteenth century after John Dent, the Member of Parliament for Lancaster, had proposed a national tax on dogs to raise money for the Royal Navy during the Napoleonic Wars. Dent argued that the tax would reduce the dog population, prevent poaching, reduce hydrophobia (a symptom of rabies) and make food more plentiful and cheaper for the masses (because wild dogs stole desperately needed provisions). A licence, signalling ownership and responsibility, was introduced in 1796 and lasted for nearly two centuries before being withdrawn finally in 1988. In truth, it had been riddled with difficulties for much of this time and had fallen largely into disuse by the time it was eventually put down.

John Dent's intervention earned him the nickname 'Dog Dent' and made him such a loathed figure that he was sent hampers of hares' legs, pheasants' tails and even dead dogs. Subsequent history has shown that the lesson of John Dent's experiences – tread carefully where pet dogs are concerned – was not lost on those that followed him.

Governments have rarely wanted to come between owners and pets, fearing the ire of what in the nineteenth century became known as the 'dog vote'. Even a government like Margaret Thatcher's – not one that usually shrank from a fight – continually refrained from increasing the cost of the dog licence, even though its administrative system ran at a huge loss. Huge numbers of owners simply ignored it. Toward the end of the nineteenth century a senior civil servant estimated that once exemptions were taken into account, it was possible that up to half the dogs in the country were unlicensed. Indeed, a London County Council official thought that the figure for the capital might be closer to three-quarters. Despite seeming ups and downs in licence numbers, the best estimates suggest that the actual number of dogs rose throughout the Victorian era.[4] Strays had long been a major issue and one response in London was the establishment in 1860 of Battersea Dogs Home. The problem continued to grow and there are suggestions that at least twenty thousand ownerless dogs were seized each year by the police, the majority of which were unclaimed and had to be destroyed.

This was a period of generally increasing anxiety about dogs. The worries were varied and included damage to property, especially sheep and cattle, and to people. It wouldn't have been Victorian times, however, without propriety also being a source of concern. Stray dogs, it was felt in some circles, were a potential embarrassment. One historian quotes a complaint about stray dogs, or 'gutter tykes', suggesting that their 'behaviour when the attractions of one of the female portion of the community turns the heads of the other sex is still more unedifying especially when such scenes take place ... in the presence of ladies.'[5] But it was rabies that was the major source of worry and by the 1870s several dozen deaths were reported each year. By the following decade there were strong pressures for an increase in police powers to seize dogs. As ever, though, there was also considerable resistance.

In the end, a policy of muzzling effectively won the day. Compulsory muzzling had been possible since 1871, though efforts were generally localised, and the response varied widely. A scheme in Bradford, which introduced muzzling and a registration scheme in 1884, seems to have caused little trouble, but the introduction of something similar in London during the following year's rabies scare became very controversial. There was considerable resistance to new powers when they were introduced in 1886, and two parallel battles – one against rabies, the other against muzzling and other forms of control – continued to be fought through the 1890s. A combination of those concerned about animal cruelty on the one hand, and those fearful of overbearing state intervention on the other, ensured that the government trod warily in mid- and late-Victorian times, with the consequence that it was 1903 before rabies was declared eradicated.

For its first 150 years or so the dog licence was relatively expensive for dog owners. In the early twentieth century organisations such as the National Canine Defence League and Our Dumb Friends League funded thousands of licence fees in an effort to support those who struggled to pay. Compliance rates continued to be low, however, and in the 1940s, in the immediate aftermath of the war, although roughly three million dog licences were issued, estimates suggested there might be as many as four million dogs overall.[6] Already on shaky ground, as governments opted not to increase the price of the licence the system began to fall apart. By 1984, dog-licence fee revenues were only a fifth of the total cost of running the scheme. Eventually a libertarian environment secretary, Nicholas Ridley, abolished the licence as part of the Local Government Act 1988.

The late-nineteenth-century laws introduced to enable muzzling and other forms of control were, with the exception of occasional legislation to deal with attacks on livestock – in 1906, 1928 and 1938 – the last major governmental intervention to deal with a dog-related issue until a now somewhat infamous law, the Dangerous Dogs Act, was passed (in just six weeks) in 1991. Earlier that year the press, and the tabloids in particular, had been full of horrific stories of attacks by pit bull terriers leading to extremely serious injuries and in some cases even death. Though there was evidence that other breeds were causing just as much of a problem, the home secretary at the time 'considered that pit bulls represented a quite different scale of menace'. The legislation, hastily passed through parliament, made possession of four breeds of dog a criminal offence. It introduced powers to order the destruction of dogs in specified circumstances, and to disqualify people from future dog ownership if they behaved irresponsibly.

To say the Dangerous Dogs Act had a mixed reception is to put it mildly. At the time it was supported by all political parties, most likely in part because of the assertive media campaign that supported the initiative. Subsequently, it was held up by some as the prime example of legislation that is passed in haste then repented at leisure, not least because it appeared to lead to relatively little action.[7] Though few prosecutions were brought it seems over a thousand animals were destroyed in the six years between the passage of the Act and the ending of mandatory destruction in 1997. The numbers of prosecutions brought annually continued to reach four figures well into the twenty-first century.[8]

From rabies to pit bulls, for over a century the focus of concern about dogs had been on different conceptions of 'danger'. The reaction was to seek to effect change by controlling dogs, generally by muzzling them or destroying them. More recently, however, the focus of control in regulatory trends has gradually shifted away from seeking to control dogs and toward influencing owners. Increasingly, in Britain and other countries, new initiatives have treated badly behaved dogs as indicative of antisocial owners. And, frankly, in modern Britain few things are considered more antisocial than owners who don't clear up after their dogs.

Tackling our indulgent sluttishness

'Turds of every size were photographed from every possible angle' said one reviewer of Thames TV's *The Case Against Dogs*. The programme, broadcast in July 1975, highlighted the dangers of children catching toxocariasis – an infection from the roundworm parasites (toxocara) which live in the digestive system of dogs, foxes and cats – through contaminated dog faeces. The programme put forward several possible reforming measures: a higher dog-licence fee; compulsory worming for dogs; greater powers for dog wardens; strict control of dogs at all times; and some form of ban on defecation in parks or public places. These preventative measures, according to the television reviewer, seemed 'sensible enough and indeed more humane than our indulgent sluttishness'.

Slowly but surely the issue of 'defecation in parks or public places' was becoming a matter of public concern. As is often the case it was a local dispute that captured public attention and provided something of a catalyst for change. In Burnley, Lancashire, a particularly noteworthy confrontation took place between 1976 and 1984. Before it was resolved a dozen dog owners had been fined, three women had chained themselves to the Town Hall railings and four people had been imprisoned. The editor of the *Burnley Express* saw it as 'possibly the biggest controversy our town has ever known'.

What sparked it all? In November 1975, members of the Burnley Recreation and Leisure Committee heard frightening news at an environmental-health conference in Eastbourne. Recent research had highlighted the dangers of children catching diseases from dog faeces. At the conference, Professor Alan Woodruff told a harrowing story about a young child who had lost the sight of an eye after the retina had been destroyed by what was referred to as an 'inflammatory mass'. Woodruff explained how researchers, armed with trowels and cardboard cartons, had collected soil samples from public parks and children's play areas, their analysis showing traces of contaminated dog faeces. He said that around two per cent of people were infected with toxocariasis. The disease was spread from animals to humans via infected faeces, and young children aged between one and four were thought to be particularly vulnerable. According to historian Neil Pemberton, one of the things that is interesting about what happened in Burnley is that this period, and the conflict that occurred in the town, 'symbolized the high-water mark of a public-health panic about the perceived threat posed by canine excrement to child health'.[9] The problem of dog shit was here to stay, but the focus on health would quite quickly subside as a source of anxiety.

Following the Thames TV programme and the Woodruff presentation two reports were passed around Burnley's council offices – *Dogs in the United Kingdom* (1975) and *Report of the Working Party on Dogs* (1976). The dog population in the country, growing at about eight per cent per year, was approaching six million and in response the authors of the 1976 report recommended a higher dog-licence fee to fund a thousand new dog wardens. The first council dog warden had been appointed in 1970 and more than fifty were in post across the country by 1976. In practice, rather than managing issues such as prosecuting dog-licence evaders or dealing with excreta, these early wardens spent their days rounding up strays – estimated to number well over a million at this point – and it was hoped that they might eventually take complete responsibility for the control of strays from a police service with more pressing priorities.

John Entwistle, Labour leader of Burnley Borough Council, said he'd received numerous complaints about dog fouling in the town's public parks, prompting the council's Public Protection Committee to investigate the available legal options to tackle the problem. Voting across party lines, the councillors decided to take radical action, passing a new by-law to exclude all dogs, except for guide dogs, in three of the local public parks. Scott Park (Burnley's first, established in 1875), Thompson Park and Queen's Park, were all close to the centre of the town and the new ruling meant that not even dogs on leads were permitted in them. Getting agreement to the plan from the Home Office took some time, but, in June 1977, notices went up on the gates of the three Burnley parks: No Dogs Allowed.

Most dog owners had not heard about the ban. The new policy seemed to have received little advance publicity and consequently many were shocked, bewildered and angry when confronted by the new signs. 'As ratepayers we are expected to contribute to the upkeep of the park, yet we are not allowed to use the facilities to the full,' said Colin England, spokesman for the local dog owners. 'If we take our dogs on the pavements and they foul them, we are liable to a fine. If we take our pets to the park we are also open to prosecution. So, it seems we have the choice of two fines if we take our dogs for exercise.'

In Colin England's view, the parks were big enough for the council to section off children's play areas from dog-walking areas, and, if it felt so inclined, the council could provide dog latrines. He also argued that dog owners were not as destructive as the vandals he claimed were riding bikes through flowerbeds and smashing up park buildings. His views on vandals were echoed by a Mrs E. Starkie. In a letter to the Burnley *Evening Star* she said, 'I have yet to see a dog using a knife on the park benches or breaking the glass in the shelters, tearing up the flower beds or swinging on the young trees! And never have I seen a dog on a bike in the park!'

In Burnley, plans to recruit a dog warden had been repeatedly cut from the council budget but now a new urgency prevailed. Local councillor James Heyes agreed that a dog warden was of prime importance, but he believed it was still in the public interest to keep dogs out of parks in order to prevent diseases and reduce the dog-dirt nuisance. 'There is nothing more annoying than walking through grassy areas and having to tread warily,' he said. Heyes and his fellow council members may have been convinced, but there was considerable opposition. A petition calling to overturn the new by-law claimed three hundred signatures on the first day, a thousand in less than a week, and eventually three thousand names. The beginning of what Pemberton calls Burnley's 'Dog War' began in late July 1977, a few weeks after the announcement of the ban, when three hundred dog walkers and their pets met in Scott Park to signal their opposition, and the Burnley Dog Owners' Action Group was formed. When a second 'walk-in' was organised, this time in Thompson Park, Burnley Council successful applied for a writ from the High Court against seven members of the Action Group's committee. The protestors were banned from taking part in meetings, processions or public discussions in the parks. Although the Burnley Seven (as they might have been but weren't called) agreed to abide by the injunction, those returning from the High Court were greeted by a crowd, estimated at over five hundred people, singing 'For he's a jolly good fellow'. The crowd, some reportedly chanting 'to hell with the borough council', then marched through Thompson Park.[10] The fight was well and truly on.

'Wot No Dogs'

In Burnley, on 5 November 1977, Councillor Mrs Sarah Ennis, a former mayor of the town, discovered some graffiti on her house:

> Wot No Dogs

Councillors had feared retribution after the banning of dogs from the town's parks, and here it was sprayed in black paint around the archway of the ex-mayor's front door. The same graffiti appeared on the steps and walls of Burnley Town Hall. The writing style seemed the same in all cases. Whatever else they had been seeking to do, Burnley's council had succeeded in provoking what Pemberton describes as 'an organized civil disobedience movement, transforming law-abiding dog walkers into criminals'. They were also drawing significant national attention to what hitherto had largely been a local issue. In addition to the graffiti, the Owner's Action Group sought to make their presence felt at council meetings, wrote copiously to the local press and would eventually take their protests to the capital. The local park rangers felt they had insufficient powers to deal with the council's new ban and were said to be surprised by the increasing amount of vandalism that had occurred since the ban had been implemented, including the stealing of official 'No Dogs Allowed' notices. The local dog owners response was to argue that it had been the presence of dogs in the first place that had helped to reduce vandalism. Letters to the local papers during the ban were four to one in favour of the dog owners, but a local poll showed an almost equal three-way split between those who were in favour of the current ban, those who felt it should be completely lifted, and those who thought it should be kept but modified.

The Burnley dog confrontation first came to court in November 1977, when fifty-five-year-old Herbert Johns faced four charges of contravening the local by-law. Johns told the court that he believed in law and order, but he didn't believe in the by-law and wouldn't abide by it. He had fought for democracy and freedom with the Eighth Army during the Second World War, but that freedom was now being denied him 'by the park rangers adopting KGB tactics'. 'What harm is there in walking a dog in a park?' Johns asked the court. 'What authority do these petty, pompous, big-headed councillors have to prevent me taking my dog into the park? This is a ridiculous situation for anyone to be in. I cannot believe that I can possibly be committed to prison for walking my dog in the park. If I had robbed a bank, all right.' As it turned out the council had all the authority they needed, and Johns was found guilty and fined £20 (£5 for each of four separate offences).

In July 1978, the High Court upheld the Council's ban. Three members of the Action Committee had challenged the by-law (the four remaining members of the Burnley Seven had agreed to abide by it) but were unsuccessful. The Judge ruled that it 'was not manifestly unjust or an oppressive or gratuitous interference with the rights of others which a reasonable council would not countenance'. In the High Court, Burnley's recreation officer, speaking of problems faced by the council, spoke of 'fouling, damage and annoyance. Parents ... expected to be able to allow their children to play freely on grassed areas; children's clothing might become fouled; toxicara canis had received publicity in recent years. Dogs damaged flower displays and dog urine could cause damage to specialized areas like bowling greens. Small children could get knocked over by over-excited dogs. Dogs had caused problems by running over the finishing lines on athletic tracks'.[11] Mr Mattock may have been getting a little carried away with his final points, but the day was won, and the case ended with the Judge making an order for a perpetual injunction, two of the owners having refused to give an undertaking not to exercise their dogs or incite others to do so. Both Frank Clifford and Mavis Thornton, the two concerned, said they would rather go to jail than obey the injunction.[12] The Council quickly made an application to have Clifford jailed and, given 90 minutes by a Judge to consider his position, he later apologised and agreed to abide with the ban.[13] With the High Court ruling in the

23

council's favour, it seemed the tide was turning on the issue of access to local parks, at least in Burnley.

The protesters were not about to give up, however. A year after having been fined £20 for his four offences, but still refusing to pay, Herbert Johns was jailed for five days by Burnley's magistrates. As unrepentant as he had been earlier, Johns said 'I will go on hunger strike if you send me to prison'.[14] Mavis Thornton, a former social worker, by now the only one of the seven who had still not agreed to abide by the High Court's ruling, was the next to be incarcerated, though her decision was more calculated than Herbert Johns' had been. If the Suffragettes had to be imprisoned before their 'votes for women' campaign was taken seriously, she thought, then it seemed likely that a Burnley dog walker might have to suffer the same fate. While lying in the bath one night, considering the likely consequences of further protest, Thornton thought about who would take care of her five children while she was in prison and she began to make arrangements. Also, knowing what was coming Thornton set about organising a sizeable publicity campaign.

Every day for a fortnight Thornton deliberately defied the High Court order by walking her three dogs – a dachshund and two terriers – in Thompson Park where 'she was greeted and accompanied by well-wishers and local and national news media representatives'.[15] Eventually summonsed, when her case reached London's High Court she was jailed. Sentencing her, Mr Justice Slade said, 'While I appreciate her sincerity, her action is absolutely misguided . . . orders of the court are there to be obeyed. I very much hope that in a short time you will realise it is misguided, and that the court will be in a position to release you.'[16] The local dog protesters were outraged and began to campaign for her release. Their protest even reached Downing Street, with upwards of twenty Burnley owners staging what was variously described as 'dog-in' and a 'silent vigil' outside Prime Minister Jim Callaghan's residence.

Thornton reported that she found the prison food as rubbery as the plates, and swearing was 'the accepted language'. While the dog-owners' group fought her cause – 'Release Mavis Thornton' graffiti appeared on an outside prison wall – Thornton ironed clothes in the workshop, cleaned the corridors and worked in the kitchens. Having eventually signed an agreement saying she would observe the by-law, Thornton was released from prison. She returned to Burnley a heroine to many, saying 'I don't regret one minute of my three weeks inside'. Bad news was around the corner, however, for she and her fellow plaintiffs in the High Court case, Frank Clifford and Kenneth Spencer, received a bill for costs of £23,500 on Christmas Eve 1979. All three were said to face bankruptcy.[17]

There was some consternation in the Home Office at the strategy adopted in Burnley, and government urged greater consultation, with councils pressed to discuss any new restrictions with animal-welfare groups before implementation. The Burnley dog-ban saga, however, was far from over. The dog owners were supported by the newly formed Pro-Dogs Group and their slogan ('Dogs Deserve Better People'), and Lord Houghton, chairman of the Joint Advisory Committee on Pets in Society (JACOPIS), looked for ways to resolve the conflict. In February 1982, the council finally reconsidered the dog ban in one of its parks. Its original application to the Home Office for a ban on dogs had succeeded because the parks were classified as 'ornamental' and thereby could be the subject of special protections. However, Scott Park's facilities had deteriorated over the years and the 'ornamental' description no longer applied. Though the council reopened Scott Park to dogs in September 1983, the other two dog-free parks remained exclusion zones (even after a further review in 2010).

It seems clear that the council's actions in Burnley became controversial in part because they were unprecedented, and the ban on walking pet dogs was viewed by many locals as an unnecessarily restrictive policy. The dog owners felt unreasonably victimised, and particular annoyance was caused by the council's barrister, Brian Leveson QC (later to find fame as the chair of the Inquiry into the British press in the aftermath of the phone hacking scandal), who described them in court as 'the kind of people against whom society needs to be defended'. In many ways Burnley was ahead of the curve. At the time that the parks ban was introduced there was no national culture of clearing up and little expectation that owners would do so. Burnley Council appeared to be at the forefront of the newly emerging concern with dog fouling – though few others were prepared to follow their strategy and ban dogs entirely from public parks. Nevertheless, Burnley's campaign, which focused on owners as well as dogs, was a straw in the wind. At the time it seems there was a reasonable level of support in government for the broad aims of Burnley Council's ban though there was no explicit encouragement to other councils to go down the same route. As Pemberton notes, 'government considered neither toxocariasis nor dog fouling sufficiently severe problems to warrant the creation of separate dog-free and dog-friendly parks, although a consensus was reached that children's playgrounds required fencing to keep out dogs and their potentially infected excrement.' In other open spaces an alternative approach was going to be necessary.

So far as the Burnley dog owners were concerned, it was the council's high-handed refusal to allow dogs into local parks that caused greatest hurt. In reality there were a large number of other spaces in Burnley – children's playgrounds, sports grounds – where dogs were also banned. Parks, however, were of great symbolic importance; they were cherished public spaces. To a degree, of course, the dispute was also about personal liberty. One resident wrote a short story about two anthropomorphised dogs, Cocker (a spaniel) and Jack (a terrier), who discussed how the Burnley dog ban was designed to scare their masters, just like a new law that had been passed in New York. 'If a dog defecates, the master is fined twenty dollars on the spot,' said Cocker, talking about the Big Apple. 'They are even forcing our canine brothers and sisters to go through the humiliating experience of wearing nappies when they are out.' 'Yes, I know,' said Jack, the terrier. 'And America is supposed to be the land of free enterprise, where everybody is free to do business.'

Burnley and the Big Apple

Burnley and New York were hardly ready-made candidates for twinning, but in the late seventies they were united in their concern with dog excrement. By contrast with Burnley's focus on public parks, in New York it was at least as much with sidewalks as green spaces. As a consequence, the administration's attention was concentrated much more closely on the dog deposits themselves. As was to be the case in England, the initial concerns centred on the health risks associated with dog faeces. A group called Children Before Dogs had campaigned widely against dog fouling on the grounds of children's health, and one parent said that the mess was so bad that children should be kept on leads. A variety of initiatives had been tested including, in 1958, the building of a concrete-based prototype toilet for dogs on 92nd Street and York Avenue. It was dismantled within a year – it is said that dogs refused to use it. Ever-optimistic, New Yorkers built another 'canine comfort station' in the 1970s on 43rd Street and Ninth Avenue, 'complete with tile walls and shingle roof'.[18]

Dog fouling had long been a problem in New York City, so much so that existing city law prohibited dogs from defecating on public property. At best this was seemingly interpreted as meaning that dogs should be led to the gutter to do their business. In practice even that interpretation was barely enforced. In 1972, a brave soul, Jerome Kretchmer, first sought to introduce a new 'poop scoop' law that would require owners to pick up after their dogs or face a $25 fine. Faced with that threat, opponents had come out in force, including PAWS (Pets Are Worth Safeguarding), DOG (Dog Owners' Guild) and the Pet Owners' Protective Association (POPA). In the battle of dog poop, and witty acronyms, Kretchmer's initiative at least had the backing of SCOOP (Stop Crapping On Our Premises).[19] Between the mid-sixties and mid-seventies the number of dogs in New York City doubled and the average dog size increased from twenty-five pounds to thirty-three pounds. Together with cuts in budgets for parks officers, police officers and street cleaners, this all led to a sense that dog fouling had become much more visible.

The consequence was the eventual passage by the City of a 'poop scoop' law in 1977. The initiative – Section 1310 of the State Public Health Law which became operational in 1978 – stated that 'It shall be the duty of each dog owner ... to remove any faeces left by his dog on any sidewalk, gutter, street, or other public area.' The new law was many years in the making and was itself the subject of huge controversy and conflict before being eventually passed. A year's grace before the law became operational was instituted because New York's officials, showing rather greater foresight than Burnley's councillors, knew that they would otherwise meet fierce opposition. As New York City mayor Ed Koch once rather astutely put it, 'people who run for office should not throw rocks at dogs'.

In a pattern that would be broadly repeated in Britain, the first year after the new 'poop scoop' law was operational in New York saw relatively low levels of formal action taken by the authorities but, seemingly, some quite significant changes in behaviour. In the first six months of operation, 7,316 warnings were given, but only 363 summonses were issued in the whole of the city (and only one third of those summonsed paid a fine). At the end of the first year of the experiment the Commissioner of New York's Sanitation Department described it as having 'proven to be very effective . . . The controversy about it has died down . . . There's a general feeling of compliance and there's increasing peer pressure among dog owners themselves to make this rule work. You can see it in the greater number of dog-walkers who are carrying bags and devices to clean up after their dogs and you can see it in the cleaner streets'.[20] One close observer of the New York experiment has claimed that it was the source of the shift in attitudes toward cleaning up after dogs around the world.[21] While that might be straining credulity, it nevertheless does appear to have been an early and significant illustration of a broad change in public attitudes to dogs and their waste.

At roughly the same time that New York City was introducing its poop scoop law, Paris was confronting its own poop problem. Where Mayor Koch's administration approached the problem with threats of fines, Jacques Chirac took another path. Despite new municipal regulations in the 1940s which stated that dogs should only defecate in the gutter, historian Chris

Pearson describes the 1950s as the 'dark years' for Paris's streets and pavements 'which lay neglected and unloved'.[22] Despite opinion polls suggesting dog mess was considered a priority public problem, it was not until the late 1970s when Chirac became mayor that things began to change. His approach, initially at least, tended to favour carrot over stick, and rather than fines and threats, persuasion, education and the provision of alternatives were the order of the day. Supplementing the gutter, the authorities built three 'canisiennes', 'a bollard surrounded by a basin that could be flushed by a pedal to carry waste to the sewer'. These were both expensive and limited in impact – being located in the touristic heart of the capital. Further experiments followed, with 'dry toilets' – 'a post surrounded by sand or grass and bordered with bushes' – and, wonderfully, with 'motocrottes' or 'poopscooters', adapted motorbikes that vacuumed up dog waste into a tank on their rear. Intriguingly, it seems that something more was required in order to stimulate the necessary cultural change, and by the late 1990s Paris began to fine owners who failed to clear up after their pets. By the early years of the new century the motocrottes had disappeared and the focus, as in Burnley and Brooklyn, was firmly on disciplining owners.

Action spreads

Back in the UK, the national publicity from the Burnley case was being studied by councillors all over the country. In Chesterfield, Derbyshire, for instance, in January 1979, the council backed down on plans to ban dogs in four of the town's parks. In Bradford, Yorkshire, later that year, the council's environmental health panel decided on a six-point code of practice for dog owners rather than more swingeing action. It was in the early eighties that central government began to take a keen interest. The approach initially was to facilitate local action via new by-laws. The Burnley experience continued to make both government and local authorities wary of banning dogs from enclosed parks and recreation grounds, and greater encouragement was given to by-laws which made it an offence for dogs to foul footways and grass verges.

In 1982, influenced by the apparent success of the faeces ban in New York City, a group of councils approached the government seeking action that would require owners to clean up after their dogs. The Home Office agreed to a set of experimental by-laws and in late 1985, with the help of the Local Authority Environmental Service Programme ('Kerb Your Dog'), these were introduced in Gosport (Hampshire), Barking & Dagenham (London), Rochester (Kent) and Coalville and Whitwick (North West Leicestershire). They were supported by advance publicity and a programme to encourage responsible dog ownership. Each local authority studied dog-behaviour patterns before fixing special waste-disposal bins in the most appropriate places. They distributed one hundred thousand hand scoops and a few long-handled scoops for dog owners who had difficulty bending. They also took out one-page advertisements in local newspapers, put up 250 posters, distributed fifty thousand handbills via local free newspapers, and offered pet-care leaflets. Though hand scoops never really took off in any significant way in Britain, these experiments arguably marked quite a decisive moment in the general shift towards Britain becoming a society that picked up after its dogs.

The number of convictions was low but press reporting of the new restrictions was felt to have provided strong publicity for the scheme. During the winter there was an increase in fouling in the experimental areas, but standards improved again during the spring of 1986. It was reported that sports players and parents were delighted with the outcome in parks, and it was thought that there was generally less hostility towards dogs as a consequence of the changes. A household survey in Rochester found that 84 per cent of dog owners and 76 per cent of non-dog owners had heard of the by-law, and almost two-thirds of dog owners and non-dog owners thought that it was successful in reducing dog fouling. Most encouragingly for those promoting new standards, 90 per cent of those aware of the scheme (including dog owners) thought that the by-law should apply to all parks, pavements and grass verges. The main criticism was of what academics would call 'displacement' – the dog fouling appeared to worsen in some nearby areas that were not part of the experiment.

The largely positive Home Office report on the experiments reinforced the trend toward recognising dog fouling as a social problem and encouraging interventions to support behaviour-change. By the end of the decade the Home Office template for by-laws was extended so that councils could make it an offence for an owner to leave dog faeces in any designated park, recreation ground and public open space. Similarly, the same was to be true for any footpath in a built-up or residential area, grass verges adjacent to highways and pedestrian areas owned by a local authority (e.g. a shopping precinct). The new model by-laws also extended such offences to include highway gutters, something of a turnabout from the fifties when the side of the road was considered the most appropriate place for dogs to defecate – picking up generally being discouraged because of the danger from traffic.

The tipping point

It was really toward the end of the century that it effectively became the assumed norm that when you went out with your dog you also took a poo bag on the walk. Something which had caused significant controversy a mere twenty years previously – on both sides of the Atlantic – was now well on its way to becoming something close to an established social practice. It reflected what were by now rapidly changing attitudes toward dog fouling and changing social expectations about the responsibilities of dog owners, all encouraged and underpinned by new local by-laws. Regulations surrounding dogs and their faeces had begun to proliferate and, more particularly, this was the point when central government really started to flex its muscles. Section 87 of the Environmental Protection Act (EPA) 1990, made it an offence to 'throw or drop or otherwise deposit, in a public open place, anything that could cause, or contribute to or tend to lead to the defacement of that place by litter'. A year later the Litter (Animal Droppings) Order 1991, extended the definition of 'litter' to include dog faeces.

There had been concern in some quarters that leaving responsibility to local authorities meant that implementation varied from 'street to street and parish to parish', and a national Litter Advisory Group, established in 1993, recommended that 'there should be a nationally defined offence based on the existing poop scoop by-law offence' and that it 'apply to ... public parks and open spaces, beaches, and publicly maintained pavements, verges and gutters of highways subject to a speed limit of forty miles per hour or less'. Government accepted that the current local controls were unnecessarily complex and a fixed penalty scheme for dog-fouling offences was proposed in order to help local enforcement. Subsequently, the Dogs (Fouling of Land) Act 1996 permitted local authorities to designate land on which it would be an offence to fail to remove dog faeces.[23] Local authorities were given powers to introduce Dog Control Orders and to issue fixed penalty notices for breach of regulations (2002 in England, 2004 in Wales). The by-laws could include dog-prohibited areas, leash laws, restrictions on walking multiple dogs, and requirements to remove dog faeces.

In general, local councils responded energetically to the new powers given to them by government, and it quickly became *de rigueur* for lampposts to carry official signage demanding that poop be scooped, and for sizeable fines to be threatened against those who failed to comply. Much of this was somewhat symbolic and prosecutions remained relatively rare. Research by ENCAMS (Keep Britain Tidy) suggested that there were fewer than a thousand on-the-spot fines imposed in all of England during a six-month period in 2004 (and over half of those were in one region: the North West). Similarly, prosecutions under the Dogs (Fouling of Land) Act 1996 never exceeded five hundred in any single year in its first decade of operation. Though a sizeable number of complaints about dog fouling were received by local councils each year – between sixty and eighty thousand from 2010 to 2015 the BBC estimated – even at their highest there were fewer than four thousand fixed penalty notices (FPNs) in any one year. Over a third of local councils responding to a survey admitted they had not imposed any FPNs in the last year and almost one sixth had not imposed any in the past five years.[24]

Slowly but surely, the spattered pavements that Alexei Sayle remembered from his youth were being cleaned up – by dog owners. Though few followed Burnley council's lead, their ban and the way they went about enforcing it, drew national attention to the issue. Subsequent campaigning, over an extended period, led other councils to make failing to clean up after a dog a local offence. It was the proliferation of these highly localised by-laws which eventually encouraged government to take more concerted national action. All this activity – combining encouragement and threat – gradually shifted social expectations and social conduct. By the turn of the century a substantial proportion of dog owners were now alive to the need to bag up. Statistical information is limited, but a 1992 survey by Nuneaton and Bedworth District Council found that picking-up rates in four parks ranged from 25 per cent in one park to as much as 83 per cent in another. An observational study in 2006 found that about three-fifths of owners cleaned up after their dogs.[25] A localised survey in Lancashire in 2010/11 found that over 90 per cent of respondents said that they would clean up the waste and either use a dedicated dog waste bin if available or take it away for disposal elsewhere.[26] Indeed, that study, published in 2014, concluded that 'in the last decade there has been a perceived reduction in the presence of dog faeces in public places in the UK'.

The new taboo

The first and crucial step in shifting attitudes and behaviour had been to establish the idea that the presence of dog shit in public spaces was a social problem. Initially, dangers to health, particularly children's health, focused concern, and this gradually gave way to a more generalised message that presented dog shit not just as something that was a source of risk but was something to be entirely avoided. Dog waste was not just unpleasant but it was rapidly becoming taboo. The means by which new social norms were established and embedded ran the typical gamut of the formal and informal. As we've seen, initially via local by-laws, and then via a number of Acts of Parliament, over a period of roughly two decades or so the general principle that dog shit should be cleared from parks, pavements and other public places became implanted in public consciousness. Though the laws and by-laws were accompanied by fines and other penalties for those that failed to comply, in practice few fines were imposed and few prosecutions brought. In truth, much of this formalised encouragement has been just that – encouragement – there to inspire behavioural change. Slowly, that appears to have been what we have witnessed.

Campaigning has been extensive. From pressure group activity, outreach by education officers (occasionally using fake turds to help explain to schoolchildren how to pick up after a dog), to council dog wardens and other officials, the range of interventions has been broad. In 1992, Nuneaton & Bedworth Council followed The Dogs Trust template ('Bag It And Bin It') by promoting a local campaign through a mascot called Oscar. (A competition to name Oscar's puppy was won by the entry 'Scoopy Doo'.) Local initiatives gave birth to such wonders as Fine Idle Dog Owners (FIDO) and Concerned Residents Against Poo (CRAP). Threatening signage (always popular with local authorities and the police) was joined by more imaginative examples, such as Twyford's 'We Want to Play But Dog Mess is in the Way', and 'The Poo Fairy Doesn't Live Here – Scoop Your Poop' put up by frustrated residents of Harwood on Bolton. Colour-coding was introduced by South Somerset District Council in 1997: green areas where dogs were allowed to foul the land without their owners needing to clean up; yellow areas where picking up was compulsory and poop-scoop bins were provided; and red areas where dogs were not allowed to enter, such as children's play areas. Keep Britain Tidy took on an anti-dog-fouling remit in 2001, and a campaign against dog dirt saw the actor Ricky Tomlinson sitting on a toilet in the middle of Clapham Common reading a newspaper with the headline 'Dog Fouling – My Arse'. The message of that campaign – 'You Wouldn't Do That, So Don't Let Your Dog' – was said to have brought an estimated 40 per cent reduction in dog fouling in specific targeted areas. Keep Britain Tidy also urged people to write to their local councillors and MPs about the dog-fouling problem. By 2002, some 94 per cent of councils employed dog wardens, with one in seven having three or more, though the majority were still preoccupied with the time-consuming duty of dealing with strays.

By the early years of the new millennium the focus was even more firmly on owners rather than their pets. By 2005, about half of local authorities had a 'shop a dropper' hotline and three-quarters were using posters and education drives to change behaviour. One potential scheme to aid prosecution, suggested by Humberside police in the early years of the new century, was to ask the public to take photographs of dog owners who failed to pick up: 'the pooper-snooper scheme'. Falkirk's Green Dog Walkers wore a green wrist band to show that they carried spare bags and pledged to clear up after their dogs. South Gloucestershire council volunteers used armbands for the same purpose, Inverness offered vet-surgery vouchers as a reward for those who picked up properly, and the Paws on Patrol scheme in Stroud, Gloucestershire, asked dog walkers to report any suspicious activity. Derbyshire County Council's *Yuk!* campaigns were conducted via the offer of weatherproof signs for residents to attach to gates, fences and walls ('Yuk! Please don't let your dog foul outside my home'), together with press releases, interviews, free poop-scoop bags and a texting scheme for people to report problems. Local councillor Carol Hart, cabinet member for public health, urged 'the irresponsible few to do the right thing for the benefit of their community'.

Just in case encouragement and threat were not enough there were also a number of shaming initiatives. In 2007, authorities in Cheltenham left dog turds in situ and sprayed coloured circles around them to highlight the problem, and in 2012, the Crosshills and Glusburn Dog Fouling Action Group (North Yorkshire) marked dog deposits with flags in a troublesome 200-metre stretch of Glusburn's Shutt Lane (known, predictably enough, as 'Shit Lane'). The number of deposits in Shutt Lane was reduced significantly by the flag initiative. One enterprising campaigner, Andrew Hawes, had the idea of dressing up in camouflage, hiding in bushes and taking photographs of culprits ('Bin Your Poo I'm Watching You'), Edinburgh used CCTV to watch dog owners, and, perhaps most extraordinarily, Hyndburn Council in Lancashire apparently used surveillance vans, plain clothes officers and wardens with night vision glasses in 'hot spot' areas[27] (it also launched a 'Poo Dunnit?' campaign, displaying banners on refuse and recycling wagons advertising a scheme with £50 rewards for residents who could prove that a person has failed to clean up after their dog).[28] Daventry District Council in Northamptonshire went as far as to threaten dog owners with fines if they failed to carry a bag to clean up the mess. All this activity didn't come cheap. One estimate suggested that the explosion in local responses to dog fouling – including signage and public information activity, dog waste bins, street cleaning and enforcement – was costing councils over £22 million a year by 2010.[29]

As was anticipated by Cocker and Jack, Burnley's two erudite talking dogs, the arenas of business, invention, technology and marketing have all played a part in cultural change. Though the pooper-scooper, de rigueur in certain parts of the United States, never really took off in Britain, and Paris' 'poopscooters' never arrived on these shores, there has been no shortage of other attempts at technological innovation in the field of canine remains. Trafalgar Cleaning Equipment Ltd targeted councils with products such as the WOLF (Walking Operator Lifting Faeces), Henry the POOVER (poo hoover) and the ROVER (Ride-On Vehicle Excrement Remover).[30] Other products, such as Porch Potty and Pet Patio Potty, were designed to keep dog fouling at home. Bob Roberts, author of a toilet-training manual for dogs, believes that all dogs can be taught to toilet at home before going on a walk, potentially removing the need to foul in public places. 'Dogs are taught to carry newspapers, do a "high five", sit down and other simple tricks,' he says. 'Why not teach a dog to defecate at home in the yard or rear garden?' Indeed, as early as 1991 the Dogs Trust ('A dog is for life, not just for Christmas') recommended 'go at home' toilet regimes and cleaning up after pets.

In 2005, the authors of the bestselling book *Freakanomics* began to think about the problem of dog shit. Despite all the efforts to eliminate the problem there were still too many miscreants. What to do? Their answer was DNA sampling. Establish a DNA file of all dogs and then 'whenever a pile of poo is found on the sidewalk, a sample can be taken to establish the offender's DNA'. This would work well, they surmised, because 'poop is in fact a robust DNA source'.[31] They admitted that the drawback with the plan was that it needed every dog's DNA on file, and the low levels of dog registration in New York made this a bit of a stretch to put it mildly. But before we dismiss the idea entirely, they said, take a look at cities like

Dresden and Vienna because civic leaders there had been giving serious thought to the idea.

Fanciful and slightly 1984-ish as CSI-style teams testing dog poop may seem, nearer home we have also flirted with such possibilities. Indeed, as early as 1995 a potential experiment in the Leicestershire village of Bruntingthorpe, population 150, caused quite a stir. According to one report, the parish council briefly considered either video cameras or DNA tests 'after an outbreak of sloppy animal manners'.[32] While CCTV was considered impractical, thanks to local biochemist Dr Ian Eperon, a DNA database for the village's thirty dogs seemed achievable. Once established, he said he hoped to recruit volunteers to collect the evidence – 'otherwise . . . it will be me'.[33] Despite the early enthusiasm, in the event the scheme 'was quietly shelved' after a local and somewhat senile collie was found to be the culprit. Though Eperon reported that he still suffered the enmity of local dog owners two years after the stalled experiment, he still believed that DNA was a practical future solution.

In 2012, the *Daily Mail* reported that Lancashire authorities were keen to explore the possibility of using a 'forensic vet' to DNA-test dog faeces which 'could then be traced back to the canine culprits and their owners',[34] and similar plans were mooted in the Isle of Wight and North Down (Northern Ireland). In the United States, BioPet Laboratory's PooPrint technology can match a dog's DNA to deposited waste, a concept which it is claimed is working well in places such as housing complexes and gated communities where residents are more contained, pets can be registered and culprits can be identified by microchips.[35] In England, from April 2016, when all dogs had to be microchipped under new regulations, the consensus was still against DNA testing. The Kennel Club, for example, which said that it 'would strongly support any effective practical measures that would selectively target the actions of irresponsible dog owners' went on to say that while DNA testing looked useful in theory there were continuing concerns over how it would work in practice. The danger, the club claimed, was that such moves would be likely 'to further penalise responsible owners, whilst doing very little to tackle irresponsible owners'.

The quiet social revolution

Just a few decades back we were a nation whose pavements and gutters were littered with dog shit. A remarkable change has occurred, however. Even if such hazards haven't disappeared, they are undoubtedly much less common. Dog waste is now picked up and tidied away in bags and bins – though all too often such bags are slung somewhere, or even hung on trees, as if the problem was thereby solved, creating what the *Daily Record* apparently nicknamed 'the hanging gardens of jobbylon'.[36] Nevertheless, as we've said, in many respects picking up after dogs represents something of a social revolution. It has been a quiet social revolution, for much of it has been achieved with minimal public debate and, Burnley notwithstanding, little obvious conflict. What made all this possible?

To a certain extent it straightforwardly reflects greater regulation – this is an area of our lives that is now more heavily rulebound. It is also clear that social attitudes and expectations have changed, and markedly so. At heart, as we observed earlier, the presence of dog waste on our pavements and in our parks has been slowly transformed from something that was seen as unpleasant but had to be sidestepped, into matter that needed to be removed. Put bluntly, where once they had simply been a

nuisance, dog turds were now perceived as a social problem –
something that we, collectively, were required to do something
about. As we've seen, Burnley Council played a key role in this
process of problem-creation. This was captured beautifully by
Mavis Thornton, one of the more outspoken of Burnley's dog
owners, who is quoted in Neil Pemberton's history of the town's
'dog war':

> I never used to notice [dog dirt] was a nuisance. It is no differ-
> ent from going in the country and seeing that sheep have done
> something or a cow. It is also part of nature. You did not notice
> it. *But you notice it now.* It has become so that if a dog does
> something in Burnley everybody notices it.[37]

The issue, initially, was presented as a threat to health, especially
children's health. The apparent impetus behind the earliest
campaigns focused on the dangers associated with *toxocara canis*.
Parks and open spaces, places where it was suggested or implied
that children might be playing, were identified as the sites where
action most obviously needed to be taken. Though the health
risks in the most severe cases of toxocariasis were indeed severe,
in practice they were very rare. Indeed, after an initial flurry of
publicity generated by a couple of television programmes, talk of
dangers to health receded considerably, including in Burnley
whose seven-year-long dispute played such an important role in
the changing management of dog waste.

The Burnley case occupies an interesting position, however.
Though it was anything but a template for future action, its ban
and the civil disobedience it provoked contributed significantly
to Britain's dog waste revolution. Most local authorities shied
away from the type of dramatic action Burnley had taken, and

those that did show interest in exploring similar bans found the Home Office to be unsympathetic. One consequence of Burnley's parks' ban, therefore, was to signal the limits of permissible reaction. Many thought the local council had gone too far, but no one of any standing argued that intervention was unnecessary. From this point on there was growing acceptance among local municipalities that this was a matter that had to be tackled.

Most of the change toward becoming a nation of scoopers was achieved with a remarkable lack of fuss. It involved a lot of activity: the provision of bins in which to deposit waste that had been bagged; increasingly ubiquitous signage pointing out the need to pick up; by-laws to threaten fines for those that failed; and, latterly, central government legislation attempting to bring a degree of coherence to it all. At heart, however, little of this involved significant enforcement activity. The campaigns and the formal interventions were still important, not least in establishing dog shit as a problem of sufficient seriousness to warrant the potential of formal action. But in the main it appears that new standards of conduct and new social expectations gradually became embedded in popular consciousness and practice via more informal means.

Establishing a social problem involves claims-making. The initial focus on health matters gradually gave way to normative concerns. Increasingly the presence of dog shit was treated as a moral indicator. Dog waste gradually became a sign of lax standards, and a failure of both civic and individual responsibility. At the municipal level, having pavements, parks and open spaces that were free of dog waste became a matter of local pride, leading local authorities to seek by-laws that would enable punishment of owners that failed to pick up. They advertised extensively, with widespread notices encouraging such activity and indicating the levels of penalty that could be imposed on miscreants. Where once the dog would have been the focus, the 'miscreants' were now very clearly human.

At the heart of much such civic campaigning lay the figure of the 'responsible dog owner' – and given that nearly one quarter of households have dogs this comes quite close to being a proxy for the 'responsible citizen'. This social construction was increasingly wheeled out when explaining and justifying policy initiatives that ranged across animal welfare and behaviour and, where owners were concerned, included such matters as picking up, bagging and disposing of waste.[38] The Kennel Club, established in the nineteenth century, and now Britain's largest organisation dedicated to the health and welfare of dogs, publishes a 'Canine Code' which, rather more accurately, is subtitled: 'A guide to being a responsible dog owner'. It lists half a dozen or so main 'responsibilities' beginning with 'Exercise your dog every day' and 'Train your dog properly'. At number three is 'Clean up after your dog'. This is presented straightforwardly as being vital to the continuing freedom to walk dogs in public open spaces. Those who fail to clean up after their dog are said to be 'the root cause of complaints to local officials' and it is this 'which will eventually lead to an increasing number of places where dogs will not be allowed to go'.[39] In considering why it is important to pick up after dogs, the code simply says, 'dog mess is unpleasant and can occasionally lead to a condition called toxocariasis in humans, which can cause serious illness and blindness,' and then details the likely fines that may be imposed for failure to comply. Those who clear up are what the Code considers a 'good owner'.

It is worth sticking with the Canine Code a moment longer for in its detail it gives a sense of just how much is involved in being a 'responsible dog owner'. As already observed, the first two responsibilities are 'exercise your dog every day' and 'train your dog properly'. The latter is aimed at ensuring the dog is 'obedient in everyday situations'. Fourth in the list is 'know where you are allowed to walk your dog'. Here it reminds owners that there may be areas where 'public space protection orders' (PSPOs) are in place which may introduce a variety of restrictions ranging from limiting the number of dogs that may be walked by one person, requiring dogs be kept on leads, through to excluding them altogether. It then informs owners that all dogs must now be microchipped, before concluding with a series of welfare-oriented bits of advice. We still place restrictions of various forms on dogs, but it is very clear that in the early twenty-first century it is the regulation and control of dog *owners* that is now considered paramount.

Beyond some health concerns, we are still left with a question about why social attitudes toward dog waste have changed? It seems quite likely that the increasing number of dogs, and therefore the increasing quantity of dog waste, has been something of an impetus. But something more fundamental seems to lie behind this story of the identification and emergence of this new 'social problem'. Crucially, it seems our attitudes and sensibilities have altered. In the post-war period we have not only become increasingly intolerant of dog mess – we require it to be cleaned up – we have become increasingly squeamish about it – we want it removed out of sight. It seems plausible to think of this as being connected to wider changes in attitudes toward hygiene and cleanliness. Just as we have become a society of indoor and private toilets and bathrooms (we will discuss this later), of expectations of daily baths or, more likely now, showers, and are undoubtedly less tolerant of a variety of bodily odours, so now we are less forbearing of the sight of dogs' deposits on our streets.

Going a step further, we might even argue that this intolerance, encouraged and inculcated in a variety of ways, could be seen as part of the continuing long-term development that the German sociologist Norbert Elias referred to as the 'civilising process'.[40] Here Elias was talking of a centuries-long set of changes in codes of conduct, involving increasing social pressures toward self-restraint in a variety of forms of behaviour.

Looking primarily at the period between the Middle Ages and the eighteenth century, Elias documented the huge changes that took place in what was considered acceptable behaviour. Central to growing 'civility' was changing 'manners' and increasing shame, embarrassment and even repugnance at a variety of bodily functions.[41] Covering manners, bodily functions, sexual relations and violence, Elias focused in particular on behaviour at the table. Slowly such things as cleaning one's teeth with a knife, blowing one's nose either into one's hand or on the table-cloth, and putting uneaten food back in communal dishes, all became unacceptable. He showed how the increasing popularity of the fork, which required a level of dexterity hitherto unknown at the table, was a reflection not of changing standards of hygiene, but of shifting standards of social conduct. Spitting gradually ceased to be something done in public, farting when others were present became increasingly shameful, and urinating in places where it had previously been quite common, such as corridors and staircases, became unacceptable. In short, customs changed and, more particularly, many human functions became associated with shame and were increasingly hidden out of sight. Initially, such changes in custom were a means by which particular social groups distinguished themselves, but eventually they became generally established social standards. Such prescriptions were gradually internalised, and it is these increasing social pressures toward self-control that Elias identifies as lying at the heart of the civilising process. We can see very similar processes at work in this generalised story of our pets' droppings. Something initially allowed or tolerated, gradually became proscribed, indeed subject to formal prohibitions and, slowly, the new practices of picking up became fairly standardised. It is in precisely this way that we might reasonably conclude that our conduct in relation to our pets is now increasingly also treated as an important mark of our civility.

CHAPTER TWO

Smoking

From the standpoint of the early twenty-first century, it is all but impossible to conceive of smoking tobacco as anything other than harmful. Indeed, it is now thought sufficiently injurious to have become firmly established as a social problem, as something requiring intervention and careful regulation. Indeed, in many contexts the only appropriate response is now considered to be an outright ban. This all represents quite a remarkable change in attitudes and behaviour. In the 1940s and '50s smoking was a popular, indeed almost ubiquitous activity, certainly for men. Just watch an old black and white movie. Almost every frame seems to include someone smoking. Fast forward to the present day and smoking is widely considered socially unacceptable and only a minority of people now consider themselves 'smokers'. Where once we were persuaded *to* smoke, now we have to be persuaded not to. Something that was not just an extraordinarily widespread and unproblematic activity, but was even considered fashionable, appears to have become largely deviant. Though dramatic, this change seems fairly straightforward to understand. As we said at the top, smoking is now known to be harmful, most obviously as a result of the identification of the risks of lung cancer, so the broad shape of what has happened in post-war Britain seems clear.

It is worth poking beneath the surface, however, to consider in a little more detail some of the matters we have already started to raise in this book. As we've suggested, among the questions social scientists tend to ask in this context is what enables specific forms of behaviour to become defined as sufficiently problematic to require intervention, and what forms of action are mobilised in support of intervention? What was involved in bringing about the significant shifts in our social routines and established practices? How and in what ways did 'smoking' become viewed as detrimental to our collective well-being? Although dog mess and smoking would ostensibly seem to have little in common, they are both areas in modern life that are now significantly more regulated and rule-bound than was once the case. In broad terms, they are both matters that have slowly been redefined, progressively coming to be seen as problematic. Both have seen gradually increasing state intervention, albeit, as we'll once again show, that governments often appeared reluctant to intrude.

In reality, so far as smoking is concerned the pace and nature of change was a little bumpier, less straightforward, and slower than one might think. The first impressive evidence of the links between lung cancer and smoking emerged in the early 1950s. Initially limits on smoking were left to voluntary agreements and it was several decades before governments intervened to any significant degree. Indeed, reform regularly proceeded in small, sometimes seemingly unconnected steps rather than giant strides, and it was a full half-century before widespread restrictions on smoking in public places were introduced. The very fact that the pace of reform was far from quick indicates the presence of competing interests, differing views and, no doubt, contrasting claims and assertions about the nature and impact of smoking. Indeed, as we will see, the scale of resistance to change has been substantial, not least and entirely predictably, from the tobacco industry which sought to limit reform at almost every stage.[1]

We should also note that although change has been profound there have also been quite distinct and identifiable limits to intervention. While we have seen some blanket bans on smoking introduced in recent times, most restrictions have tended to be partial and to contain exceptions. We remain some distance from treating tobacco like other banned substances such as cannabis (or, given the way things are changing in some countries, perhaps we ought to say we remain some distance from treating cannabis like tobacco?). It remains the case that about one in seven people smoke. This translates as roughly seven million smokers overall in the UK. Highly regulated it may be, but it is still some way from disappearing as an activity.

Smoking is good for you?

The mass market for cigarettes didn't really appear until the early twentieth century. Until at least the 1880s, cigarettes had been hand-made and were consequently very expensive. The mass manufacture of cigarettes changed the landscape and by the time of the First World War, cigarette smoking had become fairly widespread and had certainly overtaken pipe-smoking. The idea that it might be bad for the health was about as far from anyone's mind as it was possible to be. In late 1929, King George V became very ill. What appeared to have begun as a serious chest infection subsequently affected his lung. The problem spread quickly and within a relatively short time the monarch was suffering from septicaemia. Partly through good fortune it seems the King's physician was able to drain the abscess that was the original cause of the problem, enabling surgery on the lung to take place. Eventually leaving hospital in February 1930, George V went to Bognor to aid his recuperation (hence its subsequent transformation to Bognor *Regis*). The official statement from the Palace said: 'it has been realised by the King's medical advisers that, prior to the establishment of convalescence, there would arrive a time when sea air would be necessary in order to secure the continuation of His Majesty's progress'. How effective the sea air was is not known, though we do know that the same medical advisers allowed the King to start smoking again within four days.[2]

Though he may not have been thinking of Bognor, as the philosopher Bryan Magee observed of this period, the atmosphere 'was thick with cigarette smoke and I took it for granted in the way most people then did . . . There was something universal about smoking that is difficult to convey now'.[3] Like so many children at this time, for Magee it was perfectly usual to be sent out to buy cigarettes despite the fact that selling tobacco to children had been illegal since 1908. The picture cards that so often came with a packet of fags often made the trip to the newsagent a rewarding one. It was the Bristol company W. D. and H. O. Wills that first produced pictorial cards in Britain in the late 1890s. The 1920s and '30s were their highpoint, with one estimate suggesting that companies were printing as many as forty million copies of particular cards.[4] It was the paper shortages of the Second World War that effectively brought this trade to an end, by which point other forms of advertising and promotion were well-established.

A little over half a century ago advertising often carried what to modern sensibilities was the shocking message that smoking was good for you. At the turn of the twentieth century the French author Marcel Proust wrote to his mother to talk of his latest severe attack of asthma. By this point he had tried many treatments, including opium, caffeine and morphine, had had his nose cauterised (more than once) and was a devotee of smoke inhalation via anti-asthma cigarettes.[5] Though cigarettes as an asthma cure were declining in popularity they continued to be recommended at least up until the Second World War.[6] At this stage the perceived health benefits were more likely to be emphasised than any possible ill-effects. A wide variety of potentially beneficial consequences were claimed, often by members of the medical profession, happily linking their names and reputations, no doubt for a tidy sum, to the promotion of tobacco. It wasn't just medics. A widely reproduced advert from 1952 shows the famous Stoke City and England footballer Stanley Matthews with cigarette in hand, promoting Craven A, with its 'smooth, clean smoking', as 'the cigarette for me'. It should be noted that Matthews, thirty-seven years old at the time of that advert, was fit enough to carry on playing professionally until he was fifty. Crucially perhaps, he was a non-smoker. Craven A also had the racing driver Stirling Moss on their side. It was a brand he said that 'gives me all I want of a smoke – and nothing I don't!'.[7]

As is well established, not least by the market research at the time by Mark Abrams, the period from the late fifties saw the growing visibility of affluent young consumers.[8] It was also a time

Advertisement for Craven A cigarettes featuring Stanley Matthews
Source: https://wellcomecollection.org/works/u6a8gu39

when newly visible and distinctive youth cultures began to emerge and they, like female smokers, were predictable targets for the tobacco companies. Both World Wars offered a major stimulus to the cigarette market and estimates suggest that by 1949, 81 per cent of men and 39 per cent of women smoked tobacco. There was something of a dip as tax rises took effect, but in the fifties the overall percentage of people smoking increased as more women took up the habit.

Tobacco tokens

As one illustration of how unproblematically embedded smoking was in British culture in the immediate post-war years, it is worth considering the brief history of 'tobacco tokens'. In 1947, Labour's Chancellor of the Exchequer,

Hugh Dalton, faced with a range of fiscal problems, took the decision to increase taxation on tobacco by almost half. Though the measure would raise significant funds there were concerns about its impact, not least on the elderly poor. At a time when the state pension was relatively low, and smoking was widespread, the new tax was likely to hit the elderly the hardest. The government's solution was to introduce the so-called 'tobacco token', a certificate that could be applied for via the Post Office, which allowed the holder to buy tobacco at the pre-duty rise price.

Intriguingly it took over a decade for the subsidy to be repealed – a decade in which, thanks to the growing number of people smoking, the cost to government increased markedly. Some critics felt that non-smokers were missing out and should be similarly compensated. One parliamentary question in 1954 suggested it would only be fair if 'pensioners who are non-smokers should have some form of token which would entitle them to buy sweets or chocolates in place of the tobacco and cigarettes which pensioners who are smokers may obtain'. A similar question was put to Henry Brooke, financial secretary to the Treasury in 1955, asking if he was 'aware that not all old people – ladies especially – smoke, and that those who have a sweet tooth cannot afford to eat sweets at the present prices?' Although Brooke swept the question away the subsidy's time was almost up.

Though it took the decision to end it in late 1957, Macmillan's government had something of a fight on its hands. One critic described the repeal as a 'mean-spirited measure', as something the government ought to be ashamed to put before parliament, and as 'one of the worst examples of penny pinching from the poorest of the poor that we have seen for many a long day'. Hugh Dalton defended the subsidy he had originally introduced, describing it as having brought 'great comfort and satisfaction to literally millions of old people', and suggested that if pensions were increased over and above what was already proposed, in order to counteract the impact of the loss of the 'tobacco token', then the opposition to its removal would be lessened. After a stormy debate lasting almost three and half hours the government measure was eventually passed with a small majority and the 'tobacco token' finally came to an end.

In the period from the end of the First World War to the late sixties, smoking by women was generally presented positively and as being consistent with both femininity and refinement.[9] As women's social and economic roles changed, so the tobacco industry increasingly sought to exploit what it quickly spotted as a new market. As early as 1928, as the President of American Tobacco observed, 'It will be like opening a new gold mine right in our front yard.'[10] And in this the tobacco industry was remarkably successful. Rosemary Elliott in her oral history of female smoking said of the 1950s that her older interviewees tended to associate smoking with being fashionable, that there was a strong sense that 'everybody did it', and that the prevailing images in fashion magazines and films were central to promoting this. She quotes one respondent, born in 1933, saying, 'We were always at the pictures and you saw these glamorous female stars puffing away at cigarettes, with the long holders and everything, so it was quite fashionable.'

It was really only toward the end of the sixties that any cracks in the generally positive image of smoking began to appear.

Penny Tinkler, in her work on tobacco advertising and women's smoking, identifies a toothbrush advert that appeared in *Woman* magazine around 1970, which portrayed an unattractive and somewhat unkempt female smoker. Next to the image, under the heading, 'Give tobacco film the brush-off', the advert said, 'It's an unfortunate fact that smoking does nasty things to your mouth. Breath probably. Teeth certainly. Which is exactly where we can help you.' The toothbrush ad stood very much in contrast with the imagery that had been dominant through the post-war years despite the growing evidence of health-related problems.

Keep on puffing

In the 1940s, an increasing number of deaths were being attributed to lung cancer. Several potential causes were discussed with perhaps the main contender being atmospheric pollution. Those leading research on the subject, which began in 1947, were initially not at all convinced that smoking might be significant and Richard Doll, who would subsequently co-author the path-breaking paper on the subject, said had he put money on anything at the time, 'I should have put it on motor exhausts or possibly on the tarring of roads.'[11] Indeed, Doll went on, 'cigarette smoking was such a normal thing and had been for such a long time that it was difficult to think that it could be associated with any disease. Indeed, in the medical textbooks of the time the only effects of smoking that were described were tobacco amblyopia [marked by sight loss] – which is a disease that ophthalmologists now tell me doesn't occur, but which could have been produced by heavy pipe smoking in the presence of dietary deficiency – and tobacco angina: that is, angina precipitated by smoking which was so rare that individual cases were written up.'

Although the research wasn't published until 1950, both Richard Doll and his co-author, the famous epidemiologist Bradford Hill were quite convinced by early 1949 that they had found a strong association between lung cancer and cigarette smoking, and that there was little connection with the other factors they were interested in. When eventually published in the *British Medical Journal* their famous paper said, with great care not to overstate the case:

> ...it must be concluded that there is a real association between carcinoma of the lung and smoking ... The association ... seems to be specific to carcinoma of the lung. This is not necessarily to say that smoking causes carcinoma of the lung ... We therefore conclude that smoking is a factor, and an important factor, in the production of carcinoma of the lung.

BRITISH MEDICAL JOURNAL

LONDON SATURDAY SEPTEMBER 30 1950

SMOKING AND CARCINOMA OF THE LUNG
PRELIMINARY REPORT
BY

RICHARD DOLL, M.D., M.R.C.P.
Member of the Statistical Research Unit of the Medical Research Council

AND

A. BRADFORD HILL, Ph.D., D.Sc.
Professor of Medical Statistics, London School of Hygiene and Tropical Medicine; Honorary Director of the Statistical Research Unit of the Medical Research Council

Arriving in Britain from Trinidad in 1950, the year Doll and Bradford Hill's research was published, V. S. Naipaul, who would later go on to win the Nobel Prize for Literature, wrote home saying, 'Could you send me a carton of cigarettes? ... Everyone here smokes and everyone offers you, and I have fallen back into the habit'.[12] Naipaul's experience gave some sense of the scale of the challenge. Indeed, although Doll, who at one stage had smoked twenty a day, gave up as soon as the results of his research became clear, his co-author, Bradford Hill, was somewhat slower, only giving up his pipe in 1954. Intriguingly, however, he continued to keep a full cigarette box in his office. When asked by another academic why he continued to do this given the implications of his work, he was apparently horrified, saying: 'But it would be ill-mannered not to offer visitors a cigarette'.[13]

Behind the scenes there continued to be some controversy, some of which hinged on the nature of the association between smoking and lung cancer and, more particularly, the seeming inability to show a direct causal link between the two. Following on from their original research, Doll and Bradford Hill began an important longitudinal study of doctors' health which followed them for several decades. The first analysis from the study, in 1954, showed that cancer of the lung was more common when more tobacco was smoked, but officials remained reluctant to draw firm conclusions. In 1954, the minister of health, Iain Macleod, acknowledged that 'the statistical evidence points to smoking as a factor in lung cancer, but I would draw attention to the fact that there is so far no firm evidence of the way in which smoking may cause lung cancer or of the extent to which it does so.' Accordingly, the government was to put its weight behind the importance of further research. We ought to note that Macleod was hardly the best messenger, being a sixty-a-day man who chain-smoked all the way through the press conference after his statement in the House (most of the journalists in the audience smoked too). At this stage the income from tobacco was also a serious consideration for government, accounting for approximately 16 per cent of central revenue at the beginning of the decade, and there was a clear desire not to do anything too hasty. As Macleod said in a note to the Treasury prior to his Commons statement: 'we all know that the Welfare State and much else is based on tobacco smoking'.[14]

In 1956, Doll and Bradford Hill published further findings in the *British Medical Journal*. This showed that, among doctors, mortality rates were nearly 19 per 1,000 for men who smoked 25 g. or more of tobacco a day, compared with 14.5 for moderate smokers and just over 13 for non-smokers. Still government remained unmoved. In response to a Treasury inquiry, the permanent secretary at the Ministry of Health said that he thought 'the best policy is to keep the subject as quiet as we are allowed to'. Macleod, in response to a parliamentary query about a series of new reports, especially from America, said, 'If my hon. Friend is a heavy smoker and concerned about the connection between cancer of the lung and smoking, I would recommend him to give up reading'.[15]

With a growing number of negative stories around it was agreed that Robin Turton, now minister of health in Macmillan's cabinet, would make a reassuring statement in parliament. Even then Macmillan wanted it delayed, recording in his diary that 'If people really think they will get cancer of the lung from smoking it's the end of the Budget!'[16] After some back and forth a statement was finally agreed by cabinet, prompting Macmillan to note that this 'was a much better draft than the original one. I only hope it won't stop people smoking!'[17] When Turton eventually made his statement, it was said that he continued in largely the same mode as his predecessor, Iain Macleod, acknowledging the likelihood of a link between smoking and lung cancer, while showing 'a disinclination either to stop smoking himself or to wage a public information campaign'.[18]

In May 1956, Rab Butler, the Lord Privy Seal, outlined the government's thinking on smoking and the possibility of formal intervention. In the Commons he said: 'From the point of view of social hygiene, cancer of the lung is not a disease like tuberculosis; nor should the government assume too lightly the odium of advising the general public on their personal tastes and habits where the evidence of the harm which may result is not conclusive.' In effect, given the absence of overwhelming evidence of a causal link between smoking and cancer it was felt better to treat the issue as one of individual choice. It seemed many doctors agreed, and it was only with some reluctance, and no little dissent, that around this time the British Medical Association took a decision that there should be a one-day smoking ban during its annual conference.[19]

Despite further strong research evidence from the Medical Research Council published in 1957, many remained reluctant to intervene. The influence of the industry remained strong, in part through its continued funding of the scientific community, and tax revenues from tobacco were still sizeable. There were loud voices in the media also, not least Chapman Pincher in the *Daily Express* warning against 'interfering' medics, and even the *Manchester Guardian* suggesting that legislation to restrict smoking would 'run counter to British susceptibilities' not least because there was 'no evidence that smokers harm anybody but themselves'. This, as we will see, was to prove an important argument. Consequently, 'an act forbidding smoking in public places would have no more moral validity than one prohibiting it altogether'.[20]

Humbug: smoking, education and advertising

In 1950, the year that Doll and Bradford Hill's initial research was published, 62 per cent of men and 38 per cent of women smoked cigarettes. A decade later, after further research reinforcing the carcinogenic consequences of smoking had been accepted by government, the proportion of men smoking was almost identical at 61 per cent, while women's smoking had increased, with 42 per cent now smoking cigarettes.[21] A similar pattern would continue through the sixties: a small drop in the proportion of men smoking and a continuing slight increase in smoking among women. Governments continued to be unwilling to intervene directly, preferring voluntary agreements with the industry, and looking to improvements in smoking-related education and restrictions in advertising as the best way forward.

In the early sixties, George Godber, the chief medical officer, sought a plan to offset the influence of tobacco companies and played a vital role in pressing the Royal College of Physicians (RCP) to investigate the relationship between tobacco and lung cancer. In early 1962 – Ash Wednesday as it happens – the RCP's first report, *Smoking and Health*, was published. Having noted the continuing high levels of smoking that existed, it argued that 'there can be no doubt of our responsibility for protecting future generations from developing the dependence on cigarette smoking that is so widespread today'. It reviewed the evidence from a huge number of studies, showed that Britain had the highest death rate in the world for lung cancer, and concluded that smoking was also linked to the development of chronic bronchitis and coronary thrombosis. The RCP made seven main recommendations: greater public education in relation to the risks; increased restriction on the sale to children; restrictions on advertising and on smoking in public places; substantial increases in taxation on tobacco products; provision of information on tar and nicotine contents; and the development of anti-smoking clinics. Illustrating the degree of interest in the subject, the report sold ten thousand copies within days. The media reaction, though mixed, was more positive than it had been five years earlier when the MRC report was released. The *Guardian* was supportive calling the case 'overwhelming', whereas *The Times* felt that for those who smoked moderately the 'hazard is not of an order that seems to call for intervention'. Similarly, the *Daily Express* felt that those who wanted to smoke would no doubt continue to do so and that 'the vast majority of them, being reasonable in their use of cigarettes, will live long and healthy lives'.[22] Within government there remained considerable scepticism. Responding to a discussion about campaigns against smoking, the cabinet secretary, Norman Brook, asked disbelievingly: 'Does this mean that Prime Ministers should not smoke – or at least should not be seen smoking in public?' In fact, Harold Wilson, who was to enter No. 10 just a few years later, would prove to be one of the last Premiers to be seen smoking publicly.

Not everyone was convinced of the value of health education. The Health Minister, Enoch Powell, was deeply sceptical, and felt that in the context of failing to take more dramatic action such as increasing taxes on tobacco products, it was 'humbug' to continue to promote such approaches. The extensive efforts that had already been made hadn't produced 'the slightest effect' he felt. Similarly, though the Independent Television Authority did do some tightening up, 'including insisting that smoking must no longer be connected with social success, manliness or romance', Powell also felt that restricting advertising would not 'make any difference one way or the other'.[23]

The government continued with campaigns against cigarette smoking, piloting one in Edinburgh as early as 1959, with others coming later in Dunfermline (1964) and Clydebank (1965).

There were exhibitions, talks by doctors and former smokers, and handouts showing a summary of the first RCP report. Smokers were encouraged to enrol in 'curative courses'. Local organisations generally showed little interest and evaluation studies found hardly any change in smoking habits. 'These are somewhat depressing conclusions,' wrote the authors of *The Clydebank Anti-smoking Campaign*. 'In particular, one is discouraged by the growing gap between intellectual awareness and personal decision.' The authors concluded that it needed the mass media to hammer the point home. Gradually, the anti-smoking message gained greater airtime: both *Woman's Hour* on radio and a *Panorama* television special dedicated programmes to the problem, and there were a number anti-smoking films made such as *Smoking and You* (1963), *The Smoking Machine* (1964) and *Dying for a Smoke* (1967). Looking back on the period, Richard Doll said he had long recognised the importance that the media would play:

> Until the press and the radio and television became convinced of the relationship there really wasn't much hope of getting the message through to the general population. You could get through to scientists and to doctors with your publications, but not to the general public, if every time you had published a report that cigarette smoking caused disease X, the media reported that the issue was controversial and that somebody else believed that the disease was caused by something else. That continued to be the position for at least 15 years after 1950. So how could you expect the ordinary person to take the matter seriously? 'These scientists', they would say, 'They can't agree amongst themselves.' So, I never thought the public would take the matter seriously until we had a change of heart

by the leading figures in the press and broadcasting. This occurred in the early 1970s and was quickly followed by a big change in the attitude of the public.[24]

Looking back, some of the attempts at anti-smoking propaganda in this period are frankly comical. Virginia Berridge, the foremost historian in this field, tells of a record released by Transatlantic Records entitled 'No Smoking', formally described as 'A Scottish psychologist outlines colloquially and effectively the dangers of smoking'. Understandably, there is no sign that it troubled the charts. A further attempt at harnessing popular culture involved a series of leaflets supported by the singers Cliff Richard and Frankie Vaughan which sought to promote an anti-smoking message. It didn't impress everyone, however, the Education Committee in Devon for example taking great exception to its 'beatnik language':

> Always puffin' a fag – squares,
> Never stuffin' the habit – squares,
> Drop it, doll, be smart, be sharp!
> Cool cats wise,
> And cats remain,
> Non-smokers, doll, in this
> campaign.[25]

As evidence continued to mount, and increasing emphasis was placed on media campaigning, education and publicity in promulgating the anti-smoking effort, smoking rates remained stubbornly high.[26] By the late sixties, with nearly two decades of the longitudinal study of doctors completed, and with Richard Peto now Doll's main research collaborator, it was clear that the mortality rate of cigarette smokers was twice that of non-smokers of a comparable age. Indeed, doctors became the first social group in Britain to give up smoking in large numbers – the proportion smoking declined from two-thirds to one third during the sixties[27] (while the national figure dropped to just over half the population).

One of the more sizeable hurdles against greater government action was found in the formidable figure of Burke Trend, the cabinet secretary. As health secretary in 1965, Labour's Kenneth Robinson was one who was keen to pursue anti-smoking measures. Trend was not at all enthusiastic, and counselled against the paternalism implied in such action:

> ... on what grounds are the Government justified in intervening in those cases where a man's personal habits may damage only himself? And, if we accept that the Government are entitled to intervene in such cases, does this argument apply only to a man's physical habits, or does it extend also to his mental habits – i.e. to what he reads, or watches on television? In short, where does the argument, if logically pursued, stop?

Indeed, political resistance remained strong in some quarters all the way to the end of the decade. Virginia Berridge reports an incident in 1968 where a draft Bill to outlaw cigarette coupons was put before the Cabinet Home Affairs Committee. Despite considerable support from some members, Richard Crossman, who was still a significant force in the Labour Party, used all his experience to block a move he felt the government 'couldn't afford to pass when we were running up to an election'. As it turned out, Crossman found he was 'still just powerful enough to hold the thing up and finally I suggested that instead of forbidding coupons we should ration the amount of money to be spent on advertising and leave it to the cigarette manufacturers to decide how they should spend their money. I found this infinitely preferable. Harmony achieved.'[28] Precisely perhaps why seven years earlier Enoch Powell said he felt such tinkering was 'humbug'.

The end of the beginning[29]

The seventies were to prove to be an important decade. Scientific evidence of the harms of smoking was now stacking up, and would be added to, an anti-smoking lobby had come into being and was to prove increasingly effective and, slowly, political calculations began to change. Politicians on both sides of the House, from Tories such as Keith Joseph, to Labour ministers Denis Healey and Dr David Owen, began to argue that taking action against smoking wasn't necessarily the electoral risk it had widely been perceived to be in the sixties.

In 1971, the second RCP report, *Smoking and Health Now*, was published. Government action focused on three main areas: advertising and sponsorship; warnings on cigarette packets; and attempts to begin experimenting with products which would lessen the harms involved in smoking. Voluntary agreements and informal agreements remained the order of the day, including in relation to tobacco advertising – despite having commissioned research which showed that a majority of the public would have supported legislation banning such marketing. Some significant change was achieved in 1971 when, seven years after the first parliamentary attempt, agreement was reached that henceforward all packs of cigarettes would carry a health warning: 'Warning by HM Government: Smoking can damage your health'.

The Health Education Council, formed in the late sixties, had become involved in a major anti-smoking advertising campaign and by 1972–73 close to three-quarters of a million pounds was being spent annually on press advertising and TV campaigns. The Saatchi brothers, who were to play such a significant role in Margaret Thatcher's electoral success in 1979, got their first major break via the Health Education Council somewhat earlier in the decade. Saatchi & Saatchi's new-style advertisements both helped make the agency's name and signalled something of a change of approach to anti-smoking campaigning. One early ad featured a picture of a hand with tar-stained fingers, with the caption 'You can't scrub your lungs clean'. Another featured a chest x-ray with the caption 'Why learn the truth about lung cancer the hard way?' One had a quizmaster promising 'If you smoke forty cigarettes a day you, yes you, could win a case of chronic bronchitis'. For the first time women were the target. One especially hard-hitting ad showed a tiny baby in an incubator, the strapline saying, 'Poor thing. It's so weak because the mother smoked during pregnancy'. Famously, in 1973, they used a picture of naked, pregnant woman smoking, under the heading 'Is it fair to force your baby to smoke cigarettes?' Increasingly film was being used also. One Saatchi & Saatchi advert showed smokers crossing Waterloo Bridge, London, interspersed with a film of lemmings jumping into the sea, with a voice-over saying, 'There's a strange Arctic rodent called a lemming which every year throws itself off a cliff. It's as though it wanted to die. Every year in Britain thousands of men and women smoke cigarettes. It's as though they want to die.'

Around the same time the pressure group Action on Smoking and Health (ASH) was formed and took up the anti-smoking cause with brio. Its council was initially dominated by medical professionals, but with media input also. Indeed, its media-savvy approach was important to its success. In many ways ASH was in an odd position. Its initial funding from government was intended as pump-priming but, in the event, it continued to rely on central financial support for many years. Much of its job, however, beyond public campaigning was to put pressure on government. Generally speaking, ASH was also unremittingly hostile toward the tobacco industry and over the course of the seventies helped shift general policy in the field away from the harm reduction approaches which focused on safer smoking toward outright abstentionism. Again, the evidence of the slow pace of change contributed to this more forceful position.

Looking back over developments in the second half of the seventies, Mike Daube, who had been Director of ASH before taking up a university position, contrasted the magnificence of the Labour government's rhetoric with its more general practical failure. He described Labour's minister of health, Dr David Owen, as someone who appeared 'determined to face up to the smoking problem, but the image bore as much relation to reality as the glossier cigarette ads to the consequences of smoking'.[30] Even when the Labour government had planned what it felt was significant action things went wrong. In March 1976, Owen was due to front up a major announcement with the launch of a consultative document, *Prevention and Health: Everybody's business*. A day had been carefully selected when there was little else of consequence occurring, maximising the chances of headline coverage. Interviews had been pre-recorded and the stage was set. Unbeknown to anyone else in government, that was the morning that that well-known smoker Harold Wilson announced his intention to resign as prime minister, thereby gazumping all other domestic news. The decade ended with 54 per cent of men still smoking cigarettes and 44 per cent of women, up two percentage points from 1970.

Passive smoking

Mike Daube, in his analysis of policy failures in the seventies, reserved some of his most biting criticism for the medical profession. Indeed, he thought that 'those politicians who press for action on smoking could be forgiven for wondering whether, in view of the lack of support given them by doctors, the problem was indeed as great' as many were suggesting. Matters slowly began to change in the eighties. At the very beginning of the decade the *British Medical Journal* (*BMJ*) published a strong editorial describing smoking-related deaths as a holocaust aided by government. Four years later another *BMJ* campaign asked doctors to commemorate smoking-related deaths by sending black-edged postcards to local MPs. Nevertheless, voluntary agreements with the tobacco industry aimed at harm reduction continued to dominate. Alongside them educational initiatives, which used mass media to publicise messages about the harms of smoking, remained at the heart of policy.

The major hurdle holding back greater intervention was the sense that smokers were only harming themselves; that however bad their habit there was no especial social cost to what they were doing. In short, a broadly utilitarian belief held sway, one based on the idea that the state should only restrict the rights of citizens in order to prevent harm to others. It was precisely the power of this argument that helped hold back the tide of reform until the later decades of the century but then, in turn, formed the basis for a radical change of direction when evidence of just such harm began to emerge.

In the 1980s research began to show the impact of what would eventually become known as 'passive smoking'. *The Times* newspaper had first mentioned 'passive smoking' in an article in August 1973. It was reporting on findings that had been published in *New Scientist* showing that non-smokers working with heavy smokers appeared to have twice the risk of lung cancer, heart disorders, lung problems or stomach disorders. Further pieces appeared throughout the decade, and in 1981 several papers were published in the *British Medical Journal* showing that the non-smoking wives of men who smoked had significantly increased rates of lung cancer. Thirty years earlier Doll and Bradford Hill had reported that two of 649 men and nineteen of sixty women in their research sample had contracted carcinoma of the lung despite being non-smokers. By the time of the Royal College of Physicians fourth report, *Health or Smoking*, in 1983, what was variously referred to as 'environmental tobacco smoke', 'involuntary' or 'passive smoking' was increasingly on the agenda. Even then, however, it was still more often considered a nuisance rather than a danger: 'Smoking was an irritant to the eyes, the pharynx, and, not least, the psyche of non-smokers.' In 1986, the Health Education Council urged non-smokers to ask for restricted smoking areas at work, and Richard Doll put the increased risk of lung cancer from passive smoking as something between 10 and 30 per cent.

In 1988, a report from the Independent Scientific Committee on Smoking and Health, led by Sir Peter Froggatt, suggested that several hundreds of non-smokers each year in Britain died as a result of environmental tobacco smoke, and that this was a particular risk in enclosed spaces with poor ventilation. By the end of the decade, Froggatt was describing smoking cigarettes as 'arguably the greatest public health hazard in developed countries and may become so in much of the developing world'.[31] Domestically, the problems of passive smoking gained more attention when the popular entertainer Roy Castle was diagnosed with lung cancer. It was thought that Castle, a non-smoker, had most likely contracted his illness as a consequence of playing the trumpet in smoky jazz clubs. He died in 1992 at the age of sixty-two, his name commemorated in the Roy Castle Lung Cancer Foundation.

At around this time the language of 'rights' also became more prominent in debates around smoking and included, increasingly, the rights of the non-smoker. Once it could be established that smoking was not simply a matter of personal choice but something that affected others, and not just as a nuisance, the nature of the policy debate quite quickly changed – and changed in two ways. First, as Jason Hughes notes, it had the effect of inverting arguments about freedom. Where previously the emphasis might have been on people asserting their rights to smoke, now the suggestion became that others were having their right not to smoke denied them.[32] Second, arguments about *individual* freedom were overtaken by what was increasingly viewed as a collective problem, a generalised social problem, rather than something confined to particular segments of the population. A similar shift was seen in relation to policy in relation to AIDS on both sides of the Atlantic, and indeed globally. Initially, the association of the disease with homosexuality and intravenous drug use led much public debate to be framed in terms of culpability and blame, with the suffering of victims often viewed as, or implied to be, the product of their behavioural and moral failings. The identification of 'innocent victims' – most obviously children and those receiving blood via transfusions – led to a step-change in governmental concern, even if it did little to challenge the moralising language surrounding HIV/ AIDS. Rather in parallel, passive smokers were now increasingly the 'innocent victims' of tobacco smoke.

Importantly, alongside the changing scientific landscape, the social patterning of smoking was also shifting. There had been quite a marked decline in smoking by men in the seventies, and this carried on into the eighties, and increasingly included women also, such that prevalence had dropped to 35 per cent for both by 1983. Importantly, within this there were distinctive trends according to social class: middle-class people were giving up far more quickly than working-class smokers. In some respects, it was suggested that this made it more straightforward to treat it as a deviant or marginalised activity, being 'easier to mount a more consistent attack on the existence of a habit associated primarily with women and the poor'.[33] Prior to 1983, there had barely been any recognition of women smokers, and it was the RCP's report, *Smoking and Health*, that was first to devote a section to the impact of smoking on women's health. Indeed, it began the section by noting that 'the recognition that smoking in women is an important issue is perhaps one of the major developments in smoking research over the last decade'.

The eighties might arguably be thought of as the 'tipping point' where the regulation of smoking was concerned.[34] For over thirty years, ever since the original research linking smoking with lung cancer was published, activity had been undertaken either to encourage limits on smoking, or even to restrict it. The pace of change was slow, however, and many of the restrictions very limited. Although it took a long time, smoking rates eventually began to decline. Though it was still two decades away, much more radical change was beginning to be considered, and it was the identification of 'passive smoking' that enabled it. As we will also see in relation to alcohol in the next chapter, the expansion of regulation was linked to a repositioning or reconceptualisation of 'health' – focusing not simply on individual ill-health but, increasingly, encompassing the population as a whole as a result of their *potential* for ill-health.

Research showing smoking's negative impact on non-smokers was crucial in increasing the perceived acceptability of arguments for place-based bans. In its 1988 report the Scientific Committee noted that in addition to the problems relating to lung cancer, it had also found 'evidence that passive smoking is a cause of . . . heart disease and cot death, middle ear disease and asthmatic attacks in children'. It went on to conclude that 'Restrictions on smoking in public places and workplaces are necessary to protect non-smokers'. The 'discovery' of passive smoking led to an intensification of efforts to restrict smoking by place and late in the decade there was a series of legal claims against employers which focused on the long-term impact of workplace smoking. Nevertheless, for a while, and continuing the long-term trend, the approach to control remained generally voluntaristic. Over the course of the nineties this would slowly begin to change as the idea of radical government intervention slowly gained ground, with the industry increasingly powerless to restrict it. As Sarah Milov notes of the parallel changes that took place in America: 'Ironically, it was on the issue of second-hand smoke – an issue where actual uncertainty existed, where scientists of good faith disagreed on the magnitude of risk if not on the existence of risk itself – that the tobacco industry was unable to stem the regulatory tide.'[35]

You can't smoke here

We now live in a country where smoking is banned in a large number of areas: workplaces, pubs, clubs and restaurants, indeed most anywhere apart from private homes and public open spaces (though it may be restricted in the latter too). Much of this is a recent development, stemming from provisions contained in the Health Act 2006, most of which came into force in 2007. We'll discuss the lead up to, and nature of, this law later but, for now, it's worth looking in a little more detail at the rather lengthier history of smoking bans in different places. Again, they illustrate the generally slow pace, and often piecemeal nature of change.

Theatres were among the first settings for experimentation with 'no smoking' policies. As early as the fifties some British theatre administrators introduced smoking restrictions along the lines that had already been applied in countries such as Canada and the United States. When Sam Wanamaker, later famous for the restoration of the Globe Theatre in London, became the director of the New Shakespeare Theatre, Liverpool, in 1957, he decided that a ban on smoking was needed. The extent of the smoke was preventing some in the audience seeing the stage properly and the voices of actors and singers were being affected. Also, Wanamaker didn't want someone in the stalls lighting up a match and exposing the scene shifters during what was supposed to be a blackout. Wanamaker left after a memorable fifteen months of success and, though the theatre struggled on for a few years, it closed in the sixties and, ironically, was destroyed by fire in the seventies. When workplace smoking was eventually banned, the stage was one of the exceptions included in the law, allowing actors to continue to do so as long as it was required for the artistic integrity of the production, and subject to the agreement of the licensing authority.

As early as 1951, the House of Commons had held a short debate about the dangers of smoking in cinemas and theatres. Although the MP introducing the debate (Miss Burton, Labour, Coventry South) raised issues of fire hazard and discomfort, she quickly retreated from the discomfort question, recognising how unpopular any attempt to ban smoking was likely to be. The official Home Office position was that so far as fire hazards were concerned, these were already dealt with under the home secretary's regulations which prohibited smoking in projection rooms and in places in a cinema where films were handled. It was possible for smoking to be banned in the auditorium, but this would be left to local licensing authorities. As things stood, none had taken such action.

Cinemas were generally somewhat slower than theatres to restrict and then ban smoking. As early as 1964, somewhere around the release of *Mary Poppins* and *A Fistful of Dollars*, London County Council voted seventy-seven to thirty-seven to ban smoking in its 154 cinemas. Fearing the consequences for audience numbers, cinema managers refused to co-operate and the two groups compromised by limiting cigarette smoking to one deck. Who would enforce it, the usherettes, the managers or the customers? Where there was only level of seating, cinemas gradually began to experiment by making a certain number of rows, usually at the front of the auditorium, smoking rows. With television advertising restricted from the mid-sixties, the cinema became one of the ways in which cigarettes could still be promoted and, indeed, it would be 1986 before tobacco advertising in cinemas was banned. Product placement became a core strategy by this time: a tobacco company paid $43,000 (£20,000) for twenty-two appearances of Marlboro cigarettes in *Superman II* (1980), including having Lois Lane represented as a chain smoker; and Sylvester Stallone was allegedly paid $500,000 (£330,000) to use Brown and Williamson tobacco products in five feature films in the eighties. A study of the 250 most popular films of the nineties showed that 87 per cent contained tobacco use. Indeed, the films of 1995 featured four times as much smoking as those of five years earlier. One company (R. J. Reynolds) allegedly provided actors with free cigarettes on a monthly basis as part of their campaign to ensure widespread usage.[36] Tobacco placement deals declined substantially after formal agreement in 1998, though alcohol products continued to be limited only by voluntary arrangement. By that time smoking was banned in most cinemas: Rank Leisure was the first major chain to provide smoke-free cinemas in 1986, and in 1987 Cannon-ABC followed suit.

Public transport was among the first locations to provide no-smoking areas, then, as smoking declined, small smoking areas and, eventually, complete bans. Again, the timetables taken to do this varied, change was often quite slow, and the processes involved often complex. When restrictions began on buses, for example, it became traditional for the upper deck to be reserved for smoking and the lower to be smoke free. London's single-decker buses became entirely non-smoking in 1971, but it was 1985 before a ban on smoking in the front half of the upper deck was introduced on double-deckers. With sizeable drops in smoking in this period, a range of cities – from Belfast, Aberdeen and Plymouth to Darlington and Cardiff – banned smoking on their bus fleets in the eighties. London buses restricted smoking to the back of the upper deck of double-deckers and made all buses smoke free in 1991. The coach company National Express eventually outlawed on-board smoking in 1992.

To be entirely historically accurate one would have to acknowledge that when the London Underground first opened in the nineteenth century smoking was not permitted. Pressure to change the policy grew and eventually the ban was removed in the 1870s. By the 1930s there were vending machines on tube station platforms to enable sales direct to passengers. Restrictions on smoking on the London underground began as early as May 1971 when a substantial number of 'no smoking' carriages were introduced by London Transport. As is so often the case it was scandal that eventually led to change. In the early eighties, after a fire at Goodge Street station, there was a call for an immediate smoking ban on underground trains. London Underground subsequently introduced a trial ban after a fire at Oxford Circus station in July 1984, thought to have been caused by a cigarette, and that ban became permanent the following December. But the ban only included smoking within the trains themselves and smokers would often light up and discard matches on the escalators as they prepared to leave the station. There were forty-six escalator fires between 1956 and 1988 and in thirty-two cases the cause was attributed to smokers' materials. Sadly, as will be well known to many, the eventual outcome was a major disaster at King's Cross Station in 1987 in which thirty-one people lost their lives in a fire which began underneath an escalator. Poor maintenance at King's Cross also contributed to the disaster – rubbish had collected in the gaps between the treads and skirting board, fire cleats were missing and escalator running tracks poorly maintained – and the station had a history of minor fires. It was this tragedy that finally brought smoking in underground stations to an end. Similar decisions were taken elsewhere in the country around the same time. The Tyne & Wear Metro, which opened in 1980, banned smoking from the outset, and was one of the first bans of its type.

Overground rail would take a little longer than its underground equivalent to finally come around to banning smoking. During the seventies and eighties British Rail increased the proportion of non-smoking carriages in trains in line with the percentage of non-smokers: sixty–forty in favour of non-smokers in the late-seventies and seventy–thirty by the mid-eighties. In 1981, buffets and restaurant cars were made 'no smoking'. British Rail phased out smoking carriages on commuter trains to London in May 1990, though some others still had smoking carriages. It was the mid-nineties before total bans emerged in any number. There were protests but, by and large, compliance levels were high. On the first day of 'no smoking' on Network South East trains, in May 1993, over thirty members of Passengers United For Freedom to Smoke (PUFFS) protested by smoking on the 7.25 a.m. train from Clacton-on-Sea to Liverpool Street. One pro-smoker, Peter Boddington, described as 'a sixty-a-day market trader who sells cut price cigarettes', sought to challenge the ban having originally been fined £10 for smoking on a non-smoking train between his home in Brighton and London. After two years his case eventually reached the House of Lords where the judgement found in favour of the train company, Connex South Central. The rider, according to news reports, was that Boddington now travelled 'home on trains operated by Virgin where he is allowed to puff away'.[37] In 2005, the last big English train operator to allow some smoking, GNER, joined the rest in a blanket smoking ban.

With aeroplanes it was a case of 'smoke gets in your aisles'. In the sixties pipes and cigars were banned on aeroplanes, and in 1969, Finnair began providing non-smoking accommodation.

Two years later, BOAC allocated some 'non-smoking' seats after a survey had shown that a third of the airline's passengers liked the idea. Air-conditioning arguably helped contribute to smoking continuing on long-haul flights for as long as it did. In 1985, a poll of members of the International Airline Passengers Association found that nearly three-fifths favoured a smoking ban on short flights and one half supported bans on long flights. Air UK banned smoking on routes to the Channel Islands in 1987, and then on all flights the following year. British Airways had a 'no smoking' policy for domestic flights from 1988 but not on international flights. When the Canadian government announced plans to ban smoking on international, as well as domestic flights, in 1989, it was considered to be too much for the passengers to take in one step, and it was forced to back down and to phase in the plan over a period of four years.

Again, it was the influence of research evidence on passive smoking that pushed the World Health Organization and the British Medical Association to call for a smoking ban on all passenger flights in 1990. In 1993, British Airways made some long-haul flights 'no smoking' on a trial basis and extended it to all long-haul flights and European flights early the following year. It took an agreement between competing airlines before a smoking ban was introduced on intercontinental flights in 1995 (and then only for flights lasting up to six hours). The secretary general of the Federation of Tour Operators said that the move had come to fruition after four years' work and had been driven by pressure from passengers. 'There are more anti-smokers than there are smokers and it was clear more airlines were gradually banning it,' he said. 'We accepted that there were a lot more people who didn't like travelling with people who are smoking, and you can't separate people as you can on a train.' Though the majority of flights were smoking-free by 1996, as late as 2002 a number of airlines, including Aeroflot, Iberia and Garuda, still allowed smoking on some journeys.

Given the commercial interests involved, it is perhaps of little surprise that it took so long for smoking bans to be implemented on planes, trains and buses. The link between health risks and tobacco, however, made the continuation of smoking within and around hospitals simultaneously one of the strangest and most powerful illustrations of just how entrenched an activity it was and how tortuous and lengthy a process the banning of it has been. A good decade or a decade and half after Doll and Bradford Hill's pioneering research, cigarettes continued to be offered on sale inside hospitals and patients were still allowed to smoke while on the ward. The banning of smoking in the chest and heart wings of the Central Middlesex Hospital in the early fifties had been extremely newsworthy, and news was made again when twelve hospitals in South and West Dorset banned fags in 1964 (though they made an exception for old people's wards, private patients and those in single-bed rooms). In the early seventies it was still possible to see some patients smoking on wards, nurses puffing in ward kitchens, and mothers holding a fag while nursing a new-born baby. Of course, new fathers lighting up a cigar had long been something of a trope. In 1976, nearly three-quarters of hospital shops and half of ward trolleys still offered cigarettes for sale. The Department of Health encouraged the introduction of smoking policies, and the Central Middlesex was the first to do so, in 1978. Gradually the expectations changed and progressively patients' smoking was contained in day rooms or moved outside hospital buildings, though it remained possible well into the new century to see a patient in a dressing-gown holding a drip while smoking near a hospital's front entrance.

Hospital shops only stopped selling tobacco in 1992. In 2013, the National Institute for Health and Care Excellence published guidance suggesting that all NHS hospitals and clinics should become completely smoke free, should provide help to all patients who smoke, including those receiving mental health treatment, to stop smoking whilst they receive care, and preferably help them to stop for good. By 2019, it was reported that although Public Health England had said that all NHS trusts should go smoke free, a third were yet to set a date. Similarly, a report in the *Health Services Journal* in late 2019 reported that research by ASH had found that although at least four-fifths of mental health trusts had introduced a smoke-free policy, the majority nevertheless reported various levels of non-compliance. The published NHS commitment was for all Trusts to have fully smoke-free sites by spring 2020.

On one level, less surprising than hospitals is the case of prisons. Prisons are often places of exception as we will see later on when we come to discuss the subject of toilets, and one therefore expects they may be an outlier. In this case, however, they were exceptional because prisoners were allowed to continue to have the right to smoke long after bans had been introduced elsewhere. In the fifties, prisoners were not allowed to smoke in court buildings before trials, but that rule was relaxed in 1960. Thereafter prisoners were allowed to smoke in interviews with solicitors and barristers, as long as they took the cigarettes from their representatives and finished them before the end of the interview. Within prisons themselves smoking had long been a central part of institutional culture, with a large proportion of prisoners smoking, and tobacco also being used as prison currency. Surveys tended to find that the proportion of prisoners that smoked was around three to four times that of the general population. A survey in 1997 found 85 per cent of male remand prisoners and 78 per cent of sentenced male prisoners smoked, with the respective figures for women being 83 per cent and 81 per cent. In effect, only one in five prisoners didn't smoke. As recently as 2014, a survey of smoking in six prisons across Kent, Surrey and Sussex still found smoking rates of between 60 and 80 per cent, and close on two-fifths of prisoners said that their smoking increased while they were inside.[38] Why was an exception made for prisons? Intriguingly, given our interests here, it was so as not to disturb order within prison. At least initially, the idea of banning smoking within prisons was considered a very considerable threat to institutional peace and, indeed, riots in a number of English prisons greeted the government announcement that it was planning to ban smoking.

Although the Isle of Man prison was rebuilt in 2008 as the first smoke-free prison in Europe, prisons generally remained places where smoking was tolerated. Exempt from the 2006 Health Act which banned smoking in a variety of settings, it is only much more recently that prisons have shifted to become smoke-free environments. The initial exemption allowed prisoners aged over eighteen years to smoke in a single cell or in a cell shared with other smokers, though staff smoking was prohibited within prison perimeter walls. Given the by now well-established dangers of passive smoking, in 2015 the Prison and Probation Service announced the pilot implementation of a smoke-free policy in four prisons in the South-West of England. It prohibited all staff members and prisoners from smoking tobacco and possessing tobacco or smoking paraphernalia (such as lighters and cigarette rolling paper) within the perimeter walls of the four prisons. A variety of forms of support had been put in place in prisons in a bid to reduce smoking in those institutions where it was still allowed, and in 2016 the government announced its plan to make all prisons smoke free. By early 2018, around half of public prisons had reached that point. In the remainder there was at least one wing that was smoke free, and the government indicated that all prisons, rather like hospitals, were on track to become smoking-free zones in 2020.

Time to act

By the turn of the new century the big challenge for those seeking further restrictions on smoking focused on workplaces on the one hand, and pubs, clubs and restaurants on the other. Where workplaces were concerned the response to growing pressure in the second half of the twentieth century had been somewhat fragmented. A small number of places had been smoke free for a long time but in many cases, such as the Brooke Bond Tea Company, this was more to do with the nature of the business itself than concern about employees. By the early eighties, when the link between passive smoking and health became more established, it was the previous decade's Health and Safety at Work Act, placing employers under an obligation (so far as was reasonably practicable) to ensure the health, safety and welfare of all their employees, which tended to form the basis for policies to reduce smoking. By the end of the decade around two-thirds of local authorities had banned smoking at full council meetings, and a quarter had done so for committee meetings only. In 1986, Birmingham City Council introduced a policy prohibiting smoking in all sports and leisure centres, libraries and public-reception facilities. A 'no smoking' policy was introduced to a Basingstoke company in January 1988 after the staff had been given three months' advance notice of the new policy. In a similar vein, in the same year Sheffield City Council drafted a no-smoking policy affecting all thirty-three thousand council workers. By 1992, 35 per cent of companies had a written policy on smoking and four years later it was 71 per cent. A survey of five hundred major companies in 1990 found 79 per cent to have non-smoking areas and 22 per cent to operate complete bans. By the end of the nineties it was esti-mated that around 40 per cent of the UK workforce was work-ing in a smoke-free environment.[39]

In some ways, workplace bans also fitted in with wider changes taking place in the ways in which worker productivity was considered and measured. As market-based models grew in popularity from the late seventies onward, and the new 'manage-ment sciences' took hold, the ways in which we as citizens were governed came increasingly to be assessed economically. Cost-benefit analysis became the order of the day, and this was applied to the workplace in numerous ways, including in assessing the impact of smoking. The 'costs' of smoking bans included poten-tially lost business from smokers and the financial impact of smoking breaks, whereas the potential benefits were identified as including reduced cleaning and maintenance costs, reduced insurance premiums, and increased productivity (as smoking declined and health improved). An American study by the Centers for Disease Control estimated that productivity losses and medical expenditures attributed to smoking amounted to well over $3,000 per year for each adult smoker.[40] Increasingly, efficiency arguments aligned with the public health case to re-inforce the rationale for workplace smoking bans.

The calculations were different where restaurants and pubs were concerned, and with so much of their trade seemingly reli-ant on smokers, change in that sector was much slower to come.

One entrepreneurial spirit opened a café in Leicester in 1960 with a 'no smoking' rule but found it hugely challenging to keep the business going in a culture where smoking was so widespread and where food and smoking often went together. While ASH was critical of the shortage of non-smoking areas in pubs and restaurants in 1984, by 1992 the British Hospitality Association found that over half of hotels no longer allowed smoking in their restaurants and a further 30 per cent had banned smoking in at least part. Interviewed in 1991 about his career, his views of smoking and of the development of government policy, Richard Doll was asked about what he thought about people lighting up in restaurants. Though one might reasonably have expected someone so close to the medical evidence on the harmfulness of smoking to be outspokenly critical, not a bit of it. Doll said he simply attempted to ignore it and following Bradford Hill's advice felt it better both to avoid becoming involved in public education or the emotions involved in debating the subject. Indeed, he said, 'I don't mind in the least if someone in the room lights up a cigarette – it's their decision and their life, not mine.' He did admit, however, that as smoking had become less wide-spread in recent years, he'd appreciated its absence, and was now 'beginning to get irritated if someone smokes in a restaurant, because I find it actually rather unpleasant'.[41]

In 1998, a White Paper called *Smoking Kills* had offered a detailed summary of the state of smoking. Its opening sentences were stark: 'In Britain today, more than 120,000 people are going to die over the next year from illnesses directly related to smoking. And the year after that, and the year after that. Unless we all do something.' It went on to note that at time when average life expectancy is seventy-five for men and nearly eighty for women those who smoke regularly and die of a smoking-related disease lose on average sixteen years from their life expectancy compared to non-smokers. In terms of action, it committed the government to ending all tobacco advertising by 2002 and all tobacco sponsorship by 2006.

Pubs felt like the frontline in the battle. The almost symbiotic link between drinking and smoking meant that pubs would have to change in character fundamentally if smoking were to be subject to significant restriction. Again, voluntary measures were initially introduced, via a UK hospitality industry Charter in 1999, which sought to mitigate the anticipated dangers faced by hostelries and restaurants by increasing the number of no-smoking areas and erecting signage to alert customers to smoking policies. It was what ASH described as simply the most recent in 'a long history of failed attempts at self-regulation' of smoking in pubs. Despite new targets for restricting smoking, a 2003 survey found that almost half of all pubs allowed smoking throughout, and less than 1 per cent had banned smoking entirely.[42]

The steady accumulation of local, place-based smoking bans meant that by the turn of the new century there was a complex patchwork of controls and practices in place. It was clear, however, that pressure was building toward something more dramatic. Public opinion was shifting, and a 1997 survey by Stephanie Freeth found that well over four-fifths of the public agreed there should be restrictions on smoking at work, in restaurants and in other public places such as banks and post offices.[43] A 2002 London Assembly report, *Smoking in Public Places*, concluded that while further research was necessary, there was now enough public concern for it to be necessary to make significant changes. While they fell short of calling for a ban on smoking in every public place, they suggested there needed to be greater protection of choice: 'Where there are not to be total bans, non-smoking areas must be introduced wher-ever possible.'[44] In his annual report published in 2003, the chief medical officer, Sir Liam Donaldson, said 'very serious consid-eration should be given to introducing a ban on smoking in public places soon'.

There was something of a split in the media. Specialist health correspondents tended to be sympathetic; the leader writers were less so. Later that year an alliance of the thirteen Royal Colleges of Medicine called for all workplaces to become smoking-free zones because in their view the voluntary codes weren't working. The same month eighteen key members of the Royal College of Physicians wrote a letter to *The Times* with the same request, and ASH called for smokers to stop smoking in front of children. About 85 per cent of Royal College of Nursing delegates voted for a total ban on smoking in public places, and 80 per cent of Britons supported a law that would make enclosed workplaces smoke free. In opposition, the Tobacco Manufacturers' Association and the pro-freedom of choice pressure group, FOREST, pointed out that most people wanted restrictions rather than complete bans – their classic responses were a 'right to smoke', 'smoking restrictions would reduce custom', and 'smoking bans are unenforceable' – but public opinion polls suggested that 93 per cent were in favour of a smoking ban in hospitals, 86 per cent for taxis, 85 per cent for restaurants, 66 per cent in pubs and bars, 65 per cent at bus and rail stations, and 41 per cent in prisons.

The pressure for change was growing and the big question, arguably, was how long government would continue to rely primarily on self-regulation and when it would eventually be forced to concede that legislation was necessary. The health secretary at the time, John Reid, formerly a heavy smoker, had only given up shortly before taking on the job, and was seen as something of a sceptic where the idea of a comprehensive ban was concerned. Indeed, according to fellow minister David Blunkett, Reid was far from alone in cabinet in being concerned about a potential ban on smoking. While government in Westminster continued to deliberate, others moved quickly. The Republic of Ireland introduced tough anti-smoking laws in 2004, including a total ban in all workplaces. Initial proposals for England and Wales included a smoking ban in workplaces but with some exceptions, including private members clubs and pubs that did not serve food. Some individual retailers – Pizza Hut in 2003 and J. D. Wetherspoon in 2005 – announced complete smoking bans, but resistance remained strong in many areas. The dragging of English feet prompted the Welsh Assembly to quickly make it clear that it would not be following suit and would amend the rules in Wales to ensure that all workplaces were included in the ban on smoking. In mid-2005 the Scottish Parliament voted by a large majority to introduce a smoking ban in public places from March 2006. Pressure on politicians in Westminster to act was growing, but the health secretary was still not easily persuaded.

The Scottish experience, with its generally high levels of compliance, was important. During the fifteen months after the ban in Scotland became operational, only one smoker and one business had been taken to court for failure to comply, and the relatively modest total of 175 individuals had been fined. The journalist Melanie Reid was very positive, saying that Scotland felt 'like a country that's been to a health farm and come back with a clear complexion, open tubes, and a spring in its step'. A year after the ban seven out of ten people in Scotland supported it and nearly eight out of ten believed it a success.

It was clear that it was only a matter of time south of the border. After a general election, the appointment of a new health secretary and a Select Committee inquiry, a draft Bill was published, though it still included exemptions for private members clubs and pubs that didn't serve food. It was clear, not least given what had occurred in the rest of Britain, that England was significantly out of step. Distancing itself slightly from radical action, government eventually allowed a free vote in parliament, and a total ban was carried with a large majority. The Labour government announced that the ban would come into force on 1 July 2007.

Vaping

Vaping has been on the agenda since the sixties when the first patent was received for something that resembled an electronic cigarette. There are disputes as to who first used the word 'vaping', some suggesting that, so far as print was concerned, it was the journalist Rob Stepney in 1983. On a wide range of occasions patents were filed for nicotine inhaler devices, and as concerns about passive smoking grew so the activity itself spread. Really, it was only in the twenty-first century that tobacco companies became excited by electronic-cigarette products.

The first commercially successful e-cigarette came on the market in 2003 in China and such products have been sold in Europe since at least 2006. E-cigarettes have gone through a number of stages of development. The earliest were known as 'cigalikes' and resembled conventional cigarettes. They had a small disposable battery (occasionally rechargeable) and a cartridge with nicotine liquid in it. These were later superseded by 'second generation' models that are significantly bigger, have a more powerful battery and a refillable tank. More modern types still have even greater capacity and generally more than one power setting. Though smoking cessation is cited as a primary motivation, as one group of researchers have noted, 'the subculture is dominated by hobbyist vapers, usually male, who design, build and collect different devices and mix their own juices'.

A range of concerns have been raised in relation to vaping, not least that it might act as a 'gateway' by renormalising smoking or by introducing non-smokers to nicotine. Early on there had been suggestions that the chemicals involved in vaping might themselves have carcinogenic properties, though a study by Public Health England found that e-cigarettes were 95 per cent safer than conventional cigarettes. By 2013, there were 2.1 million e-cigarette users in the UK, and about two-thirds of them were current smokers who wished to cut down or stop. Heathrow Airport opened a vaping zone. While around 4 per cent of the population used e-cigarettes, they were banned from aeroplanes and football stadia together with most schools, hospitals, train companies and cinemas.

The ban

It was the beginning of the end for nicotine-stained pub ceilings and more bad news for the ashtray and cigarette-lighter trade. The new smoking signatures were dog-ends near doorways. From July 2007, smoking was banned from all contained public spaces – pubs, restaurants, private members' clubs, museums, cinemas, airports, rail-station platforms (if they had a roof), hospitals, trains, buses, taxis, company cars (but not private cars), churches, theatres, halls, conference centres, public lavatories and telephone kiosks – and the smoking age was raised from sixteen to eighteen. Smoking was not banned in private residences, hotel rooms, student rooms in halls of residence, designated rooms in nursing homes, designated rooms in offshore oil rigs, mental health units, army barracks and, as we've seen, prison cells. Smoking was expected to be permitted in working men's clubs but that was rescinded at late notice, contributing to a further decline in the fortunes of such associations.

What, then, of the impact of the ban? In the first eighteen months after its introduction local councils inspected over half a million establishments and found in excess of 98 per cent to be compliant. On the tenth anniversary of the ban a YouGov poll found three-quarters of the public to be opposed to overturning the ban, with only 12 per cent in favour.[45] The impact on smoking was predictably substantial. In 2007, the year the ban began, approximately 22 per cent of adults smoked, down from 28 per cent a decade earlier. By 2017, this had dropped to 15 per cent, with some of the largest drops in the likelihood of smoking being found among the young. Economically, one of the most obvious impacts was on pubs which, as we will see in the next chapter, have been declining in number at a very rapid rate. It is thought that around 7,000 pubs – or one in eight of the total – closed between 2007 and 2015.[46] More positively, a study that measured exposure to tobacco smoke found that it had dropped by over three-quarters among bar workers in the aftermath of the ban.[47] One of the reasons that John Reid had given for his scepticism about a potential ban when he was health secretary was the potential that it would lead to greater smoking within the home with consequent negative effects for children. In fact, certainly in the early years after the Act came into effect, the number of households not allowing smoking increased – if only slightly.

There were sceptics, and not everyone was pleased, of course. The writer A. N. Wilson, for example, was less than impressed: 'Overnight, the pubs and clubs of England became less friendly places and within months many publicans faced bankruptcy. The bleak news was followed by news bulletins, dispatched without any questioning of their plausibility by BBC newscasters, about the "improvements in public health" since the ban.'[48] Some pub landlords challenged the ban through the courts. Hamish Howitt, a non-smoking landlord at the Happy Scots Bar (though now presumably less so), Blackpool, allowed smokers to light up and said he would pay any fines that were imposed. Howitt set up an organisation called UK-FAGS (Fight Against Government Suppression) and, in November 2007, became the first person to be prosecuted under the new law. He was found guilty, fined £500 and ordered to pay £2,000 costs. Nearly five months later Howitt was back in court, fined a further £1,950 and ordered to pay £2,000 prosecution costs. Undaunted, in 2008 he stood as a prospective parliamentary candidate for the Freedom Party in a by-election in Blackpool, receiving a total of ninety-one votes and losing his deposit. Though Howitt was by no means alone in his protests, any fears of mass civil disobedience were quickly quelled. Not only did most premises comply but public opinion was generally highly favourable. Over three-quarters of the public felt positively about the ban in 2007, and this had risen slightly to 83 per cent ten years later.[49]

This was far from the end of the story, however, and the years since the introduction of the ban have witnessed a proliferation of new regulations and restrictions regarding smoking. Mental health units, which had originally been excluded, were brought within the ban in 2008, and a range of measures which affected packaging, display and sales swiftly followed. The UK became the first EU nation to introduce picture health warnings on all tobacco packaging and three years later, in 2011, passed legislation to ban cigarette vending machines and displays of tobacco products in shops, as well as further measures to deter underage smoking. Plain tobacco packaging was discussed as early as 2012 and was eventually introduced in 2015. In 2013, the Medicines and Healthcare Products Regulatory Agency announced that electronic cigarettes would be regulated, and medical journals in the UK announced they would cease publishing research funded by the tobacco industry. Proxy purchasing – adults buying cigarettes for under 18s – became illegal in 2014. In 2015 it became illegal to smoke in cars where children were present, and the following year an EU directive ensured that cigarettes could longer be sold in packs of less than 20, and also banned flavoured cigarettes. The direction of travel was pretty clear and in 2019 a Department of Health and Social Care Green Paper included a commitment to make England smoke free by 2030 – approximately eighty years after Doll and Bradford Hill's original pathbreaking research on smoking and cancer was first published.

Smoking rules

Of the things we discuss in this book, smoking is arguably one that has been altered most significantly in the post-war period. Something that was once fashionable and encouraged is now all but deviant, and is certainly very heavily discouraged. It is an area of human life that is now surrounded and punctuated by regulation, and by far greater restriction. In terms of British social order, this is a field in which there has been profound change. Whether it be who can smoke (only adults), where they can smoke (in most private and in some public spaces) and when they can smoke (less and less during working hours – and not at all in some jobs), the smoker is now minutely managed and often quite carefully monitored. As potential smokers we are all faced with a much more tightly regulated world than our predecessors faced. As we observed at the outset, in some senses therefore this would appear to be a seemingly straightforward story of growing social unacceptability and increasing control. Though broadly accurate, the picture is actually a little more complex.

Just how deviant has smoking become? Official statistics released in 2020 suggest that 14 per cent, or just under one in seven people, are smokers. This varies of course. England has proportionately fewer smokers than Wales and Scotland. Some towns, Blackpool and Hull for example, have higher rates, with more than one in five adults there smoking. It is very much a class-based activity. Whereas only around one in ten people in professional occupations smoke, it is closer to one in four in manual jobs – and this gap is widening.[50] In addition, it is estimated that over three and half million people are 'vapers', or users of e-cigarettes, divided almost equally between ex- and current smokers. To this we might add cannabis smokers. About 7 per cent of adults admit in surveys to having used cannabis in the past year, of whom around a third are classified as 'frequent' users. They can't all be baking cookies with it. Although smoking is not quite as marginal or as deviant as one might think at first blush, it remains the case that it is much less common than was the case half a century or more ago, is very obviously less socially acceptable and, as a consequence, is still in decline.

In crude terms, where smoking is concerned it is possible to see post-war Britain in three broad phases. In the early post-war years smoking was an acceptable, indeed rather trendy and largely unquestioned activity. Far from being discouraged, it was a deeply *encouraged* activity. The first half of the twentieth century saw a massive expansion in the range and diversity of cigarettes available on the market, focusing on particular groups and associating smoking with different lifestyles.[51] As evidence of health concerns began to emerge the tobacco industry increasingly promoted products such as filtered and low tar cigarettes, simultaneously seeking to create new or expand existing markets, not least among women – including introducing specialty brands. In this context, smoking was increasingly 'sold' to women as a form of self-expression – the cigarette became a symbol of women's changing social position. This was the era of the mass consumerisation of cigarette smoking,[52] marking the convergence, as Allan Brandt put it, 'of corporate capitalism, technology, mass marketing, and, in particular, the impact of advertising'.[53]

This second phase marked the growing influence of the medical profession and was one in which smoking gradually shifted from unalloyed pleasure to risky activity. The changes were eventually profound but, as we have seen, they can hardly be said to have been quick in coming. Well over half a century passed between the publication of the first significant research linking cigarette smoking to cancer and the eventual introduction of a public smoking ban. There were two major barriers to rapid regulatory reform. The industry itself used its very considerable resources to deflect attention, to challenge research and to resist change. Initially at least it was aided in this by governments that were concerned about revenue loss. As this became less of an issue, governments were still held in check by a general reluctance to intervene in what was perceived in many ways to be a private matter. The consequence was incremental change, focusing on modifications to taxation, greater public education, restrictions on advertising and sales, and a range of other efforts to mitigate apparent harms.

The largely voluntaristic, tinkering approach that governments adopted was underpinned by broadly utilitarian arguments that citizens' rights should only be restricted to prevent harm to others. Whether they truly believed this, or merely hid behind it, such avowed utilitarianism enabled governments to limit their interventionism. With the scientific endorsement of the idea of passive smoking, a third and dramatically different phase emerged in which what had hitherto been narrowly defined as primarily a health problem was transformed into a social problem. It was the conversion of smoking from a risk to individual health to a threat to collective well-being that enabled radical change, removing at a stroke one of the tobacco industry's strongest defences and, simultaneously, forcing governments to change their calculations. Importantly, sufficient time had passed for public opinion itself also to have shifted markedly. By the time the smoking ban was introduced in 2007 around three-quarters of adults supported the change.[54] This, in turn, was underpinned by changing social patterns.

Smoking was increasingly a socially divided activity, easing the task of governments wishing to portray it as dangerous and aberrant. Smoking may have declined generally, but it has not declined equally. Indeed, it would appear that our increasingly socio-economically unequal society is reflected in our changing patterns of smoking. The distinction between 'smokers' and 'non-smokers' has grown in resonance, not just as something that reflects individual choices but as an indicator of, or proxy for, other social distinctions, not least class and general social status. Smoking has become increasingly stigmatised. Just as smoking has become increasingly socially unacceptable, so have smokers. More and more the smoker is treated as a pariah. Once seen fairly unproblematically as a sign of status and pleasure, smoking has progressively become a symbol of risk and, for those continuing to take such risks, a sign of personal failing. As with so much else in this book, therefore, the control of smoking and smokers must be seen as an act of moral regulation.

Finally, we should note that one of the consequences of smoking slowly becoming a public problem is that it has become an increasingly private activity. Its health risks and its increasingly deviant and stigmatised nature have combined to push it to the corners of British society – behind closed (private) doors, in small huddles on streets or outside buildings, or in clearly designated spaces. As such the regulation of smoking has become yet another means by which our public spaces are *ordered*. While the ban means that smoking is no longer permitted in pubs, clubs, restaurants, workplaces, work vehicles, and private vehicles with children in them, it has also had an impact on public space. In effect, public space is now increasingly divided into places where smoking is permissible and an expanding number where it is not. The Health Act outlines minimum requirements, and organisations are well within their rights to extend no-smoking zones to what is referred to as their 'curtilage': essentially the land attached to the place of work. Pubs, cafés and restaurants with outdoor facilities are now required to offer no smoking spaces. Outdoor places such as football and cricket grounds also no longer permit smoking and in early 2015, two of Bristol's public squares – the Millennium Square and Anchor Square – became Britain's first major outdoor spaces to become smoking-free zones. A year earlier, a report from the London Health Commission called for smoke-free parks ('Just as smokers lungs are polluted, the lungs of our city – our parks and green spaces – are polluted by smoking')[55] and in recent times the Local Government Association has called for further restriction to ban pavement smoking outside cafés, restaurants and bars in order to make them more 'family-friendly'.[56] So far as smoking is concerned, we live in a society of increasing segregation and segmentation, with ever more finely graded boundaries – simultaneously spatial and moral – being erected to indicate what (and, therefore, who) is permissible and where.

CHAPTER THREE

Drinking

Smoking and drinking were once fairly inseparable. Most of our alcohol consumption happened in pubs, and hostelries were smoke-filled places. How our lives have changed. We now have a smoking ban which has changed the character of pubs and much besides. And anyway, we increasingly drink elsewhere. Pubs have become much less popular and, as we'll see, have changed in character, often for reasons other than the smoking ban. But what do the ways we consume alcohol have to tell us about ourselves and the current organisation of our social world? And to what extent is the story we have to tell similar to that concerning smoking?

Familiar themes are present. As has become the case generally with smoking, there are aspects of our use of alcohol that have increasingly been viewed as a problem – as something in need of intervention and control. Indeed, and thinking very broadly, this appears to be another area of our lives that is increasingly surrounded and permeated by rules and regulations. So, there are some strong echoes of the story we outlined in the previous chapter. A significant element of the regulatory environment is, as with smoking, focused on particular places. *Where* people can drink is often a focus of control efforts, especially where public space is concerned.

But, as we will see, there are also some quite profound differences between the control of drinking and the control of smoking. It is, of course, not the case that all alcohol consumption is seen as a problem – far from it (as yet). In parallel, changes in the regulation and control of drinking are complex. Some things have become more restrictive, some less so. As is the case with smoking, there have been some significant changes in public attitudes toward drinking. But unlike smoking, where attitudes generally have become increasingly negative and intolerant, attitudinal changes toward drinking are less straightforward, and are often quite specific and focused. They tend to concern such matters as where and when drinking takes place, who does it, and with what consequence. In part, that is because health-related concerns about alcohol – though significant and increasing – have tended to be less central in discussions about regulation and control. Where alcohol is concerned a much wider range of anxieties are involved.

Concerns about the impact of drinking are of course long-standing. Parliament passed an 'Act to Repress the Odious and Loathsome Sin of Drunkenness' as far back as the early seventeenth century. The nineteenth century saw the rise of a powerful temperance movement and the United States unusually, but famously, experimented with total prohibition via the Volstead Act in 1920. Prohibition was certainly discussed by politicians in Britain, though the odds were always against such radical change. Instead, governments then and since have tended to rely on instruments such as taxation, licensing controls, and legislation to restrict where, when and how much alcohol is consumed, and who it may be consumed by.

Intriguingly, in the early post-war period, as one commentator put it, 'drinking had low political salience'. In short, it was not a matter about which governments expended particular energy or around which they appeared to have especial concern. That is certainly something that has changed in the decades since, though the pattern of change is less than straightforward. In some areas, such as licensing, the general trend has been toward greater liberalisation: the hours in which alcohol is available are now generally much greater than was the case half a century ago. Booze is also both cheaper and more accessible than was the case. In a number of other ways, however, we're much more restrictive. Two examples of this – both of which we'll discuss in greater detail later – are drink-driving and drinking during working hours. Drink-driving was already a problem by the inter-war years, but it took until the late 1960s for the breathalyser to be introduced and for fairly radical action to be taken against the drink-driver. Rather akin to many of the changes in relation to smoking, the pace of change was far from swift. Moreover, we described the changes as *fairly* radical' for good reason; in a number of respects the British treatment of the drink-driver continues to be less punitive than some think it should be and certainly is the case in many other countries. Though drink-driving is now very much accepted as a problem of considerable social significance, there appear to be limits on what we're willing to do about it. And what of workplace or working hours drinking? Here there's been something of a sea change; a shift from a culture in which an alcoholic drink or two in the lunchbreak was considered a perfectly legitimate activity (or perhaps even a core part of the culture in some industries) to a position where such practices have largely, though not entirely, disappeared. In the vast majority of workplaces, lunchtime drinking is not now practised, indeed is likely frowned upon, and in many it is officially prohibited.

The culture of drinking has been changing markedly. We do it very differently from the ways in which it was done in the early post-war years. A much wider range of alcoholic beverages is now available – no longer just bitter, mild, stout and a few spirits in the pub. Indeed, as we've noted, pubs are no longer the centre of our drinking universe. Sales via supermarkets, convenience stores and off-licences now far outstrip pub sales. We're now drinking much more at home, and pubs have fast become places where people go to eat and where drinking is often not the financial core of the business. At the same time, however, concerns about drinking have grown markedly in the post-war period. Certainly, it has become a much more regular focus of governmental activity. It is no longer possible to say that it is a matter of low political salience, though as we've indicated, the reasons for this are not straightforward.

Before setting off we should pause to take a look at what we actually do. How much do we drink, how do we drink, and who drinks?

Boozing

How boozy are we compared with previous generations? The answer, of course, very much depends on who we compare ourselves with. There are historical eras – the late Middle Ages and during the eighteenth-century gin craze most obviously – where levels of alcohol consumption were much higher than at any part of the past hundred years. The broad pattern in the twentieth century is of uneven but overall decline in alcohol consumption until around mid-century, whereupon the trend reversed, and alcohol consumption increased pretty consistently until the millennium.

Why the decline in drinking in the first half of the century? The temperance movement that came into being in Victorian times was undoubtedly still having an impact. A huge change occurred during the First World War as new restrictions led to a substantial drop in the amount of beer and other drinks consumed. Then, although levels of alcohol consumption once again increased at the end of the war, these proved somewhat shortlived as the financial consequences of the Great Depression began to bite. The Second World War had less of an impact on alcohol consumption than the Great War, and it was in its aftermath that per capita consumption really started to take off. Despite average intake more than doubling between 1950 and 2000, we were still some way short of late-nineteenth-century levels of alcohol consumption by the time of the arrival of the new millennium. The last twenty years have seen considerable drops in overall levels, though Britain continues to be toward the top of the European league table for drinking.

To what extent are changing drinking patterns a function of cost? There is now solid evidence that the price of alcohol is linked with consumption levels and that it has a particularly strong influence on levels of heavy drinking.[1] In crude terms – the absolute cost – the price of alcohol has increased over the past century. But if we think about 'affordability' – the price of alcohol compared with average income – it is clear, relatively speaking, that the price of alcohol has dropped, and dropped markedly. Calculations done by the Office for National Statistics in 2007 suggested alcohol was over 60 per cent more affordable than it had been in 1982, and the relative price of alcohol has continued to decline since.[2] This trend is fuelled by 'off-trade' sales – from off-licences, supermarkets and corner shops – where prices are particularly low. Off-trade beer, for example, has become nearly three times as affordable in the last thirty years.

As this indicates, the last half-century has also seen a huge shift in where alcohol is sold, with the share of overall business via what are known as 'on-trade sales' (pubs, clubs and restaurants) falling from over 90 per cent of all sales in 1975 to just over 50 per cent by 2010. By 2014, on-trade sales of beer were, for the first time, lower than off-trade sales. More and more alcohol is consumed in the home. As most readers will no doubt be aware, that great British institution, the pub, has been in long-term decline, something only exacerbated by the coronavirus pandemic.

So, booze is cheaper, is now bought at least as frequently from supermarkets and off-licences as pubs and clubs and, until recently, consumption levels had been on the increase. But who is drinking and do these general patterns hide other, more particular trends? About one-fifth of the adult population now say that they don't drink at all and the number of teetotallers is on the increase. Increasing numbers of young people are now likely to report not drinking, but this age group is also the most likely to engage in 'binge drinking' (heavy episodes of drinking) – a subject we'll also return to later. Nevertheless, youthful alcohol consumption has been in long-term decline – both in terms of the proportion drinking and the amount they drink. A variety of explanations are offered: the possibility of a 'backlash' against adult drinking patterns and youthful consumption in previous generations, greater awareness of the risks and consequences of drinking, together with general health consciousness.[3] In short, attitudes are changing.

Alcohol use (and abuse), of course, has some significant social consequences and many of the changes in the ways in which we regulate and control drinking have resulted from growing concerns about these consequences. In 1985, Alcohol Concern estimated that alcohol cost society about £1.5 billion a year in terms of lost hours, decreased production, unemployment and early death. By 2014, the total annual cost to society of alcohol-related harm was estimated by government to be £21 billion a year, of which £3.5 billion was the cost to the National Health Service, £11 billion the expense of tackling alcohol-related crime and £7.3 billion the lost working days and productivity costs.

Off with the King's Head: the rise of supermarket booze

So far as British drinking culture is concerned nowhere is the scale of change more visible than in the not so gradual decline of the pub. One needs to cast one's mind back a little to capture just how central the pub was to British civic life. As the Mass Observation study conducted in the mid-twentieth century noted, 'of all the social institutions that mould men's lives between home and work in an industrial town ... the pub has more buildings, holds more people, takes more of their time and money, than church, cinema, dance-hall, and political organizations put together'.[4] Half a century later and so imperilled had the public house become that in 2009, the Leeds North West MP, Greg Mulholland, established an All Party Parliamentary 'Save our Pub' Group. Described by the Chair of the group as 'the most precious of all our institutions', it is possible that the public house is now in irreversible decline. Indeed, this general picture of the pub may be one of the few things that unites political voices across the spectrum. London's Labour Mayor, Sadiq Khan, described them as being 'at the heart of the capital's culture' at roughly the same time as UKIP said that it believed 'that the pub is the beating heart of our communities'.

The decline of the pub in post-war Britain's cities, towns and villages has been precipitous. From an estimated 87,000 licensed houses in England and Wales in 1914, there were 68,000 pubs in 1982 and 47,000 in 2019, despite the fact that there are far more of us of drinking age – and until the turn of the century we were drinking more and more. Calculated as the number per head of population, there are now only one third the number of pubs in England and Wales there were a century ago.[5] The decline is not uniform and certain types of pub have survived much better than others – not least the so-called 'dry-led' pub where food accounts for a very significant part of its revenue (at least one third) but which still contains a bar and is still considered a drinking establishment.

There are a number of reasons for the decline of the pub. Tastes have changed. In 1970, beer accounted for over 70 per cent of all alcohol consumption, but by the turn of the century it was down to less than half. Over the same period, wine consumption had almost trebled.[6] Drink-driving laws have certainly affected the ability and willingness of drinkers to venture out in rural areas where the 'local' may be some distance away. More recently, the 'smoking ban' has undoubtedly affected the attractiveness of the pub for some of its former clientele. Crucially, our lifestyles have changed. We've already noted how much alcohol consumption now takes place in the privacy of the home. Alcohol is cheaper in supermarkets, off-licences and corner shops, and is easily accessible. When surveyed, almost half of publicans thought cheap supermarket booze was one of the main causes of pub closures.[7] We simply no longer need or rely on the pub the way we once did. Finally, as pub profits have fallen, in many parts of the country the value of the real estate has led to the property being sold for other forms of use or for redevelopment. Though the decline is a long-term trend, concerns about the vitality of the public house go back a long way.

While the image of *Coronation Street*'s 'Rovers Return' and *Eastenders*' 'Old Vic' may suggest that the spit and sawdust local boozer went unchallenged at least until the 1980s, in reality nearly half a century earlier reformers were intent on changing the nature of the public house. The inter-war years saw the emergence of the pub improvement movement which sought to respond to declining sales, the continuing threat of the temperance movement, and the spectre of greater state interference (of which more later). Part of pub improvement focused on civility and trying to shift pubs away from their traditional working-class, male focus, encouraging a wider clientele, women not least, and offering meals as well as drinks. As we will see, the encouragement of civility (defined in various ways) has been a regular focus of regulatory efforts. There were other – somewhat more unusual – reform initiatives, including the work of the Committee for Verse and Prose Recitation ('Poetry in Pubs') which organised readings and performances in an attempt to change the general tone of establishments. Safe to say it was changing what was on sale that eventually had a far greater impact on the general tenor of pub life.

Arguably the biggest alteration in the pub business has been the movement towards pub meals, not least since the new 'restaurant and residential licence' was introduced by the 1961 Licensing Act, and pork scratchings, pickled eggs, crisps, peanuts, the ploughman's lunch and the cheddar-cheese sandwich gave way to chicken in a basket and scampi and chips. Part of the revolution began in the 1950s, when Frank and Aldo Bernie opened

107

their steakhouses, and the family-friendly Bernie Inn was born. Beefeater arrived in 1974 at the Halfway House in Enfield, north London, and Harvester launched its first pub in Morden in south London in 1983. There are claims and counter claims as to which hostelry first badged itself as a 'gastropub', but it seems they began to appear in the nineties. It was 2001 before the first pub – the Stagg Inn in Titley, Herefordshire – was awarded a Michelin Star,[8] but they have proliferated since. Overviews of the industry suggest that food now represents somewhere between one third and one half of all revenue,[9] and the general trend continues to be toward increased food takings and decreased 'wet sales'.

This was also the period when the shift toward managed public houses, as opposed to tenancies, began in earnest. One historian of the pub describes the period from the late 1950s onward as 'one of an unprecedented rate of change', not least as a consequence of growing concentration of ownership.[10] The period between 1955 and 1972 saw the emergence of the brewing industry's Big Six who owned about 75 per cent of the nation's pubs and controlled half the rest. The Monopolies Commission estimated that by 1967, the six largest breweries[11] were responsible for 70 per cent of all beer production. The number of breweries in Britain in the twentieth century fell from 6,290 to only 115 by 1989.[12] Greater profitability was facilitated by a shift toward keg beer and lager sales. Barely existing at the beginning of the sixties, lager accounted for 45 per cent of the market by 1986. So far as the big breweries were concerned, among the attractions of keg beer was that it kept longer than real ale, was easier to handle, was a more consistent product and was simpler to transport. Maybe so, but as *Which?* put it in a report in 1972, it was 'bright, chilled, fairly fizzy, moderately expensive, bland tasting beer of average strength' (names such as Watney's Red Barrel, Double Diamond and Skol will be enough to induce a shiver in readers of a certain age). Writing in the early seventies, Christopher Hutt, author of *Death of the English Pub*, commented that whereas in the past landlords might have watered down their beer in the pub cellar, now breweries were doing it for them. In 1971, the *Sunday Mirror* claimed that five particular beers were 'so weak they could have been legally sold in the United States during the era of prohibition'.

In 1962, Sainsbury's became the first supermarket to obtain a licence for selling alcohol, and others swiftly followed suit. The liberalisation of the licensing laws in 2005, something we'll come to later, provided further stimulus, with the number of supermarkets and other stores having permission to sell alcohol increasing by over a quarter between 2008 and 2010 alone[13] and doubling in the decade from 2003 onward.[14] Researchers calculated the mean distance from buyers' homes to the nearest pub and off-licence had shifted, people having to travel further to find a pub but finding that local supermarkets with off-licences and convenience stores were increasingly close at hand. The same was true of density: on average the number of pubs within a one-kilometre radius had declined by one in the same period, whereas within the same area there was one additional restaurant selling alcohol and two new convenience stores.

These days, just under one third of alcohol is purchased in pubs and other on-licensed premises, with the remainder now bought in supermarkets, off-licences and convenience stores. Indeed, a small number of large grocery retailers (Tesco, Sainsbury's, Asda, Morrisons, Aldi and Lidl) account for close to half the market, with convenience stores accounting for at least a further 10 per cent.[15] A survey in 2009 found that buying alcohol was now a core part of the supermarket experience. Wine had become the drink that was most often bought, being both women's first choice as well as being what was referred to as the main 'compromise item' when men and women were shopping together.[16] They can also generally sell beer and other drinks much more cheaply than pubs and bars. Indeed, one estimate suggested that in the quarter century from 1987, the retail price of beer in pubs and bars had gone up by 187 per cent, whereas in supermarkets and off-licences it had gone down by 52 per cent.[17] By 2004, almost half of British adults had a drink at home at least once a week. One study, based in a Cumbrian city and a Staffordshire town, found that home was the most common drinking venue (72 per cent of the sample), followed by friends' and family's homes (63 per cent), pubs (60 per cent), restaurants (53 per cent), hotels (28 per cent) and clubs (23 per cent).[18] Drinking at home had become more accessible, more affordable and more popular.

Regulating a deadly foe

Historically, there have been two main regulatory instruments: licensing and taxation, of which the latter is arguably the longest standing. In the early eighteenth century, as concerns about levels of gin consumption heightened, legislation was introduced to impose a £20 licence on all gin retailers and, additionally, a two-shilling excise duty on every gallon of compound spirits. Although there was some small drop in consumption, producers soon got around the new restrictions by producing raw spirits and the new law, only introduced in 1729, was repealed in 1734. Two years later, in an attempt at prohibition, the Gin Act brought in an annual £50 licence on any retailer selling gin in quantities under two gallons, and also imposed a 20 shillings per gallon duty. In practice, most retailers ignored the regulations, few of the new licences were taken out, and even government-sponsored attempts at recruiting informers failed to have the hoped-for effect. The Act was repealed in 1743 and new legislation brought in more realistic licences and taxes.

Historically, taxation has regularly been used as a means of attempting to affect what and how much alcohol is consumed. In the early nineteenth century, concerns over high levels of smuggling led to a lowering of levels of taxation on spirits, but subsequent increases in consumption led the authorities to begin to explore means by which beer-drinking might be encouraged as an alternative to spirits. Though the Victorian era saw the rise of the Temperance movement it was 1910 before any significant tax increases were introduced. The annual report of the Commissioners of Excise suggested that the threefold increase in beer duty not long after the outbreak of the First World War led to an increase in the consumption of spirits as people switched away from beer – albeit temporarily.[19] During the Second World War taxation levels on beer increased significantly once again, just as the strength of beer began to decline. Nevertheless, beer sales rose.

Although by the 1970s the state of concern in some quarters about levels of alcohol consumption stimulated support for the use of taxation as a means of discouraging over-indulgence, government views were largely unfavourable. In 1981, in a document entitled *Drinking Sensibly*, the Department of Health rejected the systematic use of taxation as a means of regulating consumption, and although duty on beer would continue to rise for a few more years, duty on wines and spirits had been static or falling for some time. By 2016, wine duty was only three-quarters of the level it had been at the end of the seventies and the duty on spirits had effectively been halved.[20]

According to the Fabian social reformers Beatrice and Sidney Webb, licensing developed 'not in any abstract theory, but in a practical necessity of the state'. It was felt to be a practical necessity for a range of reasons: because of the harms thought to be associated with alcohol consumption, both socially and to the individual; as a consequence of the everyday and political difficulties associated with prohibition; and, as a means of managing an industry whose tax revenue was of increasing importance to governments. It was really in the nineteenth century, and the rise of the temperance movement and growing concerns about the impact of alcohol, that the first significant attempts were made to use licensing to control consumption. In effect, licensing can operate in three ways: through the power to award a licence; the ability to withdraw it; and, through the authority to establish conditions that set the terms under which the sale of alcohol may occur. Though all three avenues have been important, the twentieth century saw a gradual reduction in emphasis on the use of powers of award and withdrawal, so that by the beginning of the twenty-first century much licensing operated through the setting of conditions.

Early attempts to introduce a licensing system began in the 1860s, though it was the period around the First World War that saw major shifts in regulatory practice. An Act of Parliament in 1872 was the first to impose an age restriction on alcohol sales, banning pubs from selling spirits to anyone aged under sixteen. The 1904 Licensing Act forced a reduction in pub numbers and the Central Control Board (CCB), established by the Defence of the Realm Act at the outbreak of the First World War, then added substantially to these closures. The CCB introduced restricted opening hours for pubs – initially 12–2.30 p.m. and 6.30–9.30 p.m. – and from 1916 one of the most radical experiments began when the government began to buy up pubs in a number of areas including Enfield Lock in north London, Cromarty and Firth in Scotland and, most famously, around Carlisle in Cumbria. As David Lloyd George, then minister of munitions and later prime minister, put it in 1915, 'We are fighting three great foes; Germany, Austria and Drink: and as far as I can see the greatest of these deadly foes is Drink.'

What became known as 'the Carlisle experiment' was one of the most significant government interventions in relation to drinking in the first half of the twentieth century. Here, in the area around the Cumbrian town, where there was a concentration of munitions-related industry, the brewing and retailing industry was nationalised. At the time, there were four main breweries in Carlisle and around four hundred pubs in the area. All were nationalised at a cost in compensation of around one million pounds.[21] Subsequently, and now under overall state control, fifty-three pubs and two breweries in Carlisle were closed during the twenty-seven months of the war after July 1916. The supply of drink was restricted, there was complete Sunday closing, and the sale of spirit 'chasers' was stopped. Perpendicular drinking – standing up at a bar – which was believed to lead to greater consumption, was discouraged, and greater emphasis was placed on the selling of food and non-alcoholic drinks, as well as encouraging a greater variety of patrons, especially women, all in the belief that it would lead to greater sobriety and civility. Even at this early stage, part of the official concern with alcohol was linked to ideas of (in)civility and, as we will see, in the post-war years this became an ever-increasing preoccupation. Though nationalisation was not a policy that would spread any further, many of the policy changes associated with the Carlisle experiment were indicative of things to come elsewhere.

What happened around Carlisle was important, not least in sending a message to the private brewers that a greater focus on reducing obvious signs of drunkenness was considered desirable. Although by the end of the war there was little appetite for extending the experiment, the 1921 Licensing Act continued the general trend toward increased controls. The Act ended various restrictions, on the strength of alcoholic drinks for example, but also included a range of new ones, not least in banning the buying of drinks 'on the slate', i.e. on credit. The end of the war did not see a return to earlier drinking arrangements, and tighter regulation, including compulsory afternoon closure and limited Sunday opening, to five hours, continued. Some reports suggested that convictions for drunkenness had fallen by over 70 per cent in Carlisle during the war, and by between 80 and 90 per cent in Liverpool and Portsmouth – ports with a solid reputation for formidable levels of consumption. More generally beer consumption had almost halved by the early 1930s and there was a substantial decline nationally in convictions for drunkenness in the same period. Lloyd George's government had outlined both prohibition and nationalisation as potential policy solutions to the perceived problems associated with drink, not least the threat to those industries crucial to the war effort. In the end, although there were limited experiments with nationalisation, both that and prohibition were used more as a symbolic threat, encouraging the industry itself to reform both its output and its product.

The brewing industry was also affected by the Second World War, but the changes were not nearly as dramatic as those linked to the Great War. By this point the temperance movement was of declining significance and more generally it seems attitudes toward alcohol consumption were beginning to shift. Indeed, the government, perhaps not all that surprisingly given Churchill was prime minister, saw the availability of alcohol as important to the war effort, both for the morale of the troops and of civilians. This is not to say that drinking was considered unproblematic and, indeed, thanks to dangers in the blackout this was the period when the issue of drink-driving (or as we'll explain in a later chapter, *drunk*-driving) started to become a recognised problem. The post-war Labour government made occasional changes, not least expanding state control in certain, limited respects, primarily through increasing taxes on alcohol, but there was no uniform reduction of opening times or any rationing of beer. A 1945 Planning Act increased local authority licensing powers in areas extensively damaged during the war, and further Acts early in the 1950s introduced new local licensing arrangements in all new towns and reinforced local authority licensing powers in other areas.

No doubt the fact that alcohol consumption generally had been in decline for the better part of half a century facilitated this relative post-war tolerance. Using advertising campaigns under the slogan 'beer is best' (building on the success of the earlier 'Guinness is good for you' campaign) and wider efforts of the brewers involved in the pub improvement movement to reposition the pub, it was true that beer consumption did begin to increase after the war. The impact of any increases didn't come close to returning alcohol consumption to early century levels, and the difficult financial climate and the new licensing arrangements limited the effectiveness of the brewers' plans 'to re-establish the pub as the centre of social life'.[22] The movement to promote the 'improved public house' was also initiated by a small number of influential brewers, leading to the closure of many smaller public houses and the building of larger hostelries, particularly in suburban areas. Despite such initiatives, small, tenanted pubs remained numerous and there was little evidence of significant change in habits, or clientele, until at least the 1950s. Although the Licensing Act 1953 increased local authority powers it was the early 1960s which saw the first significant change to the licensing laws since just after the Great War. The direction of travel was one of liberalisation though the pace of change was generally slow.

The Licensing Act 1961 increased opening hours and formally regulated the ten-minute drinking-up time. It introduced a new type of licence – the 'restricted on-licence' – for hotels and restaurants, thus rapidly increasing the number of places selling alcohol. It also reduced restrictions on off-licensing, increasing their number and enabling them to open in daytime. London's weekday opening hours were extended to 11 p.m. (10.30 p.m. elsewhere); and dancing clubs were permitted longer opening hours. The 1961 Act also ended the compulsory pub closures on Sundays in Wales – before 1961 only bona fide travellers could be served alcohol – and local referenda were introduced to rule on Sunday opening. It was not until 1996 that the last bastion of Sunday closing, Dwyfor (Gwynedd), finally voted to end Sunday closure.

The broadly liberalising measures were a further contributor to the social trends which underpinned many of the changing drinking patterns observable from the late fifties onward, not least the increased visibility of women, youth and the middle-classes in pubs. Generalised concerns about 'youth' that were growing at this time also focused on their alcohol consumption, though this didn't translate directly into regulatory activity until much later in the century when drinking and disorderliness became much more formally linked. The more major concern

116

was connected to health and safety issues and to drinking and driving in particular – something we shall come to shortly.

The slow but general liberalisation of licensing continued in the following decades. Afternoon closing was scrapped in 1988, and Sunday restrictions were removed in 1995. The 2003 Licensing Act shifted responsibility from licensing justices to local authorities and, at least as importantly, also introduced a presumption in favour of granting licences. More controversially at the time, the 2003 Licensing Act removed statutory closing times, heralding the prospect of twenty-four-hour drinking. In practice, however, the changes brought about by the new regime, which came into effect in 2005, were considerably less signifi-cant than had been anticipated. Although some pubs extended their hours, in most cases the extensions were not lengthy, and although alcohol consumption was spread over longer hours, before long overall consumption actually began to decline. The presumption in favour of granting licences had very clear limits, reflecting the fact that by the time of the new century it was issues of misconduct that had become the central overriding concern of licensing.

We'll get back to matters of crime and disorder shortly, but first we must return to the 1960s and the point at which one of the most significant health and safety-related concerns – drink-driving – hit the top of the agenda.

Health, safety and security

As consumption began to rise in the 1950s, and more steeply from the 1960s, so concern about alcohol also rose. By and large, and with one very significant exception – drink-driving – central government preferred either to leave it to local authorities, or to present it as the responsibility of those selling and consuming alcohol. Once again, broadly utilitarian thinking dominated governments' approaches to regulation. In this sense at least there were some quite strong parallels with post-war policy in relation to smoking which, similarly, sought to focus as much as possible on either the consumer or voluntary agreements with the industry itself. With the temperance movement having largely lost any political traction it had enjoyed, increasingly the approach to alcohol regulation became one of dealing with its associated harms. Although health issues appeared to be of rising importance in the post-war period, where guidance on so-called 'sensible drinking' (or its reverse) increasingly came to the fore, such matters rarely dominated the approach to controlling drinking.

Sensible drinking

A medical model of alcoholism – which found expression in the Victorian concern with 'habitual inebriates' – re-emerged in the post-war period. It did so against a background of official inaction: medical services were close to non-existent, the main medical bodies showed no particular interest in the issue and, rather remarkably from a contemporary perspective, the Ministry of Health considered alcohol consumption 'neither a problem nor a health related issue'.[23] The situation was a little different in the US where a strong psychiatric profession led to the idea of alcoholism becoming a more significant social issue in the fifties. Much influenced also by the World Health Organization, similar ideas gradually gained ground in the UK and, again influenced by US developments, the Alcoholics Anonymous (AA) self-help movement also began to spread, the first UK group being set up in Croydon in 1952.

As late as 1956, it was admitted that no statistics were available on alcohol-related disease – one inquirer being directed to the National Temperance Society as their best bet for information. It was 1957 before the chief medical officer's annual report mentioned alcoholism, and it took decades before government began to take anything approaching a serious policy interest in alcohol. Although the disease model was more firmly established within the Ministry of Health by the mid-sixties, there remained reluctance within government (both by the Ministry of Health and by the Home Office) to be seen as having lead responsibility for the 'problem'. A public health approach began to emerge in the seventies and, with that, there began a discernible shift in which the focus moved toward general patterns of conduct and, increasingly, prevention. According to a leading expert, the growing importance of alcohol issues and policy was a consequence of 'rising alcohol consumption, the perceived economic costs of alcohol misuse, and the interplay of competing interests',[24] governmental, medical/professional and the industry itself.

By the late seventies, the Royal College of Psychiatrists was urging that efforts be focused on trying to ensure that overall average alcohol consumption across the population did not increase from current levels. Two methods were proposed: one using taxation to increase the cost of alcohol, the other establishing limits to what might be considered 'safe drinking'. From today's perspective the safe limits seem generous indeed, being four pints of beer, four doubles of spirits or one standard-sized bottle of wine a day! Rather than being some carefully calibrated medical judgement it seems this was simply a back of an envelope attempt to begin a long process of changing attitudes and the general approach toward drinking. It was the first step in getting citizens to measure and monitor and thereby control their drinking.

Government was still reluctant even to go as far as promoting a prescribed drinking limit. In seeking to encourage sensible drinking, and therefore to distinguish such conduct from problem drinking, it also rejected taxation as an appropriate lever for changing behaviour. The solution was to pass the buck and to encourage citizens to self-monitor – to engage in a form of voluntary surveillance, primarily through the notion of 'standard drinks' or 'units'.[25] Introduced in the late eighties, 'units' were roughly equivalent to half a pint of beer, a glass of wine or a single measure of spirits, and guidelines published in 1987 suggested that safe limits were twenty-one units for men and fourteen for women with 'too much' now defined as thirty-six units a week for men and twenty-two for women. Though this standard appeared to be a product of scientific assessment from the Royal Colleges and Health Education Council, twenty years later a member of the Royal College of Physicians admitted the figures had been 'plucked out of the air', were simply an 'intelligent guess', and had been produced because there was 'a feeling you had to say something'.[26] As with much we have been studying, the aim here was to offer guidance on forms of behaviour characteristic of a responsible citizen: a self-monitoring, self-governing individual who has internalised messages about appropriate conduct (in this case about alcohol consumption but it could equally be about smoking or, indeed, about care of pets).

Governments increasingly promoted safer practices through widespread advertising of indicative limits, and Tesco was the first of the supermarkets to introduce warning labels on booze in 1989. Ignorance nevertheless abounded, and research in 1990 suggested that only 15 per cent of people knew that a pint of beer had two units. The following year the Royal College of Physicians proposed that alcoholic drinks should carry a health warning to combat deaths, diseases and alcohol-related injuries. The early nineties saw the emergence of more formalised 'sensible drinking' messages: initially men should consume no more than twenty-one and women no more than fourteen units per week. In recognition of the dangers of excessive drinking in a single session, the message was changed to focus on daily guidelines, now becoming a maximum intake of two to three units per day for women and three to four for men. Toward the end of the century government advice about how the responsible citizen should behave became increasingly detailed, the advice including: two alcohol-free days after heavy drinking; avoidance of continued alcohol consumption at the upper level; and that groups such as those engaging in potentially dangerous activities (operating heavy machinery, for example), and pregnant women, should drink less or nothing at all. On the positive side, government suggested that intake of up to two units a day could have a moderate protective effect against heart disease for men over forty and post-menopausal women.[27] In the years to come some of the language changed – 'sensible drinking' became 'drinking responsibly', for example – and guidelines were updated as new medical knowledge emerged. Some more focused concerns also emerged, among which arguably the best known are the actions increasingly taken against the drink-driver.

Don't drink and drive

There will be few readers who can remember a time before the 'breathalyser'. Introduced over half a century ago, this new technology allowed for accurate testing of breath-alcohol levels (reflecting the amount of alcohol in the blood) and radically changed the relationship between alcohol consumption and the driving of motor vehicles. The breathalyser was slow to come, however, arriving decades after concerns were first raised about drink-driving. Moreover, although it was the first serious attempt to control alcohol consumption by drivers and proved an important and influential reform, it was a limited one; drink-driving is still treated in a more liberal manner in Britain than is the case in many other countries (indeed, it is treated in a much more liberal manner in England than it is in Scotland).

It had been an offence to be drunk in charge of a carriage on a highway as far back as the 1870s, though it was 1925 before motor vehicles were treated as a separate category. At this stage, however, the focus of concern was the 'drunk-driver', and what was meant by 'drunk' remained clouded in mystery. How was alcohol intake to be assessed? An editorial in the *British Medical Journal* in 1927, which argued against alcohol testing, said:

> The mere fact that it was proved, or admitted, that some alcoholic liquor had been taken a short time before the occurrence of the circumstances which led to the charge was, in a country like this, where so many people are in the habit of taking alcoholic beverages, clearly insufficient.

In the thirties, alcohol was a major contributor to over seven thousand road deaths a year, as well as a great many more serious injuries. Half the victims were cyclists or pedestrians. Until the Road Traffic Act 1934 there was little in the way of speed limits on the roads, there were no driving tests, car insurance had only been introduced in 1930, and a powerful pro-motoring ideology still held firm. Although a British Medical Association report in the mid-thirties suggested that a large number of accidents, many of them fatal, resulted from something much less than complete intoxication, the regulation of drinking and driving remained unchanged all the way to the late sixties, and even then didn't go nearly as far as many reformers hoped.

Government concern about 'the grievous toll in death and injury on the roads' from drink-driving was expressed in the Queen's Speech in 1954, and increased penalties were introduced in 1956, but such were the loopholes in the law the 'intoxicated driver' was still often able to avoid prosecution. In the fifties the legal situation was likened to a comic opera – a blood test could only be taken with the driver's consent, but intoxicated drivers were often unwilling or even in no fit state to give consent. Despite a survey in 1955 finding that three-quarters believed drivers suspected of drink-driving should be subjected to compulsory testing for alcohol, the Home Office, the Ministry of Transport and motoring organisations such as the AA and RAC continued to resist greater intervention. Among those pressing for change were the British Medical Association (BMA) and the Pedestrians' Association, the latter shifting its stance quite radically in the post-war years.

Within Whitehall, the arrival of Ernest Marples (who we will meet again several times later in the book) at the Ministry of Transport signalled the beginnings of a change in official attitudes. Marples had been shocked by the scale of deaths on the road – the sixty-six people killed on Christmas Eve 1959 represented a doubling of the previous year's tally – and began to press the reform case on the Home Office. Marples staked his reputation on the need for more road safety and encouraged civil servants to look closely at the model of controls in Scandinavian countries: Norway had been the first country to introduce blood-alcohol testing as early as 1936. A new Licensing Act in 1961 briefly mentioned drinking and driving and regulations were introduced to limit the possibility that motorway service stations would apply for the new restricted on-licences government had introduced. Blood-alcohol tests became admissible in court in 1962, and the appropriate test changed from being 'incapable of having proper control' to 'a person shall be taken to be unfit to drive if his ability to drive properly is for the time being impaired'. The intention was to shift the focus from 'drunkenness' to drink-driving. Barbara Castle, the Labour minister of transport, was at the forefront of debates now, and her indefatigable nature was required in the face of considerable personal abuse for her part in attempting to introduce stricter controls. In parliamentary debate in early 1966, she opened her speech by observing that during the Second World War 'Hitler did not manage to kill as many civilians in Britain as have been killed on our roads since the war at the hands of our own citizens'.[28]

With road deaths reaching almost eight thousand in 1966, the Ministry of Transport and the Home Office finally accepted the need for reform. The Road Safety Act 1967 provided the decisive change. The introduction of the breathalyser is a clear example of the arrival of greater restriction and regulation in citizens' lives in Britain. But it was a change that was hard-fought, with powerful lobbies ranged against it, and which successfully limited reform in important ways. Government initially appeared willing to embrace the idea of random breath testing, for example, but the plan was eventually scuppered by powerful opposition. Motoring organisations, predictably enough, were not keen on such 'intrusion' and neither was the licensed trade. Crucially, the police service also represented a major hurdle. Ever since motor cars became relatively common, the policing of traffic violations had been a major source of contention.[29] It brought the police into conflict with the middle classes – a section of the population that they might otherwise have had little to do with and with whom they might have enjoyed a more straightforwardly positive relationship. By the sixties, police concern about the negative impact traffic policing was having on public relations was particularly acute and they were not keen to see anything worsen the situation. The Police Federation, which represented the rank and file, saw random breath testing as far too risky and the Labour government, initially quite keen, soon backed off. The Act therefore introduced breath tests under three limited conditions: suspicion that a driver had been drinking alcohol; had committed a traffic offence; or had been involved in an accident

In addition to shying away from random testing, the government also compromised on blood alcohol levels. The new offence introduced by the Act was 'driving or attempting to drive with more than a prescribed concentration of alcohol in the blood stream, regardless of whether or not driving ability was impaired'. The crucial question here is the definition of 'prescribed concentration'. Although one body of expert opinion pressed strongly for the limit to be set at 50 mg per 100 ml (as it was in some other countries), it was eventually agreed that the blood alcohol concentration (BAC) would be set, significantly higher, at 80 mg per 100 ml.

A year after the Act became operational the new minister of transport, Richard Marsh, announced that road deaths had been reduced substantially and the Act had resulted in 23,971 convictions. It was true that there had been a variety of other changes to traffic regulation that may also have influenced things, but to most observers it appeared that the Act had an initial and quite substantial impact, albeit one that wore off quite quickly. Indeed, research suggested that within a year of the new legislation many drivers had returned to their old patterns of activity so far as drinking was concerned. As one academic observer at the time put it, 'The British driving population learned that a moderately drunk driver who managed to drive in a manner that avoided attention of routine police patrols had little to fear from the Road Safety Act'.[30]

By the mid-seventies it was clear that the Act was having a diminishing effect, with over half of all drivers killed in road collisions found to have alcohol in their blood. However, it was concerns about alcohol abuse more generally that brought the whole matter back on to the political agenda. The government response to these wider anxieties, the Blennerhassett Committee, reported in 1976, and among its recommendations it suggested the tightening of a variety of procedures, though it again resisted calls for the BAC to be reduced to 50 mg per 100 ml. It also recommended that the police should no longer be restricted in the circumstances under which they could request a breath test, though the lowest requirement – that an officer have a suspicion that a driver had alcohol in their body – was seen by many as allowing close to unrestricted opportunity for testing, something it was clear still raised significant concerns.

A brief experiment in Cheshire in 1975 illustrated the problem. The chief constable, concerned about the level of traffic accidents locally, instructed his officers to breathalyse all drivers in cases where there had been either an accident or a road traffic violation – carefully avoiding the widest of the three circumstances (suspicion a driver had consumed alcohol) in which officers had the right to administer a screening test. The result was a tenfold increase in tests in the local area, a doubling of convictions and a 60 per cent decline in accidents resulting in death or serious injury. Success you might think. Because of the potential for controversy, the experiment was conducted without publicity. It proved impossible to keep quiet, however, and quickly drew criticism from the AA, the RAC and members of the local council – the major accusation being that the constabulary was using random testing. In the event his threat of resignation was enough to get the police authority to back its chief constable, though not to save the short-lived experiment. Brief it may have been, but it appeared to confirm two important truths: increased enforcement did at least appear to have a short-term deterrent effect; and random breath testing remained too controversial in some quarters to make its more widespread adoption likely.

Though government continued to drag its feet – a series of publicity campaigns in the late seventies (such as 'Think Before You Drink Before You Drive'), the changing of drink-driving to a summary offence only (confining it to the Magistrates' courts), and some increases in penalties – the courts began to apply the existing law more confidently than they had previously. But it was not until the early eighties that full evidential breath-testing (i.e. without the need for blood or urine samples) was fully introduced – and even this was not implemented until 1983.[31] Toward the end of the decade further extension to the law was proposed as a consequence of the inability to prosecute drink-drivers for the fatalities or serious injuries resulting from the accidents they caused. A specific offence of causing death by careless driving whilst under the influence of drink or drugs was proposed and came into being via the Road Traffic Act 1991.

In the mid-eighties the House of Commons Transport Committee made a number of recommendations for reform but once again came out against random testing. A backbench Bill also failed in 1988 and although it appeared the proportion of public supporting such a change in the law was growing there seemed little likelihood of change. Indeed, despite widespread international evidence of the impact of such procedures – a large number of other countries use random testing (including Australia, Sweden, France)[32] – the Home Office continued to be at the forefront of official resistance, as was the Association of Chief Police Officers. International examples and pressure also failed to alter the main measure of excess alcohol. In 1988, the European Commission had proposed harmonisation of BAC limits of 0.5 mg/ml in all member states. At that time only Finland, Sweden, Portugal and the Netherlands already operated BAC at that level. Belgium and France followed in the mid-nineties, and five more European countries followed suit shortly thereafter. By the early twenty-first century, of the fifteen EC member states only the UK, Ireland and Luxembourg had a BAC limit as high as 0.8 mg/ml. More recently, gradual devolution of powers has enabled Scotland to change its limits, a new reduced BAC level of 0.5 mg/ml coming into force in late 2014. Several further attempts have been made to reduce the limit in England but, as yet, without success.

The 1967 Act is arguably one of our great public health success stories. Road deaths have declined markedly since the introduction of the breathalyser. In 1979, the year in which such matters were first accurately assessed, around 1,600 people were killed and a further thirty thousand injured in traffic incidents in which a driver or rider was over the drink-drive limit. By 2015, this had dropped to roughly two hundred killed and eight thousand injured.[33] This would be a very sizeable decline by any measure, but during a period in which traffic numbers roughly trebled, it is even more spectacular. Although governmental activity in this field has come in waves – the high points being the late 1960s, late 1970s and late 1980s – a huge and fairly sustained effort has been made via legislative changes, enforcement efforts and public education campaigns to bring about behavioural and attitudinal change.

In this it appears to have been successful. The research evidence points to education – knowing and understanding the law – together with effective enforcement, having been central to the shifts that have happened. The British Social Attitudes Survey for 2015 found that three-quarters of people thought that the amount drivers were allowed to drink should be reduced, with only one in ten people against. The National Travel Attitudes Survey in 2019, for example, found that over four-fifths (81 per cent) of people now think that someone shouldn't drive if they have drunk any alcohol.[34] The proportion of drivers reporting that they believe they have driven while over the legal alcohol limit at least once in the past year has remained generally stable over the past decade at around 7 per cent. Unfortunately, survey data are not available for the earlier period. Nonetheless, there is every reason to believe that the numbers are much smaller now than would have been the case a half-century ago.

The changes then have been profound but, importantly, they have also had their limits. Evidence from around the world has gradually built up to suggest that a reduced BAC threshold would further reduce the problem, especially if linked with more effective deterrence via random breath testing. In Britain, however, the use of breath testing is on the decline, largely it seems as a consequence of police budget cuts.[35] The current resistance to both random testing and to reductions in the BAC limit may indicate something about contemporary attitudes toward alcohol consumption in general, or drink-driving more particularly but, arguably, really tells us more about the continuing power of certain lobbies to shape the nature and pace of reform.

Fighting drunk

If health concerns had been a significant factor affecting alcohol-related regulation in the 1960s, then from around the mid-eighties the focus moved toward crime, security and, subsequently, antisocial behaviour. Governments became increasingly preoccupied with such concerns, and a wide range of regulatory reforms, including those focused on drinking, were justified because of their supposed benefits in reducing such problems. At roughly the same time as this shift of emphasis around alcohol was taking place, the industry itself was also undergoing some substantial changes. The monopolistic practices of the big breweries – not only their hugely dominant position in relation to both the production and sale of beer, but also their control of pubs – came under increasingly critical scrutiny. The Monopolies and Mergers Commission recommended that the 'big six' brewers should be forced to sell close to two-thirds of the pubs they currently owned – a huge change, not least as it was one that was brought about by direct intervention rather than licensing. Some negotiation meant that it was closer to half of their existing stock that the brewers were eventually forced to divest, a great many of which were bought by companies such as O'Neill's and All Bar One – Pubcos as they were known – none of whom had much experience in the production side of the business and were all about sales. What emerged, as one observer has put it, was a 'proliferation of theme bars and superpubs on the high streets of towns and cities across the country . . . and it was these outlets that were starting to become the focus of increasingly vociferous complaints about the drinking habits of young people'.[36]

The newly reshaped industry also began another significant change, rebranding its products (both drinks and pubs) and seeking to reshape its markets. Some of this, particularly where young people were the focus, was stimulated by the arrival of late eighties' rave culture and the attraction – temporary as it turned out – of ecstasy to a new generation. The drinks industry needed to compete, and it did so in two main ways. One was to offer different types of drinking establishment – most obviously pubs that would attract a youthful clientele, and by design would be unattractive to other age groups. Loud music, limited seating (which promoted what was now referred to as 'vertical drinking' – the late century equivalent of the 'perpendicular drinking' discouraged during the First War) and a variety of other features, such as 'happy hours', all of which helped to maximise alcohol intake. In addition, the products themselves changed. The keg beers of the 'big six' era disappeared, as lager sales rocketed, especially branded, 'continental' strong lagers, along with other innovations such as alcopops and the promotion of 'shots'. 'Never before had the industry so explicitly sold drunkenness as the aim and point of drinking' as one historian put it.[37]

The first substantial law and order, youth-related concerns in this period focused on what became known as 'lager louts'. Indeed, such was the regularity with which this particular folk devil was the focus of negative news stories that a Home Office researcher described 1988 as the year of the lager lout.[38] The eighties had seen the growing availability of relatively cheap alcohol, often purchased in supermarkets, and associated with a range of perceived social problems: violence in and around football matches, the spread of rave culture and acid-house parties, and the generally growing visibility of outdoor drinking and associated disorder. Great play was made of the fact that much of the disorder that occurred seemed to happen in smaller towns and cities, and rural areas – a change from the usual focus on the main Metropolitan centres. One such was Coventry, in the West Midlands, which experienced regular problems. On Christmas Eve and New Year's Eve 1984, large crowds on the streets led to considerable city centre damage, and the *Coventry Evening Telegraph* headline was, 'Bottled up on the streets of fear'.

In the late 1980s, Coventry's response to its disorder was to apply to the Home Office to designate the city centre an 'alcohol free zone'; in essence banning all public drinking and confining the consumption of alcohol to pubs, clubs and other licensed premises. The proposal was accepted in 1988 and Coventry became part of a new experimental scheme alongside a small number of other towns including Bath, Chester, Scarborough and Aldershot. Being the first, however, and launching the new zone with great publicity, Coventry became the poster town for this new approach. The council also spent around £10,000 on new city centre 'Alcohol Free Zone' signage. Enforcement was a police responsibility, with offenders being given an initial warning in case they were unaware of the ban. As with so many other areas we focus on in this book, the reality was that control was generally exercised without the need for formal enforcement, and few arrests were made or prosecutions brought.

At the time of the experiment, the Home Office conducted some small-scale research showing that prior to its introduction there were quite high levels of anxiety about crime in Coventry and that around half of people surveyed viewed public drunkenness as a problem (or, as the government researchers rather starkly put it, 'drunks, winos and tramps were the most commonly avoided group'!). This figure reduced after the introduction of the ban and surveys suggested the general atmosphere in the city centre had improved. Indeed, the ban was popular with the police and seemed to work reasonably well in other places it had been introduced, leading home secretary, Leon Brittan, to announce in 1990 that the new by-law was being made more generally available 'so that other towns can take action to sweep the drunken louts off the streets'.[39] The changes were made permanent in 1992. Broadly speaking they seemed to be received favourably, members of the public offering generally positive views of the way in which the new regulations were policed, and the police themselves saying they were subject to relatively little hostility. In a short space of time, drinking had become the latest focus for imposing restrictions on behaviour in public spaces, and has continued since. According to one estimate in 2012, London had over seventy zones in which there are restrictions on alcohol consumption.[40]

Public drinking bans were very much a sign of the times. The Coventry-style prohibition was merely one of the first and better publicised law and order initiatives. In the years that followed, misconduct and disorderliness associated with drinking, and youthful drinking most obviously, became the dominant frame of reference in alcohol-related regulation. In the early 2000s, such concerns coalesced around what was increasingly referred to as 'binge drinking'. There was evidence in the 1990s that concentrated single-session drinking was growing, and by early in the new century further studies showed that weekly consumption by the young had increased markedly over the previous decade. The industry changes that introduced and promoted bottled beers, ice lagers, white ciders, alcopops, ready-to-drinks (bottled spirit mixers), flavoured alcoholic beverages (such as

Bacardi Breezer), happy hours, shots, two-for-one deals, together with 'fun pubs', dance bars and so forth, helped fuel what one chief constable memorably called a 'drink-punch-smash-vomit culture', with the police's role described as one of 'mop and bucket'. By contrast with the 'sensible drinking' messages coming from government, 'determined drunkenness'[41] appeared the order of the day for some of the young.

The official reaction to the emergent youthful patterns of drinking was intriguingly mixed. On the one hand, the general liberalising approach to licensing that had been in evidence for some time, and which no doubt in some small ways helped facilitate the changes to youthful leisure that were evident, was continued. Thus, on the surface at least, what appeared to be one of the most far-reaching reforms of licensing was introduced in 2003. In this case, at least in some circles, it was believed that relaxation of licensing restrictions would help facilitate the wider aim of reducing alcohol-related crime and disorder. As we noted earlier, the Licensing Act removed licensing justices, gave responsibility to local authorities and introduced an assumption in favour of granting licences. Statutory closing times were removed, and this introduced the prospect of late night/early morning drinking becoming fairly standard. In the event, the impact on opening times was much less dramatic than many had believed would be the case, academics in one instance calculating that on average Saturday night drinking time was extended by only twenty-one minutes.

The overall aim of the new law was to attempt to change British drinking culture, stimulating a more relaxed, 'continental' feel to the streets of our towns and cities. The Home Office was clearly not entirely convinced that improvements would be quickly seen, and it substantially increased its funding for a number of 'Alcohol Misuse Enforcement Campaigns' and some increased policing initiatives focusing on nightlife hotspots in 2004 and 2005. It is worth reiterating before we move on that while this was in one sense a liberalising measure, it was underpinned by a hope that it would eventually result in diminished problems, i.e. in effect in greater (self)-control. Fundamentally, we were being encouraged to change our relationship with alcohol. Although the Act introduced a presumption in favour of granting licences, the grounds for refusal were made very clear, and they focused almost entirely on orderliness. Refusal would occur when there were good reasons to suspect that granting one would be inconsistent with the Act's main objectives which were: to prevent crime and disorder; to promote public safety; to prevent public nuisance; and the protection of children from harm; and (in Scotland only) the protection and promotion of public health.

In terms of broader issues of regulation and control, the 2003 Act was very much in line with the spirit of the times. Managing order or preventing disorder were at its heart, and public health was barely mentioned. The Act expanded police powers to confiscate alcohol from young people and to close premises where there was disorder or where disorder might be anticipated. Fundamentally the Act was not about alcohol but about other forms of social behaviour – and social problems – it was believed to be connected to. So dominant was this mindset that listing other alcohol-focused crime and disorder measures introduced around this time could go on for pages, but included: increased powers of confiscation and 'test-buying'; the outlawing of 'proxy-buying' (for those under-age); 'designated public place orders' allowing police officers to stop drinking and confiscate drinks; 'dispersal orders' allowing police to move rowdy drinkers on; the banning of alcohol consumption on all London transport; and 'Early Morning Restriction Orders', enabling local authorities to introduce a complete ban on alcohol sales between midnight and 6 a.m. in specific locations. In myriad ways in the early twenty-first century the regulation of drinking became central to the construction of the responsible, non-violent, pro-social citizen.

Drinking and work

> My drink in those days, in the bar at Yorkshire TV, was a gin and double Cinzano Bianco, and I used to buy the first round because I wouldn't expect anyone to buy that, and I would sip it and when anyone offered me a drink I would ask for a Cinzano or a gin, and by the time I'd finished my first gin and double Cinzano three rounds would have elapsed and I'd have another gin and double Cinzano, and by the end of the lunch break I would have had a third. So, this meant that at least seven rounds had to have been bought for this to happen. And then we all went and did good work again in the afternoon. Astonishing. (Comedy writer David Nobbs talking about the 1970s when writing for *The Les Dawson Show*)[42]

There is enough alcohol being drunk at lunchtime in David Nobbs' tale to qualify for what more recently has come to be called 'binge drinking'. It seems remarkable not only that he drank that much but that he was seemingly able to carry on working effectively afterward. From today's perspective, however, it is not just the quantity of alcohol drunk that is surprising but the simple fact that it was done at work, at lunchtime, and that this was seemingly considered a mundane, even unremarkable activity. As the journalist Deborah Orr wrote a few years ago:

'like smoking on planes and transporting toddlers in cars without tying them up first, a little inebriation to break up a working day is one of those things that in a generation has moved from normal to, "Oh my God, can you believe we ever did that?"'

Precisely. And one doesn't have to be in David Nobbs' seven rounds territory. The scandal that surrounded Downing Street in the pandemic also illustrated elements of this change. The furore was of course largely about the alleged failure to follow the rules about social gatherings that had been set by the government. But it was clear also that the more straightforward revelations about drinking at work – all exacerbated by tales of wine fridges and suitcases of booze – were a source of considerable consternation and surprise. Was it really permissible in this day and age for people to be boozing at work? For many, any kind of alcoholic intake during the working day is now considered completely unacceptable.

A YouGov poll in 2016 found something close to a two to one majority against lunchtime drinking at work (60 per cent versus 32 per cent).[43] Again, something of a social revolution in attitudes and behaviour seems to have occurred. Up to at least the 1970s, drinking for many was an embedded part of the working routine, especially at lunchtimes. Drinking together was often seen as something positive, not least in terms of team bonding and sharing ideas. Many organisations had onsite bars or staff clubs where alcohol was available at favourable prices. In that era a lunchtime drink (or two or three) was regulated more by desire and affordability than workplace policies.

In *Diary of a Dog Walker*, Ed Stourton writes about joining ITN in 1979, when virtually all the staff spent lunchtimes in nearby pubs and restaurants. Increasingly, however, the focus gradually turned towards the negative features of drinking, such as alcohol abuse, absenteeism, days lost to sickness, increased accident rates and lower productivity. As Stourton said, in 2011, '*Private Eye*'s perennial caricature Lunchtime O'Booze should really be renamed "Lunchtime No Booze".' In early 2017, Lloyd's of London announced that it would no longer tolerate lunchtime drinking by its employees.[44] Anyone working for the insurer was prohibited from drinking alcohol between 9 a.m. and 5 p.m. Monday to Friday. Failure to comply risked gross misconduct proceedings and loss of job. An internal memo circulated to staff announcing the new policy captured the zeitgeist of this new alcohol-free work environment:

> The London market historically had a reputation for daytime drinking but that has been changing and Lloyd's has a duty to be a responsible employer and provide a healthy working environment. The policy we've introduced aligns us with many firms in the market. Drinking alcohol affects individuals differently. A zero limit is therefore simpler, more consistent and in line with the modern, global and high-performance culture that we want to embrace.

According to one insider, initially at least the ban only affected 'the nine-to-five, admin types', and that the 'brokers are drinking as much as ever – that's how the deals get done'.[45] The decision by Lloyd's, which generated considerable publicity, prompted a range of recollections of work-time drinking habits from earlier times. Pete Brown, a British writer whose work focuses mainly on alcohol and the drinks industry, recalled his years of working in advertising in the 1990s. One regular feature at work he reports was the 'Jolly Trolley' – laden with food and drink, it appeared during the afternoon whenever someone was leaving, had been promoted or had a birthday and, of course, when new business was to be celebrated. In short, at a minimum once or twice a week. But often, no-one needed to wait for the Jolly Trolley to appear as lunchtime client meetings tended to feature something very similar. Booze was expected and was so unexceptional it was never commented upon. At some point in the years that followed it all changed. As Brown put it: 'sometime in the early noughties I was in a lunchtime meeting with Pret sandwiches and cans of Coke and I remembered the lunchtime booze trolley for the first time in many years. I realised that not only had it disappeared; if anyone suggested bringing it back now they would be censured for suggesting something so inappropriate.'[46]

Like David Nobbs' and Ed Stourton's memories of working in television in the seventies and eighties, the culture of drinking that existed among journalists in Fleet Street at this time is well-known (hence Lunchtime O'Booze). As Janet Street-Porter described it, 'The all-day drinking culture was so ingrained that people would pop out for an early morning pint around 11.30am, then a full hour and a half at lunchtime. By 12.30pm on Fridays, my column filed, the afternoon was written off – starting with lunch at Wheelers in Soho, drinks at the Colony Club alongside Francis Bacon and Denholm Elliott, on to the French pub on Dean Street around 6pm, followed by a nightcap at Gerry's drinking club down the road – until I fell into a cab home at 9pm.'[47] Professional sports were replete with similar stories. Tony Adams, the captain of a famous Arsenal football team in the eighties and early nineties, was far from alone in football, as was later discovered, as a self-confessed alcoholic.[48] The George Bests, Jimmy Greaveses and Paul Gascoignes of the footballing world were the more extreme examples of what until at least the end of the last century appeared to be a generalised drinking culture in British football. And it wasn't just football. David 'Bumble' Lloyd, the former Lancashire and England cricketer, and now well-known broadcaster, described making his England debut at Lord's. Coming in at the first lunchtime, his refreshment was a pint of lager with his lunch, before then resuming batting, successfully he felt, in the afternoon session.[49]

In a wide range of jobs a drink at lunchtime was a perfectly unremarkable thing – at least for men. So long as jobs got done, few considered it in any way unusual. One study of five UK industries in 1981 found at least one quarter of all men reported lunchtime drinking during the previous week (very few women did so), and more than half the men working in vehicle manufacture reported drinking at lunchtime as, perhaps predictably, did over 70 per cent of those working in breweries. Up until at least the 1980s, British civil servants had access to bars during their lunchtimes, and an inquiry by one peer (a teetotaller) found that in 1981, the league table of civil service drinking was topped by Century House, an outpost of the Foreign Office which housed MI6 staff, which had sold £32,500 worth of alcohol during lunchtimes the previous year. The Foreign Office itself was second, having recorded a similar £31,300 in sales.[50] In the House of Commons in 2018, total sales in the Smoking Room and the Strangers Bar were £630,878. A World Health Organization report published in 1996, printed a series of specimen alcohol at work policies that were in operation in the UK in the late twentieth century. Some workplaces – health care facilities and airports, for example – banned the consumption of alcohol 'on site' and 'when in uniform', but many others were far more liberal. A typical policy from the insurance industry simply noted that it was 'a disciplinary offence to be under the influence of alcohol to the extent that duties and responsibilities cannot be performed'. The same report quoted Kent County Council's policy advice as being that 'moderate drinking of alcohol is acceptable. It is equally acceptable for people not to drink alcohol at all if they do not wish to'!

One of the early signs of change occurred in the Royal Navy where the rum ration (the 'tot') came to an end. It had been introduced in 1655, when Vice-Admiral William Penn captured Jamaica, and the ritual of sailors queuing for two tots a day – one at noon, the other at dinner time – lasted for over three hundred years. Eventually, in 1969, after a seven-year investigation by the Admiralty Board it was recommended that it should end, the suggestion being that it was 'no longer compatible with the high standards of efficiency required now that the individual's tasks in ships are concerned with complex, and often delicate, machinery and systems on the correct functioning of which people's lives may depend.'[51] The last day of this ritual was 31 July 1970, though it was reprised for one day in 1981 when Prince Charles and Lady Diana Spencer married. A 1979 Think Tank report stated that 'so far as possible alcohol and work should, like alcohol and driving, be kept apart'.

Gradually, other occupations followed suit. In 1979, British Steel introduced breath testing at the Clyde Bridge works in Glasgow, though initially these were optional. Bus and coach drivers were covered by drink-driving legislation and in the eighties London Buses banned drinking during office hours for all employees. In 1988, the oil company Conoco (UK) introduced formal policies to prevent the misuse of alcohol when dealing with dangerous substances. After the 1989 *Exxon Valdez* disaster, when the tanker crashed and spilt nearly eleven million gallons of oil, many oil companies introduced a 'no alcohol' rule and screened employees. But the vast majority of companies had no alcohol policies in place by the end of the eighties. The percentage of businesses banning all drinking during working hours (including lunchtimes) rose from zero (in the fifties) to nearly 20 per cent in 1990 and then, according to one report, to well over half by 2007, though this is most likely an overestimate.[52]

Employers were increasingly recognising the financial and other impacts of heavy drinking. Though inappropriate consumption could lead to dismissal, at this stage case law appeared still to treat moderate drinking as relatively unproblematic, seeing drunkenness as the issue – and then one that was equally a health problem as much as a disciplinary one. Indeed, much of the literature in this area focuses on 'problem' drinking behaviours, and on the impact of *excess* alcohol on employee performance, paying less attention to drinking per se – and it is arguably in relation to the latter that the biggest cultural shift has taken place. An ACAS (the Advisory, Conciliation and Arbitration Service, a public body which advises on workplace rights, rules and best practice) code of practice from the mid-eighties reinforced this sense that there was a responsibility on employers to view alcohol misuse as a medical issue and to respond accordingly. In one of the more colourful stories at the time, it was reported that the principal timpanist with the Manchester-based BBC Philharmonic Orchestra was sacked after being found to have drunk a gin and tonic, two glasses of wine and two pints of bitter at a birthday lunch prior to a live broadcast. Apparently, the wheel of his kettledrum slipped noisily off stage during the performance, and he missed a cue and a complete passage of the flute concerto the orchestra was playing.[53] Though the tribunal described the decision as 'harsh', he nevertheless lost his appeal against being drummed out of the orchestra.

As a junior health minister in 1987, Edwina Currie criticised the culture of alcohol use in the country's boardrooms, suggesting that while it was quite appropriate that companies should increasingly be introducing alcohol policies, it was hypocritical not to focus equally on the conduct of those in positions of responsibility.[54] In 1991, in its *Health of the Nation* document, the government made a commitment to encourage employers to introduce workplace alcohol policies and evaluate their impact.[55] A survey of personnel officers in different industries in the early nineties found that over four in five favoured a ban on staff drinking. Support was particularly strong in manufacturing and construction industries.[56] The Transport and Works Act 1992 made it a criminal offence for certain workers to be unfit through drink and/or drugs while working on railways, tramways and other guided transport systems, and required all employers to show 'all due diligence' to avoid alcohol-related incidents. It was in the aftermath of the Vietnam War that testing for alcohol and drugs was introduced by the US Department of Defense, and gradually spread to other industries. Having become more common in the USA from the mid-eighties, British employers followed suit, especially when linked to an American company. British Airways began spot checks in 2001, pilots being forbidden to drink eight hours before flying (and only moderately twenty-four hours previously). By 2003, about 10 per cent of companies were using random drugs and alcohol tests.

A BBC News report in 2006 picking up on these shifts noted that the 'lunchtime pint – a cultural tradition in its own right – [is] disappearing. A survey from law firm, Browne Jacobson, [found] that 57% of businesses now ban drinking during the working day ... [and in] many parts of the country, particularly outside London, an ever-higher proportion ... don't allow staff to drink.' Seemingly, in the West Midlands the proportion was closer to three-quarters.[57] That the relationship between drinking and work should have begun to change in the eighties, and to have picked up pace since, is hardly a surprise. It is, in significant part, a reflection of wider socio-economic changes we have already come across, characteristic of a period in which market-based thinking and what is often referred to as 'new public management' were increasingly dominant. An era in which terms such as 'competition', 'downsizing' and 'performance measurement' became much more central to almost all public sector occupations, as many others, ever greater emphasis was placed on 'efficiency', on 'outputs' and on workplace discipline, encouraging increasing micro-management of the workforce. Though often far from being a central, or even explicit, target of such practices, one consequence has been that drinking during working hours has slowly become unacceptable.

We lived in markedly changed times where work is concerned. Working hours' drinking habits, apparently deeply ingrained two generations ago, have changed out of all recognition. The lunchtime drink, or three, is no longer part of everyday working culture. It happens of course and is less unusual in some walks of life than many others but is now very much the exception. Working lunches are now a radically different beast – assuming people even take lunch breaks at all. In short, a combination of health and safety concerns, growing legislative restriction, and significant shifts in the organisation and management of workplaces, have produced some remarkable changes in attitudes and expectations where the relationship between drinking and work is concerned.

A place to drink

Once again, it is time to reflect a little on what this brief foray into some aspects of our drinking habits tells us about ourselves and the nature of our post-war world. Predictably enough the picture is not a simple one. We have often thought of ourselves as a nation that has a somewhat problematic relationship with alcohol: drinking too much overall; bingeing and misbehaving, especially when abroad; and generally conducting ourselves in ways that contrast unfavourably with the café culture of our continental European neighbours. While this picture contains some important and uncomfortable truths it is far from being the full story. The UK comes somewhere around midway in European countries in terms of average alcohol consumption. Some of our neighbours consume more than we do, some experts consider many of the supposed benefits of a continental café culture to be vastly overstated, and we are far from alone in having problems of alcohol-related disorder. Nevertheless, until relatively recently British drinking levels were on the rise, with liver deaths having increased between three- and fivefold since the 1970s compared with a three- to fivefold decrease in both France and Italy.[58] And, similarly, the often drink-fuelled behaviour of our football fans, particularly in the latter decades of the last century, was sufficient for hooliganism to be regularly referred to as the 'English disease'.

Superficially at least, and certainly so far as licensing is concerned, we appear to have become gradually more permissive in the post-war years. The range of opening hours is greater. Arguably the choice of places in which one can drink has increased, the availability of places where alcohol can be bought has mushroomed, the range of drinks on offer is wider, and often cheaper and, as we say, until recently, the amount drunk was greater. Alcohol continues to be a core element in many social and leisure activities. All this occurs within a general regulatory environment that is much more complex than was previously the case. Restrictions have proliferated. But the nature of regulation has also changed. As the temperance movement withered in mid-twentieth century, alcohol regulation was increasingly viewed as a matter concerning the whole population, or significant parts thereof, not just that sliver (however big) who experienced or displayed particular problems. As we have seen, government action was focused not just on strategies to tackle the consequences of 'irresponsible drinking', but increasingly included proactive means for encouraging 'sensible', 'responsible' or some equivalent form of drinking. Given that only one-fifth of the population is teetotal, this translates directly into what is more broadly considered to be 'sensible' and 'responsible' citizenship. Policies have been wide-ranging, including such things as minimum pricing, further restricting the advertising of alcohol, encouraging the greater availability of lower-strength drinks, providing clearer information about the strength of drinks, and increasing the number and spread of accreditation schemes that promote and reward responsible behaviour (such as Best Bar None and Purple Flags). At the same time as general advice and encouragement for the population as a whole, aspects of the control of drinking have become much more targeted – on problem groups or problem behaviours: on young people, youth culture and so-called antisocial behaviour; on women, pregnancy and health; on the drink-driver; on safe and productive workers; and on issues of crime and disorder.

As we briefly mentioned earlier a group of European researchers have constructed scales to measure and compare the extent of formal social control with regard to alcohol across fifteen differ-ent European countries. The scoring mechanism includes points for production licences, restrictions on sales in various places, personal controls (e.g. legal age limits), marketing controls, drink-driving controls and national prevention programmes. The UK was ranked as having 'average alcohol control' in the 1950s and 1960s. From the sixties on the majority of European countries began a move toward stricter alcohol control. The UK itself moved from 'average' toward 'high' alcohol control from the seventies onward, and by 2000 only Sweden and Finland ranked higher in terms of their overall measures for alcohol regulation.[59] Compared with three-quarters of a century ago we may be consuming more alcohol, but we are doing so within a signifi-cantly more complex environment, and one which is character-ised by a wide array of rules and regulations which restrict what we can do and where and when we can do it or, alternatively, proffer guidance on what is considered appropriate and respon-sible behaviour.

So far as Britain is concerned, what we might think of as the 'moral order' of drinking has shifted significantly. In line with the changing way in which we are regulated and governed, both our practices and our attitudes appear to have changed markedly in the post-war period. Most obviously, considerably less of our drinking takes place in public in pubs and clubs, and much now happens in the privacy of the home. When we do go to the pub, we're much less likely to drive there, not least because driving home again afterwards is increasingly impermissible. Where once many workers would have thought nothing of taking alco-hol with their lunch, this is now generally exceptional. Though for many workers it is formally disallowed, for a great many it has simply become culturally unacceptable. Furthermore, it now seems that the flood of generalised health-related information about alcohol and its consequences, together with other social and economic changes, have begun to have an impact on drinking patterns more generally. The long post-war rise in overall average consumption has not only stalled but has begun to reverse. So-called 'binge drinking' is in decline, including among the young, and the numbers of young people reporting themselves to be teetotal has grown markedly. As commentators have long observed, drinking cultures are not static; both behaviour and attitudes can and do change, often very substantially. As is frequented noted by campaigners, alcohol is at least as dangerous as many other substances that we restrict much more severely, or even attempt to ban outright.[60] That we are heading toward a future of even greater legal and social intolerance of boozing seems more than likely.

CHAPTER FOUR

Queuing

Many commentators have observed that queuing is almost a national pastime for the English, who automatically arrange themselves into orderly lines at bus stops, shop counters, ice-cream vans, entrances, exits, lifts – and, according to some of the baffled tourists I interviewed, sometimes in the middle of nowhere for no apparent reason. (Kate Fox, *Watching the English*)

Fox is absolutely right that the queue has long been thought of as something that is peculiarly British. It is not that queues, or lines, don't exist elsewhere, merely that for a complex set of reasons they are thought to be particularly visible and frequent on these Isles, or at least have become presented as such. In what follows we will look in a little more detail at how the British actually queue, examine how these arrangements actually come about (they are far from *automatic*), how they might have changed in the past half-century or more, and how they relate to some of the emerging themes in this book.

As to how they form, just consider children's playgrounds. Swings, climbing frames, slides and all the rest. Are there queues to use the equipment? The answer is likely a bit of a mix. Yes, here and there. Sort of, if a slightly messy but partly organised set of kids roughly *taking turns* is a 'queue'. But also, no, it's all a bit of a free for all. So, there are very unlikely to be small kids in lines, waiting in a traditional queue. That's just not how kids behave or, importantly, are generally expected to behave. But there may be a system of taking turns depending on how old the kids are and, perhaps crucially, whether there are parents present. At least two things are of importance to us in this illustration. First, it is context specific. Playgrounds appear inherently disorderly – though even they have an order to them. They are designed precisely to allow children to do their thing in a *relatively* free manner – to play. Second, they are children and, as a consequence, are still in the process of learning, including learning to queue. This is something that they will pick up as they mature. They will learn, partly by imitation and practice, and partly by instruction. If we had used primary schools as our illustration, then our answer to the question would likely have been different. There are plenty of occasions in school when kids are asked to line up, and it is in school as much as anywhere that the concept of queuing is acquired. As with everything else we encounter in this book, queuing is learned behaviour and is socially patterned. And though relatively stable and predictable, it is not fixed. Its patterns and protocols shift and change. And it is thinking about both the patterns and changes that is our concern here. So, before we begin, please form an orderly . . . oh, you know the rest by now.

Queuing and British culture

As is regularly observed, one of the first to comment on the supposed British obsession with queuing was the Hungarian-born British journalist Mikes György, better known as George Mikes. In his faux-anthropological book, *How to Be an Alien*, he turned his humorous eye on British culture. His chapter on 'Sex', for example, consisted of a single sentence: 'Continental people have sex lives: the English have hot water bottles.' He was also the originator of the observation that an 'Englishman, even if he is alone, forms an orderly queue of one'. Indeed, his short chapter was entitled 'The National Passion', with queuing in his view being one of the few things to excite the members of this 'otherwise dispassionate nation'.[1]

At the top of the chapter we met Kate Fox, a more serious anthropologist than Mikes, but another whose starting point was to examine 'the unofficial codes of conduct', or what she refers to as the 'grammar', that governs everyday life. Queuing being one of those things that, certainly since Mikes' time, had been associated with Englishness, is something that Fox focuses on in some detail. One of the phenomena she considers is the response to the death of Princess Diana in 1997, and the public displays of grief and mourning that it prompted. Huge numbers turned out, a sea of flowers, messages and mementoes was left, and at least some commentators interpreted the reaction as indicating a marked change in the ability of buttoned-up Brits to display their emotions. Such were the numbers waiting to sign books of condolence, totalling forty-three in the end, that waiting times still stretched to seven or eight hours. The numbers of people wanting to take photographs, in the pre-selfie age, was sufficient for the police to create photographer-only lines.[2] All of which moved Kate Fox to observe that, despite some occasionally unusual characteristics, 'the English paid tribute to Diana in the most English possible manner, by doing what we do best, queuing'.

There can be little doubt that the scale of the reaction felt unprecedented at the time, and it certainly was extraordinary in its international reach. But in truth, in some of its basic features, the public response was far from unprecedented. We can see this if we cast our minds back a few years earlier to April 1989 and the dreadful Hillsborough stadium disaster in which ninety-seven Liverpool football fans lost their lives. In the aftermath the city of Liverpool became a focus of mass grieving. From late in the day of the tragedy itself both Hillsborough in Sheffield and Anfield, Liverpool's football ground, became sites of large-scale, ritualised mourning. Flowers, scarves and other tributes were left, initially on the gates of the football grounds, and subsequently within Anfield when the ground was opened to the public. Within days the whole of the pitch in Liverpool was covered in floral tributes, and there were huge queues of people waiting patiently to pay their respects, often for much of the day, for the seven days that the ground was kept open. During that week it was estimated that over a million people – twice the population of the city of Liverpool – visited Anfield.

There may have been something of our national character in evidence in the scenes outside Buckingham Palace after Diana's death as Fox was implying, but we really shouldn't get too carried away at the 'Englishness' of any of it. As the coronavirus lockdown was eased in Moscow what quickly re-emerged? Yes, the queues to enter Lenin's mausoleum. Over a hundred thousand people viewed Lenin's body in its initial temporary mausoleum in the first months after his death. The more permanent granite mausoleum was built in 1930 and Lenin has lain there ever since. As the Russian anthropologist Konstantin Bogdanov noted, 'all subsequent funerals of party bigwigs followed more or less exactly the format of Lenin's internment, and notably the leave-taking ceremony, which always took the form of a queue'.[3] Entombed now for close on a century, the three-month closure during the pandemic was one of the longest periods the former Russian leader had been without visitors. As soon as it became possible once again, queues formed for the renewed visits, though as one observer noted, the pandemic-linked restrictions meant they'd never seen a queue so short.

Although the standard outsiders' picture of Indian railways is one of apparent chaos and confusion, the Metro system in Delhi is rather different. As one set of observers describe: 'At the Chandni Chowk Metro station, passengers disembark onto a grey concrete platform awash with white light and ride elevators upwards. As they drop their tokens and move towards the street exit, others prepare to descend down. The process is highly regimented. There is a queue at the ticket counter; there is a queue where the gate is opened; and there is a queue at security, as passengers are patted down, and their bags fed through a machine. Passengers accept this serial queuing with good humour. Indeed, many find the exacting attitude to be exemplary.'[4] Of Caracas in Venezuela, the *New York Times* journalist Simon Romero said, 'Revolutions come and go. Construction frenzies reshape this city's skyline and then go bust, leaving white elephants as testament. Oil prices rise and fall and rise again. But one thing, at least, endures: the lines.'[5] And he quotes a local journalist observing Venezuelans' tendency to queue: 'We're attracted to lines like flies to honey; we actually love them'. In reality, perhaps no-one loves them but, like the British, the

Russians and the Venezuelans, they can become an habituated part of everyday life.

Kate Fox says that she was drawn to study queues having read a newspaper article in which it was suggested that queuing was in decline and that somehow or other the English were losing the knack. Feeling that this didn't accord with her everyday experiences she set out to examine current practices and in so doing she found plenty of evidence not just of the continuing ubiquity of queues, but of their complexity. Queues, she noted, are little mini-dramas, 'full of intrigue and scheming, intense moral dilemmas, honour and altruism, shifting alliances, shame and face-saving, anger and reconciliation'. As the Harvard-based psychologist Leon Mann observed in the late 1960s, queues are miniature social systems, which deal with the problems of norms and rules that face all social systems, often reflecting cultural values of egalitarianism and orderliness.[6] With that, let us turn briefly to issues of morality and ethics.

First come, first served?

Back to the humourist George Mikes who we met earlier in the chapter. Talking in general, Mikes said, 'A man in a queue is a fair man; he is minding his own business; he lives and lets live; he gives the other fellow a chance; he practises a duty while waiting to practise his own rights; he does almost everything an Englishman believes in doing'. Though the masculine language may be outmoded, Mikes hits on an obvious but important point about queuing: it has a rationale. People tolerate queues for a number of reasons. We understand that we are not alone in wanting whatever it is we are queuing for: food, tickets, stamps, entry to a theatre or football ground, even to see the preserved body of a former leader. In a physical queue we see the human manifestation of a lack of balance in supply and demand: in short, there are more of us wanting a particular service than there are people offering it at that place and time. Consequently, there needs to be a system for dealing with this problem, and this is why the queue has occasionally, if pompously, been referred to as a 'fairness management facility'. That is to say, so long as we can see some sense of order and predictability to the queue – some sense that things are *fair* – within reason we will put up with it. As Mark Wexler puts it, the 'social system of the queue involves repressing the "me-first" ego of the individual and calling upon the leaderless queue to maintain order'.[7] At heart this is what tends to be referred to as 'distributive justice'.

The phrase 'first come, first served', or 'first in, first out', captures how we generally think things should work (there are exceptions as we'll come to later). As a consequence, failure to behave by the rules of queuing tends to be considered selfish, arrogant, rude and an affront to order. The boundaries of the acceptable are often tested by practices such as saving someone's place for them while they head off to take care of other shopping or another task. This can be acceptable, but its legitimacy very much depends on the circumstances. Indeed, even when it is tolerated it is often annoying. A Mass Observation diarist in 1948 summed up the frustration: 'That tripe shop is the most unreliable ever. Women keep dodging out to "just go to pikelet shop", run over t'fish shop, just fetch us eggs and so on, so that when one joins it, it may seem twenty strong, but when all the missing women return there are thirty ahead of me.'[8]

All of which brings us to the thorny subject of 'queue-jumping', those occasions of failure to adhere to what are thought to be to be the norms or rules. As ever, it is deviant activity that shows us where the boundaries of the acceptable actually lie. The renowned American sociologist Charles Cooley writing in 1902, in his book *Human Nature and the Social Order*, examined the social bases of a series of human emotions. When examining 'hostility', he used queue-jumping as one of his examples:

> Suppose one had to stand in line at the post office, with a crowd of other people, waiting to get his mail. There are delay and discomfort to be borne; but these he will take with composure because he sees that they are part of the necessary conditions of the situation, which all submit to alike. Suppose, however, that while patiently waiting his turn he notices someone else, who has come in later, edging into the line ahead of him. Then he will certainly be angry. The delay threatened is only a matter of a few seconds; but here is a question of justice, a case for indignation, a chance for anger to come forth.[9]

Queuing, in short, is rule-governed behaviour, and adherence to those rules is affected by the sense that they apply to all and not just to some. Stanley Milgram, the American psychologist responsible for one of the most (in)famous studies of obedience, also had an interest in queues. His best-known experiments in the 1960s examined how obedient volunteers would be to instructions to give electric shocks to other volunteers making errors in word recall tasks (in practice they were members of the study team and they feigned the impact of the non-existent electric shocks). Despite exhibiting considerable reluctance to do so, almost two-thirds of the volunteers administered what would have been fatal levels of electricity had they been real.[10]

Milgram's interest in 'obedience' also led him to experiment with queues, though thankfully with rather less controversy. In a study in New York, he used graduate students to 'queue jump' in order to study the reactions of those waiting in line. In each case, in the 129 instances studied, a student would approach a queue which on average had six people in it. Approaching the third and fourth person in line the student was then instructed to say: 'Excuse me, I'd like to get in here' and then insert themselves. If they were told to leave the queue they would do so, otherwise they would remain there for a minute before leaving. In about two-fifths of cases, some sort of objection was raised. In about one in ten cases some sort of physical response was forthcoming; in the remainder people responded verbally or through non-verbal reactions, such as dirty looks or hostile gestures.[11]

Though objections to queue jumpers were expressed by both, it was those behind the person who had pushed in who were more likely to react than those in front. Of course, we should not be surprised by this given that they are the ones most directly affected – being those who now have to wait longer. However, the fact that those in front also tended to object, and do so quite frequently, shows that it is not just losing one's place in line that causes concern, but the general fact that the rules have been broken. The norms of this small and temporary social system have been challenged. In fact, one of the most interesting findings from his research on queues was reported by Milgram only very briefly and in an almost throwaway manner. Milgram's team observed all of the interactions, looking not only at the process of queue-jumping, but also at the behaviour of the five graduate students who were doing the hard work. What they discovered was that the students who were hired to push their way into queues found the experience highly uncomfortable. Indeed, he reported that many of them 'procrastinated', pacing near a queue they were planning on jumping into, sometimes for up to half an hour, before they summoned up the courage to do so. Some even reported feeling nauseous. Arguably, Milgram was potentially learning just as much about obedience here as he did in the remainder of his experiment. With all the backing of senior academics, and the knowledge that they weren't going to disadvantage anyone to any significant degree, and at worst only temporarily, the students still felt incredibly awkward about what they were being asked to do. For these students at least – and arguably for a great many of us – the rules of queuing are deeply ingrained.

Queues can be annoying, hugely so. But, a lot of the time, despite the fact that they stand between us and the immediate satisfaction of some particular desire, we are prepared to accept them. We do so because they also protect our interests; they defend us from those who come after us. Our status in the queue is determined by when we arrived – after some and before others – not by other attributes we bring with us, such as our wealth or social standing. We are simultaneously the victim and the beneficiary of the queue. We create order to avoid the price of disorder. And, as the sociologist Erving Goffman observed, all of this requires 'queuing discipline' among all those in line.[12] Now, with all these allusions to equity and democracy we need to pause once again before we get too carried away. So far, we've discussed the ethical principles of queuing; the general assumptions that underpin our standard conception of the queue. Leaving aside the problem of queue-jumping, we also need to acknowledge that queues do not always operate in the standard form: treating everyone the same, as equals. There are plenty of examples, some positive, others less so, and a number of exceptions to the general rule of queuing that we are prepared to accept. The hospital Accident and Emergency Department is one of these. There, as

Richard Larson puts it, queues generally work on a 'worst come, first served basis'.[13] We will all have our details taken when we arrive, but it is assumed that those who have the most urgent needs will tend to be seen first. Though not everyone is happy to put up with this, as anyone who has worked in, or spent any time in A&E will testify, it is a broadly understood and accepted principle.

Queues may seem, and indeed are, a mundane feature of everyday life. But as small social systems they are potentially also highly instructive. Studies of queuing have been conducted all around the world. People wanting to understand everything from human emotions to business ethics have used queuing behaviour as an illustration. At this point, however, we must come back to the alleged 'Britishness' of queuing. Even though it is perfectly clear that queues can be found pretty much anywhere, it is seemingly impossible for the Brits to shake off their reputation – deserved or otherwise – for queuing. A couple more recent examples. In *Rules Britannia*, a 2007 book ploughing a similar furrow to George Mikes' post-war classic, author Rohan Candappa said, 'Nothing is more British than queuing.' Not just something we are associated with but, seemingly, are good at: 'Indeed, if queuing ever became an Olympic sport Britain would undoubtedly win gold every time.'[14] A OnePoll.com survey in 2008 found that the three most typical British traits were described as 'talking about the weather', 'great at queuing' and 'sarcasm'. A 2016 audit of 'Britishness' commissioned by Tetley, who else, based on an analysis of the British Social Attitude and OnePoll surveys listed the top forty British traits. At number five was 'finding queue-jumping the ultimate crime' and, hot on its heels at six, was 'forming a queue for pretty much anything'. The year previously, Debrett's, which badges itself as the authority on business and social etiquette, said: 'Even today, grumbling in a queue is one of the great British joys – there is a liberating anonymity in conversing with someone whose back is to you; the grumbler in front will turn enough so that you can hear them but not enough so that you exchange eye contact and graduate to actual personal interaction and the implications of intimacy that that might entail.'[15]

So, there you have it. Like it or not, we continue to believe, or at least be told, that we are a nation that queues and, much of the time, just loves to do so. To understand this a little more we have to think a little more historically, beginning by taking a look at some of the ways that queuing has changed since around the time of the Second World War.

A not so 'golden age'

Much of the post-war history of queuing has been analysed beautifully by the cultural historian Joe Moran. The first, and important, question he asks is why did so many people comment on the British propensity for queuing in the 1940s? The very act of asking this question almost makes the point in itself. The war and the rationing of foodstuffs and other goods had made queuing a visible, everyday experience – for women at least. Indeed, much of this was already well embedded before the war. As *The Times* noted in January 1939, 'If there is one thing for which our nation may claim credit it is the patience and orderliness of its voluntarily formed queues ... When once a queue has begun to gather, it is a bold man or woman who would seek to enter it anywhere but at its latter end ... the queue is quite capable of dispensing its own justice.'[16] But this was the period when two conceits took hold. The main one was that we were a nation of queuers, not just from necessity but because it was part of our culture and character. The second, and related to this, was that we were somehow *better* at it. Not only did we think we had the 'best police in the world' we believed we had the politest and most orderly queues. Though still repeated today, certainly about queues if less so about the police, these are still conceits – things we like, or are persuaded to believe about ourselves.

The forties was a world of shortages and privation. But it was a set of privations that were accepted in the war. As the historian Peter Hennessy observed, 'selling rationing to the people during the war was the most successful Government public relations exercise I have ever encountered ... It succeeded in giving its huge apparatus, which forcibly pre-empted the usual laws of supply and demand, a human face'. And like queues more generally, selling it required that it be based on some sense of fairness. As a Ministry of Information report noted in 1942, 'people are willing to bear any sacrifice if a 100 per cent effort can be reached and the burden fairly borne by all'.[17] Petrol was the first thing to be subject to rationing, and foodstuffs followed. Bacon, butter and sugar were the first to be restricted, followed progressively by meat, cheese, eggs, milk, tea and others. Many of these restrictions would last for much of the remainder of the decade.

The end of the war brought expectations of a brighter future, in which there would be 'homes for heroes' and, eventually, an end to rationing. But as diarist Nella Last of Barrow observed in 1945: 'Queues were everywhere, for wedge-heeled shoes, pork pies, fish, bread and cakes, tomatoes [and] emergency ration cards at the food office.'[18] In this period, and perhaps for the first time, queuing became a matter of politics; a shorthand, symbol or indicator of wider social ills and a nudge to indicate to the frustrated citizen that the brighter future they hoped for might arrive more quickly if their vote was cast in one direction rather than another. Moran reports that the Mothers' League began a campaign against queuing in 1945 and in response the Ministry of Food went so far as to send staff to join queues to see what all the fuss was about. Much focused on perceived unfairness. There were those such as the elderly and the infirm, and women with babies and young children, who straightforwardly felt that queuing disadvantaged them. But the wider problem was that queuing, not least for basic foodstuffs, increasingly came to be viewed as unfair and unnecessary now that the conflict was over. After five years of war it was hardly a surprise some relief was expected and that queuing and rationing were a source of dispute. According to Mass Observation, shortages were listed as the 'top civilian grumble' in early 1946 and two-thirds of people questioned felt they were going short of essentials.

Continuing restrictions were bad enough, but the fact that they appeared to worsen stretched many to breaking point. What brought things to a head was bread and flour, which were rationed for two years from 1946 to 1948. The wartime government had avoided such a restriction, feeling that the costs in terms of physical well-being and morale would be so great that it was unthinkable. Indeed, as one account has it, it was a policy that both the government and the British people had been taught to dread. Nevertheless, Attlee's post-war Labour government felt it was necessary in order to drive down consumption, and it paid a great price as a consequence. If selling rationing during wartime was one of the greatest PR exercises ever, then selling bread rationing in the years after was one of the less impressive. Churchill described the Labour government's announcement of the new restrictions as 'one of the gravest announcements that I have ever heard made in the House in time of peace'.

Campaigns against the new restrictions sprang up immediately, not just via the Conservative opposition, but also the press sympathetic to the Conservatives, among housewives' groups and, of course, bakers. The British Housewives' League, founded after the war, began its life with a campaign against queuing. 'We the housewives of Great Britain are now in open revolt against bread rationing,' said Irene Lovelock, the League's leader. 'The rich people will not suffer, the middle class, the poor people, the ones with children, they're the ones that's going to suffer.'[19] Towards the end of the Second World War the League became a formidable organisation, reaching a peak of one hundred thousand members, rounding up signatures, and, in the early fifties, leading a successful campaign against identity cards, which were connected to the queuing system.

The British reputation for queuing might somehow have been cemented in the post-war years but it was hardly a period when anyone should have actually confused compliance with enjoyment. The British regularly formed queues, but there was plenty of evidence that, at least some of the time, they were not in the slightest happy about it. Here is Edie Rutherford, a Mass Observation diarist, writing in 1947: 'It looks as if several national dailies are saying queues should be abolished. Well, I have said all along, and still say, some of us just have not the time to queue, so we don't. It has been unfair all through the war years that the women who have loyally gone to work have had to go without extras. While the women who went on calmly living domestic lives have stood around to get the plums.' And as another contributor to the Mass Observation study put it in 1948, 'Queuing is a necessary evil, and the only fair method to ensure equal distribution of scarce commodities. At its [most] nauseating in butchers' shops; at its most depressing in fish shops'.[20]

Petitions proliferated and as one historian noted, 'women and especially housewives, frustrated by queuing, shortages ranging from curtains to cosmetics, and the difficulties of providing family meals out of diminishing rations, emerged as a leading group opposed to austerity'.[21] There is even evidence that bread rationing had an impact on three by-elections in 1946. All registered swings to the Conservatives, and although Labour maintained large majorities in two, there was a swing of over 20 per cent to the Conservatives in Bexley, a seat that Ted Heath won for them in the 1950 general election.

Many charges were laid at Labour's door. First, that the country they were presiding over in peacetime now faced shortages and rationing worse than those often found in both the war and the pre-war years. Second, that they were a government of micromanagement, introducing ever more minute regulations and controls over everything from house building to the sale of flour. Restrictions on bread, and the queuing that was linked to this most unpopular of policies, became a political wrangle over liberty. Churchill's Tories increasingly positioned themselves as the housewife's friend, bemoaning the unacceptability of wartime controls in peacetime. As the Conservatives put it, 'controls breed like rabbits ... when you ration one thing, like bread, the substitute for it, like potatoes, will become scarce and may be rationed in turn'.[22] Shortages, restrictions, rationing, queues, red tape, anxiety, socialism on the one hand; freedom from an overbearing state on the other.

Moreover, it was successful. The public unhappiness with rationing and restriction, and the way it was exploited, enabled

Churchill to recover much of the ground he'd lost to Attlee at the end of the war. By the time of the 1951 election Churchill had honed his message that linked restrictions and waiting in line with Labour's failures: 'Why should queues become a permanent, continuous feature of our life? The socialist dream is no longer Utopia, but Queuetopia. And if they have the power, this part of their dream will certainly come true'.[23] Queues were presented both as a sign of a society failing to return to prosperity, and also an indicator that Labour favoured a drab form of equality rather than rewarding individual effort and merit. In the aftermath of their election victory, and with Conservatism now increasingly linked to 'affluence', queuing was still called on as a symbol of everything that was to be avoided and all that would be risked if ever Labour was re-elected. Indeed, as Moran notes, it was really only in the aftermath of the end of rationing in the mid-fifties that queuing finally, and quietly, slipped off the political agenda.

We've been queuing a long time

As we've seen, so entrenched had queuing become in wartime and in the immediate post-war years that it seemingly became lastingly attached to British national character. Indeed, as the Mass Observation diarist B. Charles wrote in December 1945, the experience was so profound it felt new:

> There were two queues in the post office. This queue business is simply amazing. I can't think how it was that there were none of them prior to the war. When I was coming home on the tram I spoke to a naval officer and his opinion is that, now people have become so 'queue-minded', they just fall into a

queue instead of hanging about the counters of the shops, as
they used to do before the war. He thinks the vast majority of
people are so determined to get all they can that they queue so
as not to miss anything. I feel sure, too, that a great many
women *like* queuing: the queue is, really, the 1945 edition of
the Mother's Meeting.[24]

Of course, it was not as if queues were absent in pre-war Britain.
When King Edward VII was lying in state, in 1910, estimates of
the number of mourners ranged from a third to over half a
million. A similar number paid homage at the tomb of the
Unknown Warrior in 1920 and, two years later, the queue at St
James's Palace to see Princess Mary's wedding presents averaged
four thousand a day with a few hundred turned away. 'The queue
has visibly established itself as a standing feature of London life,'
wrote a correspondent of *The Times* in 1922. 'There are queues
regularly recurrent, such as those of the theatre, the tramway, the
omnibus and the railway booking office; and occasional queues
generated by episodes as diverse as the display of Royal wedding
presents and the clash of heavyweight boxers.'[25] The writer went
on to say that queues in the twenties displayed an incredible
degree of patience. People arrived with camp stools, sandwiches,
sewing, newspapers, crossword puzzles, card games, knitting or
books. Sooner or later the theatre doors opened, an unfilled
omnibus arrived and the gates to Wimbledon tennis courts were
unlocked. One correspondent wrote to *The Times* saying that
throughout the thirties they had 'queued obediently at cinemas,
marshalled by commissionaires and even sometimes by the
cinema manager'. The manager would likely be on patrol in the
foyer during especially popular films, the commissionaire keeping control outside. Indeed, 'friendly commissionaire could be

relied on to let us know how long we might have to wait, or indeed whether we were wise to wait at all'. In 1936, over eight hundred thousand mourners walked past King George V's coffin at Westminster Hall over a four-day period, and, in 1952, over three hundred thousand paid their last respects to King George VI over three days (without a weekend to raise numbers).

It wasn't all voluntary, however. In 1936, the London Passenger Transport Board sought powers to introduce a by-law requiring people 'to enter tramcar trolley vehicles or public service vehicles in the order in which they stood in such line or queue'. The by-law was introduced in 1938, together with signage (Please Queue). London Passenger Transport Board accompanied the new rule with a statement: 'Londoners accept the queue. They ask for queues to be organised. The queue makes for a quicker getaway. It allows 274 tramcars to leave Blackfriars in one hour; a tramcar every thirteen seconds. The queue gives everybody an equal chance. "First come, first served" is a popular motto. It is only another way of saying "Please queue".'[26] The first prosecution under the law came in May 1939, when a man was fined ten shillings (a sizeable sum in the thirties) plus ten-shillings costs for jumping a queue of seventy people in Waterloo Road, Lambeth.

With queuing having worked as a political symbol for the Conservatives in 1951, they used it again in 1955. As Moran reports, 'they produced pamphlets with photographs of long lines of housewives and captions reading "Queues, controls, rationing – don't risk it again!".'[27] By this stage, however, with rationing having come to an end, the sense of queuing for everything had also begun to disappear. By 1957, an editorial in *The Times* commented that 'the worst features of the queue have subsided since the war'.[28] Indeed, with the promised arrival of the idea of 'self-service' shops, it seemed possible grocery queues might disappear altogether. Though an increasingly affluent and consumerist society meant there was never any hope of a queue-less utopia emerging, so far as politics was concerned the symbol of the queue had lost its power. It would be the seventies before it returned and, again, it would be the Conservatives who would exploit it most successfully.

For a party that would go on to preside over record unemploy-ment levels the Conservatives' use of Saatchi and Saatchi-designed campaign posters featuring lengthy unemployment queues and the strapline 'Labour Isn't Working' and 'Labour Still Isn't Working' was more than a little ironic. In fact, the general election occurred at the end of what was in many ways a miserable decade punctuated by an oil crisis, petrol rationing, the three-day week, power cuts and the 'winter of discontent' with its empty supermarket shelves, garbage piling uncollected in the streets and a gravediggers strike meaning bodies went unburied in Liverpool. Once again, the queue – this time the dole queue – became the go-to symbol of national problems and of political choice. Joe Moran sums it up:

> As queuing ceased to be an explicitly political issue in the 1950s and 1960s, it became a way of subliminally addressing historical problems through shared daily routines. What had once been held up as an example of the best of the national character could now be seen as symbolic of the 'British disease' at its worst.

In fact, from the seventies onwards the management of queuing, and the proliferation of techniques to manage citizens via queu-ing, would become an ever more central part of British civil life.

As we will see, it was also the point at which in many respects the association of queuing with fairness was at least partially fractured.

Queuing for groceries in the modern age

The curse of the grocery queue was supposed to be radically transformed by two things: the end of rationing and the introduction of self-service. It will only be readers of a certain age that will recognise just how significant a shift self-service made to the process of shopping. Anyone born before the 1960s will be familiar with the dominance of old-fashioned counter service. Customers would make requests for the things they wished, either by asking for them or handing over a list, and shopkeepers and workers would then retrieve, weigh or measure the goods, and wrap them. Indeed, in large department stores, even up to the 1960s, cash was handled centrally, and systems of pulleys or pneumatic tubes were still used to transport payments and change back and forth from elsewhere in the shop (often the basement). Most shops were decentralising by this point and by the seventies there were no more than a couple of dozen left. The last of the pneumatic systems, apparently, was at Fairhead's department store in Ilford, which removed it in 1991.[29]

There can be no doubt that the rise of the supermarket and the arrival of self-service were the 'pivotal retail innovations of the twentieth century that transformed the process of selling and the act of shopping'.[30] Supermarkets and self-service stores altered the British high street, though supermarkets caught on much more quickly than self-service. The fifty or so supermarkets that existed in 1950 had risen tenfold to well over five hundred by 1961, and to 3,400 by 1969.[31] Arriving in the forties, thanks to the ending of rationing and easing of building restrictions, by 1967 supermarkets accounted for 20 per cent of all grocery sales, and smaller self-service stores took a further 30 per cent of the market.

One of the very first shops to experiment may have been Spooner's department store in Plymouth, which reportedly had 'a special feature ... the "Piggly Wiggley"[32]. There are no assistants in this department where all articles are specially lowered in price.'[33] It was Co-operative Societies that were at the forefront of the self-service revolution, not least because of the relatively high proportion of their customers who were registered for rationed goods, and therefore had to queue. Under the headline 'The Gospel of Self Service', *The Grocer* promoted such changes arguing that 'British housewives are sick of queues'. The first Co-op experiments began in east London as early as 1942 and there were up to six hundred stores operating on partial or full self-service lines by the end of the decade. Sainsbury's converted its first grocery to self-service in 1950, but still only had three by 1954. Developments on the two sides of the Atlantic proceeded at very different speeds, the British and American economies being barely alike at that stage. As one observer put it, associating 'the freedom, the plenty and the overflowing abundance of wealthy American "self-service" with the subsidised, rationised and controlled economy of England is like comparing heaven with purgatory'.[34]

The expansion of self-service, which picked up quickly in the fifties, was largely driven by two imperatives. One was a desire to limit what appeared to be the ever-rising costs of labour, the other the need to reduce the problem of consumer dissatisfaction with the lengthy queues that were so often found in traditional grocers and other shops. Indeed, in its earliest days in

Britain, the new self-service experience was marketed in the media as a 'no queue' approach to shopping. A retailing manual in the late 1940s said, 'self-service has the advantage of eliminating the queue, of reducing overhead costs, and of allowing shoppers to make their purchases at high speed, or in leisurely manner, as they wish, without impeding the movements of other shoppers.'[35] Indeed, the Union of Shop, Distributive and Allied Workers (USDAW) found that 'customers were less irritable because they did not have to wait in queues'.[36] Market research found self-service to be generally positively received and no doubt anticipated improvements to the shopping experience were a major impetus behind its introduction and spread. Commercial interests were also to the fore, and there are suggestions that those involved in the promotion of retail refrigeration might have had quite a substantial hand in encouraging negative claims about queuing, thus boosting the search for new ways of shopping.

The idea of increased freedom and choice, supposedly core characteristics of supermarkets and self-service shopping, were also the primary means by which people (women mainly) were persuaded that it was in their interests to reorient how they went about their shopping. Professor Paul du Gay asks how one persuades people to adopt new technologies, in this case a technology relating to shopping, when it is new to them and its use flies in the face of their normal assumptions and practices? More particularly, he asks 'how do you get them to see something that they have conceived of as work, undertaken for them by other people for a wage, as something they should do themselves, for free?' Indeed, perhaps even to view the whole shift as boosting their own freedom?[37] Indeed, not everyone was happy about such changes. Allegedly, Lord Sainsbury was once waylaid by a

171

judge's wife in Purley telling him he 'had no right to expect the customer to do the work the assistants had done in the past'.[38] In this connection, the answer to du Gay's question is largely by trying to promote ideas associated with organisation, ease, hygiene and modernity; to persuade 'housewives' – and that was the way it was seen – that this was an attractive new world. Speed, primarily by doing away with lengthy queues, became one of the key selling points for this seductive, rational new world. Evidence is far from plentiful, but research in 1950 found that a high proportion of those using self-service felt it was quicker and that they had not experienced excessive delay at the checkout.

There was another aspect of the change in shopping that had to be carefully managed. It was felt that the advent of self-service reduced the sociability of shopping, at least for some. Queuing could be a source of annoyance and frustration, but it could also be an important meeting place. An interviewee in one study described her experience thus: 'if you were waiting you would chat to the other people in [the queue] – who were waiting and then again, you'd chat to the people over the counter; but, yes, I mean once or twice you did used to have to wait because people did like to chat and they would do so even, you know, even at the expense of holding other people up and I suppose in one sense that was a disadvantage of that type of shopping but in a way it . . . was nice that people felt that they could do that and I don't think people used to get very irate about it really.'[39]

Though starting from the early post-war years, self-service operations (stores and supermarkets) accounted for 15 per cent of grocery turnover in 1959, rising to over 60 per cent by 1969. This was in some ways a hard-fought battle and, as du Gay puts it, 'it is difficult to overestimate the amount of work that retailers and related trades engaged in to try and convince their publics of the benefits of "going self-service"'. When Tesco opened its first self-service store in 1947 it quickly had to return to counter service when customers complained of the trouble involved in shopping for themselves. Customer surveys found that the ability to select goods for oneself, to see everything that was available, and to save time, were the three most common reasons given for favouring self-service shopping. As one woman told Mass Observation in 1959, 'Well, you can walk round and everything's out for you to see, everything out in front, and you're not waiting in a queue to be served, you can just pick what you want and get away.'[40]

In her history of modern shopping, Rachel Bowlby notes that in this period when self-service was still relatively new there were those who felt that there would continue to be resistance to the changes it heralded. Indeed, she quotes one writer of the planning of shops and shopping in the late 1950s saying that one could 'safely assume that the development of self-service will not affect seriously our plans for the foreseeable future'. The problem, the writer felt, was that shopping 'is not for many women one of those chores to be done as quickly and easily as possible. Shopping is more than buying an article.'[41] In short, shopping was felt to serve a social function as well as satisfying consumer needs. In 1963, in a widely circulated report called *Shopping in Suburbia*, supermarket shopping was still presented as unfamiliar and somewhat alien. Nevertheless, by the end of the decade, she suggests, efficiency had generally won out over conviviality. Reflecting the changed times, the Consumers' Association's magazine, *Which?*, published a report which took for granted that supermarkets were now the norm and that shopping had changed, with most women making it clear 'that general food shopping was something to be carried out efficiently'.

Queues had by no means gone away of course, in some respects they had merely changed in style and location; they had shifted from counter to checkout, and possibly from small grocers to larger ones. As one supermarket shopper observed, all it meant now 'is a queue in one store as opposed to queues in four or five shops'.[42] Though supermarkets were now an increasingly embedded everyday experience for many shoppers, queuing and time-delays were a continuing bugbear. Earlier in the decade, *The Times* reported that the Director of the Consumer Council had told the Supermarkets Association that a 'major source of dissatisfaction was the waste of time at checkout points where all time saved in going round the store was lost'.[43] A series of reports in the early seventies continued this theme. *The Grocer* called on opinion poll data to show that over half of women using supermarkets and self-service stores disliked long queues at the checkout more than any other feature of that form of shopping. On its 'Women's Features' page in February 1968, *The Times* similarly observed that as 'every busy woman knows, the greatest deterrent to weekend shopping in the supermarket emporia is that the time saved in serving oneself is lost 16 times over in that slow moving shuffle to meet the cashier'. It went on to report on an innovation from a Wallsend Co-operative store in the north-east of England where each cashier had three bays into which they could send goods on a conveyor belt. The shopper went to one of the bays which then allowed the cashier to charge for the goods and give any change required. They could then move on to their next customer while the first continued packing their shopping. As it noted, generally by the time the third customer had been dealt with, 'the first bay is clear and the lightning procedure begins all over again'. So impressed were they, that all they had left to say was 'London supermarkets please copy'.[44]

Increasing effort went into both reducing the time spent queuing and changing perceptions of queues. From softer, 'more restful' lighting at checkouts to the placing of promotional and advertising materials, a range of means were used to try to distract or otherwise engage the shopper in the queue. Perhaps some shoppers could be persuaded to alter the time they shopped, again through various promotions, in order to spread the load? In the end, as *The Times* feature had indicated, there was really nothing for it other than to try to make checkouts more efficient. The Wallsend-style multi-bay packing approach became more widespread in the seventies, some tests suggesting it improved efficiency by as much as 30 per cent, as did the introduction of a 'magic eye' system that controlled the movement of the conveyor belt when the shopping had reached the person on the till. Cash handling was another issue, with both speed and accuracy being required. Again, at least part of the answer was automation, first via an 'automatic change computing sales register. This machine computes the exact amount of change due to the customer and indicates it. A further extension is the use of a coin-dispenser which dispenses change automatically to the shopper.'[45] And to the present day where the throughput of customers is all but a branch of science. From computerised cash registers in the seventies, universal product codes and barcodes in the eighties, to the logical conclusion of self-service, the self-scan checkout. Safeway introduced the first in 1995 and by 2020, small supermarkets and many other shops had all but done away with staffed checkouts, effectively leaving everything to the shopper. The judge's wife in Purley must be fuming.

On a waiting list

As we noted earlier, from the early 1980s, politics shifted markedly in Britain, not only with the arrival of Margaret Thatcher to power for over a decade, but with the increased stress placed on the culture and ideology of the market and the private sector. Not only were governments on both sides of the Atlantic increasingly business-oriented and keen, wherever possible, to privatise public services, but public services were increasingly subjected to private sector-style management procedures. Under the banner of 'new public management' (NPM), in Britain the initial stress was upon what were referred to as the 'three E's': economy, efficiency and effectiveness. Performance indicators and league tables were the new game in town, auditors the new referees. The revolution heralded by self-service shopping was about to reach a whole new range of outlets. The post office, schools, universities, police forces, the list is long, and all became subject to attempts to do more for less through that horrible phrase 'driving up performance'. If changes in post offices, banks and building societies illustrated many of the consequences of this new culture, then the management of hospitals was emblematic of one important element of the politics of queues at the end of the century.

For as long as we have had a National Health Service the issue of waiting lists has been a concern. When the NHS began its life in July 1948, there were worries that there would be queues outside hospitals and GPs' surgeries, not least because of the large number of people with chronic conditions. Though this fear wasn't realised, the issue of waiting lists has been with us

ever since. Before the end of the forties means were being explicitly sought both of explaining waiting for treatment to the public
and how, if possible, to reduce the problem. In 1963, Enoch
Powell acknowledged the difficulties the health service faced,
saying, 'I cannot but reflect sardonically on the effort I myself
expended, as minister of health, in trying to "get the waiting lists
down". It is an activity about as hopeful as filling a sieve . . . In a
medical service free at the point of consumption the waiting
lists, like the poor in the Gospel, "are always with us".'[46] In fact,
hospital waiting lists were relatively stable through the sixties,
and it was in the seventies when financial pressures grew that
debates over waiting lists – and over the role of private medicine
– began to intensify. Even so it was hardly a hot topic. The *British
Medical Journal*, which had published two letters on the subject
of waiting lists in the fifties, and three in the sixties, still only
published a dozen in the seventies.[47]

According to the historian of health care Sally Sheard, there
'is a clear relationship between the emergence of health economics as a distinct academic discipline and profession in the United
Kingdom, and rising concerns for NHS efficiency and effectiveness'. One of the biggest early impacts health economists had
was in switching emphasis away from how many people there
were on waiting lists toward how much time people had to wait.
The arrival of the emphasis on the three E's changed thinking
around waiting lists, though the generally poor quality of NHS
data meant it would be some time before they could easily be
used as a management tool. By the mid-eighties statistics were
beginning to appear which allowed practices in NHS districts to
be compared. The nineties saw the full flourishing of management tools such as performance indicators, league tables, a
system of star ratings for individual hospitals and Prime Minister

John Major's 'Citizen's Charter'. Indeed, the NHS had its own 'Patient's Charter', which both included a right to treatment within two years of diagnosis and promised to prioritise waiting times over numbers of patients on waiting lists.

Queues in the NHS were now firmly a cross-party political matter. In seeking election in 1997, Tony Blair's New Labour published a card with five pledges on it, one of which was 'Cut NHS waiting lists by treating an extra 100,000 patients as a first step by releasing £100,000,000 saved from NHS red tape'. Long heralded, it was only at the turn of the century that waiting times finally overtook waiting lists as a major method of monitoring NHS performance, and a series of major investments, and new promises, were made in an effort to reduce the queues. Given how often politicians have declared war on every social problem from poverty to drugs, it was perhaps a surprise that we had to wait until the new century before the then health secretary, Alan Milburn, declared a 'war on waiting'![148] The image of the queue was now firmly established as a primary means by which citizens were asked to engage with the politics of health care. Put slightly differently, and paralleling arguments we have made elsewhere, we might also observe that, in this context, the queue was increasingly becoming a means by which the consumer of health care was encouraged to think and act – and increasingly as citizens we were being persuaded to think and act as 'consumers'.

The efficient queue

Banks, building societies and, quintessentially, the Post Office, were the site of a related range of queue-related reforms in the second half of the twentieth century. Post-war welfare state reforms added unemployment benefits, pensions and family allowances to the range of things to queue for in the Post Office. *The Times* reported in August 1946, that the minister of national insurance had visited Stepney post office in east London to 'greet the many women who went there to draw the new family allowances'. Mrs Hall, a mother of six, was the first to be paid having been at the head of a queue that had formed soon after 7 a.m.[49]

If anything, things worsened in the 1960s, with already inefficient and somewhat overrun post offices under even greater pressure once they effectively became banks too. The introduction of the Post Office Giro banking service in 1968 brought significant new business. However, already employing over forty thousand counter staff, and having increased its headquarter's staff, the Post Office was determined not to hire any extra workers. Their head of operations estimated that business would increase by 3–4 per cent but said he did not anticipate any lengthening of queues.[50] The post office was one of many casualties of the energy crisis in 1973, which saw limits placed on petrol use. Deliveries became almost impossible and by mid-December there was only one post office open in London together with a small number in the provinces, and then only for three hours. At the London post office huge wartime-like queues developed when a ban on forthcoming parcel deliveries scuppered hopes of posting Christmas presents.

December 1975 saw a flurry of letters to the editor of *The Times* on the subject of the seemingly increasingly infamous post office queue. One correspondent summed up a common experience: 'Every time I visit a post office, I am faced with the problem of which queue to join: invariably the one I choose proves to be the slowest to move, particularly if it was the shortest. When eventually I reach the counter and start a lengthy transaction, I am conscious of those behind me realizing that they too joined the wrong queue.'[51] The solution to this all-too-common problem was to be found in American banks and post offices, he said, and it was simply to install a guiding rope with an explanatory notice, inviting people to join a single queue, and then proceed, in turn, to a counter whenever one becomes free. Just as supermarkets and self-service had eventually crossed the Atlantic so 'queuing tape' would also eventually arrive in the UK. In response the head of Post Office services said that this form of 'single queue system' was already operating in one head post office in London and that this would help them 'find out how our customers feel about it and whether there are any snags for them or for us'.[52]

Sir, The Post Office is in the middle of a witty advertising campaign touting the bewildering array of services to be had at any post office. The humour is, of course, that one cannot buy anything at all, not so much as a stamp, at a post office for the interminable queues to be found there.

Might the Government not insist that the Post Office provides service at all times within operating hours, so that we do not have to wait more than, say, four minutes to be served? Only when the Post Office is offering its existing services efficiently should it be allowed to offer new ones.
Letter to *The Times*,
2 May 1984

Sir, Perhaps [your correspondent] would like to consider the staff on the other side of the fence or glass who have to master and deal with the vast variety and number of transactions the Post Office offers; the long queues of impatient customers (caused by lack of staffing) ... The Post office not only handles more services and transactions than any other public-service business but also has to contend with a fast growing bank (Giro) and its customers.
Reply, *The Times*, 5 May 1984

The general secretary of the main union representing post office workers also wrote to respond to the letter of 2 May. The reasons for post office queues, he said, was the result of the implementation of 'severe' financial targets and their insistence on substantial cost reductions. 'The government has imposed upon the Post Office a 5 per cent real reduction in running costs over a three-year period, but at the same time has removed from post office counters many of the types of transaction which help meet the overheads.'[53] The more general complaint, which was a widespread one at this time, was that commercial imperatives were now considered far more important than other aspects of running a public service.

As Joe Moran observes, the Post Office was an enthusiastic adopter of new queue management techniques, and he points to a 1988 Monopolies and Mergers Commission (MMC) report on Post Office Counters, by this point a subsidiary of the Post Office, which examined current performance standards and monitoring. As an illustration of the nature of the new managerialism in this period of history, the assessment of the work of Post Office Counters is a tour de force. At this time, quality of service was assessed in three ways: via 'speed of service', 'office style' and 'convenience/accessibility of the office network'. Speed of service meant 'waiting time' and was measured in two ways:

a. A percentile of the waiting time distribution, determined from a sample of customer waiting times to indicate the percentage of customers that are served within a given time period of joining the queue; and

b. Average waiting time, an estimate of the average time within a period that customers spend waiting for a counter clerk to become available to serve them.

In order that all this could be centrally monitored the poor old Branch Manager had, using daily sampling, to record (a) the number of customers entering the office during the sample period (obtained by taking readings from customer counting devices before and after the target customer is served); (b) the queue length (again, before and after the target customer is served); (c) waiting time before target customer is served; (d) the number of counters open and with clerks serving or available for service; (e) the number of counter clerks scheduled to be available for serving. In the name of economy, efficiency and effectiveness the post office queue had become a site of Orwellian surveillance and microscopic management.

Because 'quality of service' was influenced by both the manner in which people joined queues and by what service they wanted, this meant that it was imperative not only that clerks were efficient, and sufficient in number, but that some control was exercised over customers.[54] Considerable experimentation had been undertaken by Post Office Counters into what was now officially referred to as 'customer queue discipline', not least in comparing the differential impact of single queues, multiple queues and special service queues. Future policy was to convert multiple queues into single ones and to introduce quick service positions for shorter transactions wherever possible. Though endorsing the single queue system, the MMC noted that some form of 'customer signalling system' to indicate a counter clerk was free was vital in increasing queue speed and maximising 'effective counter position occupancy'.

Queue flow into cash flow

In 1987, *The Times* had reported that there was good news for post office customers complaining about queues. A new 'package of reforms is set to sweep away years of anger and frustration'. On the way out were old work practices and dowdy interiors to be replaced by extra staff and new décor. Union objections to part-time workers having been overcome, it would be possible, it was said, to have more flexible working, allowing greater coverage during the busiest periods, such as Thursday mornings when pensions were traditionally paid, and at lunchtimes. Other innovations, according to the newspaper report, would include 'fast service points, electronic stamp machines ... and extra Girobank facilities'. Potentially the greatest shake-up would come when computerised counter transactions became possible.[55] The spectre of privatisation haunted many public bodies in the eighties, and given the circumstances it can be of little surprise that the Post Office was such an enthusiastic adopter of queue management techniques.

The widespread implementation of the single queue formation was accompanied by a range of other queue technologies, from things as mundane as the metal poles and 'queue tape' that became increasingly ubiquitous, to the electronic call forward (ECF) signalling systems whereby cashiers pushed a button when they were free, and an automated game show voice called out 'Cashier number two' or similar. Indeed, it is all but impossible now to think of queues in places like airports without the accompanying tape – what would departure halls, with their check-in and luggage deposit queues, look like without tape? Seemingly mundane, queuing tape emerged from cybernetics which first saw life in the US from the late 1940s on. The term 'cybernetics' was initially associated with the American mathematician and philosopher Norbert Wiener but subsequently spread widely across a range of disciplines from computer science, electrical engineering and robotics to medicine and psychology. Also known as 'systems thinking', cybernetics was, as the famous psychologist Jean Piaget put it, essentially a theory of models that deal 'with relations of means to ends ... with regulatory modulations (positive and negative feedbacks ...) and generally with the acquisition and trans-mission of information'.[56] The term 'cybernetics' was drawn from the Greek for 'helmsman', 'pilot' or 'governor', and can be thought of in that way: its focus is upon the ways in which systems can be regulated, adjusted and controlled, generally by using feedback. Of course, the crucial thing is that what is really being controlled, regulated and governed here is *us*, the citizen (or consumer if you will).

This alerts us, if we need it, to the fact that the management of queues is not some simple benign act. In the case of the Post Office, it was focused on those three E's, trying in an increasingly pressured environment to squeeze greater profit out of every-thing from space to employees and customers. As the architect Adam Sharr puts it, the queue, 'formerly a symbol of democratic consent, has instead become managed: contained and controlled by tape within which people are assumed to behave as predicta-ble pinballs'.[57] Queuing tape is not a neutral phenomenon. It is, as Sharr puts it, also 'an instrument of control'. This is not the voluntary, almost spontaneous form of queue which illustrates the informal workings of a micro-social system with its demo-cratic underpinnings but, rather, something in which the partici-pants are externally managed, or are encouraged to manage themselves, largely as they cannot be trusted to behave in ways that will produce the greatest economic benefit. As the report on Post Office Counters cited earlier suggested, 'queue discipline' is something that needs to be encouraged and enforced. As customers, it seems, we have to be minutely managed in order for utility to be maximised.

As our experiences of queue tape, call forward systems and the like in post offices, banks, airports and so many other places illustrate, huge efforts are now expended in trying to manage and organise us so that spaces are used in the way that businesses value. We line up how and where we are told, and we make our way to check in our luggage or pay for our goods as quickly as possible. And if we can possibly do it all ourselves – be self-managing and save on staff – then so much the better. But that is far from the end of it. If there have to be queues, if we must stand in line, then this is also an opportunity for further exploitation. In short, in further horrible parlance, queues can be monetised. Which brings us back, as if we'd been in a queue the whole time, to the dear old Post Office. Under increasing pressure in the early 1990s it announced yet another new innovation: Postshops. Under pressure from WH Smith and a range of other retailers, the Post Office decided that it would create internal stationery shops within its main branches, in particular seeking to persuade waiting customers to shop as they stood in line. Indeed, in neat circularity, this then also became a further reason to try to reduce queues, as freeing up space through shorter lines could produce yet more room for retail opportunities.[58] And in post offices and innumerable other locations, if shopping was impossible there was still the opportunity for 'in-queue marketing'. As Tensator, a company specialising in 'queue management solutions' (and claiming to be the inventor of the 'original retractable queue barrier') put it, such merchandising and marketing can help turn 'queue flow into cash flow'.

The Wimbledon queue

'Part of the reason that Wimbledon attracts such great attention is that it is a bone fide, certified British tradition,' tennis champion Arthur Ashe once said, 'and British traditions are just a bit more traditional than anyone else's.' The Wimbledon championship is well known for many things: grass courts, strawberries and cream and, these days, its queue. Though from the early twentieth century it attracted crowds in sufficient numbers to need managing, its 'overnight' queue arrived in the mid-thirties when Fred Perry, a working-class Englishman, won three successive Wimbledon Singles titles. In 1934, the first two thousand in the overnight queue secured a place in the free-standing area on Centre Court. Some of them had brought folding stools and picnic boxes. Signs were erected and a refreshment trolley visited the queue.

It has been in the post-war period that the Wimbledon queue has become famous. In 1952, over two hundred people were already in the queue by 10 p.m., and, in 1969, over three hundred were in the queue at dusk before the Newcombe–Laver men's final. For many years the person responsible for Wimbledon's organisation was the club secretary, Chris Gorringe, widely known as 'Clockwork Gorringe' because of his efficiency. In his book, *Holding Court*, he described 'the nicest contact I have had' as being 'with people in the overnight and early morning queues'. In charge from the 1970s, he oversaw the gradual formalisation and increasing regulation of the Wimbledon queue, covering everything from ticket touting to public safety.

So sophisticated, and so formalised, has the whole operation become that the All-England Tennis Club now publishes a thirty-page booklet called *A Guide to Queuing*. In addition to queuing it covers security, the provisional programme of play, accessibility and wheelchair procedures, maps, eating and drinking, advice to spectators and conditions of entry to the grounds. One recipient described it as 'the most British thing I have ever been given'. The guide also includes an extensive 'code of conduct', advising those who are planning to queue on how they should behave:

- Temporary absence from The Queue for purchase of refreshments or toilet breaks etc should not exceed 30 minutes
- Overnight queuers must only use tents which accommodate a maximum of two persons, and one person should be present at all times. Gazebos must not be brought to The Queue
- Unattended items will be removed and may be destroyed by the police
- Barbecues, camping stoves or fires are not permitted in The Queue or in Wimbledon Park
- Smoking/vaping in The Queue is strictly forbidden
- Anti-social behaviour likely to cause annoyance or offence to other queuers will not be tolerated. Loud music must not be played at any time
- Excessive consumption of alcohol and/or drunken behaviour will not be tolerated

- Do not play music or ball games etc. after 10 p.m.
- All litter should be put in the refuse bags/bins provided
- Any take-away food deliveries must be arranged for collection at the Wimbledon Park Road gate only and must arrive before 10 p.m.

Queue-jumping: the new normal

As we have seen, queuing in many circumstances is something that is now carefully managed and controlled. Not only has it become a key means by which the performance of organisations is assessed and audited but increasingly it is exploited as a means by which the person queuing can themselves be managed and, wherever possible, sold more goods or made in some way a more efficient user of whatever service is being offered. Increasing efficiency and maximising profit are the watchwords of this management 'science'. But there is one further aspect of queuing in our modern exploitative age that is worthy of comment and that is the rise of queuing inequality; in essence the creation of formal systems of queue-jumping. What is often referred to as 'multilevel queuing', where there is some combination of standard and priority queues, is yet another opportunity for supplementary revenue creation and, consequently, is found everywhere from theme parks to airports. Far from all being in it together, we have slowly learned or been persuaded to accept that money buys you the ability to avoid the queue altogether, or at the very least join a quicker one. From priority boarding on planes to 'VIP' access at concerts, the social contract of 'first come, first served' now comes with its own small print.

Theme parks were among the first to experiment with

multilevel queuing. In the late 1990s the Disney Corporation tested 'virtual queuing', essentially a computerised ticketing system which allowed visitors to book times on selected rides and then, rather than stand in line, use the time they would have queued to do other things (spend their money most obviously). The FASTPASS system now operates in Disney themes parks around the world. Subsequently, a number of theme parks such as Universal Studios in America and Alton Towers and Thorpe Park in England developed priority access packages which allowed visitors to purchase access to shorter queues. At Alton Towers, for example, four separate packages are available from 'Bronze' (one Fastrack access on each of four rides) through to 'Platinum' (unlimited Fastrack on all rides).

There are various euphemisms for such multilevel systems including 'priority queuing', 'speedy boarding', 'queue skips' and, for economists, 'waiting line segmentation'. Of course, transport systems like planes, trains and cruise ships have long had different 'classes' of travel. Originally, this was a guarantee of different standards of comfort and perhaps access to different services. The avoidance of various forms of queuing has now become a central part of the 'first', 'business', 'premium' or [insert your own preferred synonym] experience, especially where airlines are concerned. In their study of the social order of airports, Steve Woolgar and Daniel Neyland give the following wonderful example of the experience of a flyer with an Upper Class ticket for a Virgin flight from Heathrow Airport. The account captures just how different the experience of flying (or for our purposes let's call it the experience of social order) is for those who can pay to jump the queues:

... the 'limo' picks me up from my home ... The driver asks if I have done this ... before (no) and, as we set off, he explains the routine. He has an electronic pod thingy in the front of the car, on which he consults the details of my booking. 'Yes, you're in there, seat 6K, is that alright?'

Nearing the terminal at Heathrow, the driver takes a turn down an alleyway entrance in amongst the multilevel car parks, which I have never seen before. Forty yards down the road we come upon a sign illuminating a kiosk 'Virgin Upper Class Drive Through Check In'. The car stops and a uniformed Virgin clerk approaches the car ... She looks at my passport and hands it back. Over her shoulder another uniformed person is (cursorily) incanting a series of questions about whether I have packed my bag myself, are there sharp objects etc. I give the right responses and the car drives me round to the main entrance to the terminal ...

The other side of Fast Track [security] presents ... [a] confluence with the lower classes. Before actually entering the departure 'lounge' I am forced into a queue which turns out to be a second check on passports. Some of my companions from Fast Track evince visible irritation at this development ...

The lift up to the lounge on the second floor has a padded bench seat in it ... The Upper lounge is organised ... for luxury, privilege and convenience for the busy executive ... There are no (or few) announcements in this space. Instead, staff individually approach passengers and remind them when the time comes for their departure.[59]

As the economist Michael Sandel has noted, 'in recent years, selling the right to cut in line has come out of the shadows and become a familiar practice'. This is now an established and, in many ways, accepted part of our social order and in his book *What Money Can't Buy: The Moral Limits of Markets* he describes many of these new queue-jumping opportunities. Some, like express lanes on freeways and 'concierge medicine' (for same day or next day appointments with a doctor) are still rather American but others, like some modern forms of ticket sales, are to be found much more widely.[60]

Official queue-jumping – what Sandel describes as the 'tendency of markets to displace queues, and other nonmarket ways of allocating goods' – is now so pervasive an aspect of our culture that we often fail to notice it. Even when we do, and feel unhappy about it, criticism rarely seems to have an appreciable impact. It is true that formalised ticket-touting (the euphemism is 'secondary resale') has been the focus of some attempts at increased regulation. Sites such as Seatwave and GetMeIn closed after investigation by the Competition and Markets Authority, but the general fleecing of concertgoers remains rampant. More generally, the idea that paying 'extra' buys you the ability to avoid standing in line is largely uncontested and seemingly uncontroversial. We know it is unfair, but we accept, or have been convinced to accept, the apparent normality of it. As one group of researchers studying theme parks noted, 'When priority queues are introduced the long-held principle of [first come, first served] is abandoned and feelings of injustice and inequity come to the fore.' They found that the presence of priority customers reduced satisfaction levels among those in the main, standard queue. Their enjoyment was reduced by seeing others queue-jump. One might think that, for those concerned with profit, the solution to this would be to hide the priority queue – and, indeed, this is what some theme parks do. But this potentially creates another problem, for those who have paid to jump the queue are not always happy that they can't see the main queue; the inability to estimate how much time they have saved potentially reduces their perception of the value of their priority ticket. Certainly, where theme parks are concerned there is little getting away from the sense of inequality.[61]

The end of the line

We should by now have got over the conceit that we Britons are a distinctive nation of queuers. We are hardly alone in lining up for certain goods or services, to pay for our food in supermarkets and the like. Like all widespread social phenomena, no doubt our history of queuing differs from those in other countries and, similarly, there are no doubt some characteristics of queues that are peculiarly British. As we've seen, it seems highly likely that the general association of queuing with the British national character was established around the time of the Second World War, and despite widespread changes since then, it is an association that has proven difficult to dislodge. But we are hardly uniquely orderly. As we acknowledged in relation to drinking, in some parts of the world Britons have a reputation precisely for their apparent disorderliness.

Many of the examples we've used in this chapter illustrate the long-held sociological observation that queues are akin to mini-social systems; they have rules and expectations, may involve negotiation, and are often shaped by broader forces. Examining when and how we queue therefore becomes an instructive way of thinking about our wider social worlds and how they are changing. What might we say, therefore, about the changing moral order of the queue in post-war Britain? Rationing may have ended well over half a century ago but, in some ways, queues have proliferated, especially if we include in our calculation that modern horror, the online queue. If there has been a fundamental change in queuing, however, it is that it is something that is increasingly analysed, managed and manipulated. We see this is a variety of ways.

Grocery shopping offered one series of examples. Much of what has occurred in grocery shopping, from the rise of the supermarket to the advent of the self-checkout, has at least in part been an effort to reduce or mitigate queues. At first the aim was to circumvent the seemingly never-ending counter-queues. The arrival of self-service, though it took a while, largely put paid to the worst of those. There followed the gradual mechanisation and then computerisation of the checkout to speed up the queuing process. As observed by management and organisation scientists who study such matters, waiting in line involves two issues for customers: one is how long they wait; the other is how long they think they wait. Time spent in a slow-moving queue is sometimes referred to by sociologists as 'thick time' – in essence time that is perceived to drag. Increasingly a range of techniques have been utilised to help 'thin' queuing time, via music, material to read and displays of relatively cheap goods, all of which is intended to distract the queuer from the queuing and, of course, to part them from more of their money.

With supermarket shopping, one of the problems of queue management concerned the issue of 'justice': how to enable customers with relatively small quantities of goods to avoid getting stuck behind those doing the weekly shop (in the bank or post office the equivalent was how to ensure that the customer with a single, simple transaction didn't find themselves in a queue behind the shop owner cashing up for the week). An initial solution was to create checkouts for the quicker customer (a small basket; eight or fewer items; or something similar). Then the single queue with multiple checkouts became de rigueur. In-shop efficiency aided by new technology has now taken this to the obvious next step: increasingly the shopper is also the checkout person (the citizen-bagging-cashier-checkout person). Not only does this reduce the number of staff required, but it means that a false sense of queue minimisation or absence is created: time is thinned for the shopper as they are fully occupied in scanning and bagging their own goods. As the marketing phrase had it, queue flow is turned into cash flow! To do all this, however, we as citizens have to be trained. Not in the formal sense of attending classes or seminars, but informally through guidance, signage and gradual experience – just as that significant chunk of the population that has a pet dog had to be trained to pick up after them. Slowly a new breed of citizen consumer has emerged: one who has learned how to scan, where to place goods, when to bag, how to pay and, crucially, one that has entirely imbued the idea that this is now *their* responsibility, not that of trained staff. We are largely obedient to these new expectations, having learned and internalised the new rules of the grocery.

In addition to the focus on profit maximisation and increased efficiency of supermarkets and other shops, there is another related set of ways in which queuing and efficiency have increasingly become linked in post-war Britain. The managerial revolution that took off in the eighties, and which brought with it a preoccupation with the measurement of performance, increasingly treated the queue as a useful indicator of efficiency. We saw in some detail how minutely Post Office managers were required to collect and report data on queue times in their branches, the

Post Office having become one of the many sites where 'single queuing' was now favoured and queue tape was ubiquitous. Not only are we queuers increasingly trained and managed, but queuing has become one of the means by which we are invited as consumers to assess the service we are provided with – and thereby becoming a means, potentially, through which those providing the service are assessed. The clearest example of this is the health service, where waiting lists and, eventually, 'waiting times' have gradually become a core means by which we are invited to understand health service performance.

Queuing, then, is increasingly formalised, and in many areas has become a social phenomenon that is analysed, evaluated, managed, structured and organised. We, the queuers, are studied and subsequently encouraged, through a variety of means, to organise ourselves in particular ways – ways that will increase throughput, maximise profit and reduce frustration or the sense of 'thick time'. Indeed, it is not just queuing that has become increasingly formalised, but queue-jumping too. Though reforming queuing in places like supermarkets and post offices was largely about increasing efficiency and therefore revenue, it did not fundamentally alter the underpinning sense that some form of justice was at play. Indeed, it was designed in ways that convey a sense that justice and fair play were not being compromised. This is not the world of priority queues, however. There, rather than some expression of equality and democracy, queues reflect power, in this case financial power. If the reform of queuing in many sectors was an indicator of the reach of the managerial revolution in the latter decades of the twentieth century, then priority queuing and its offspring are a reflection of the triumph of what many economists refer to as *neoliberalism* – an ideology in which the market and selfish individualism come to

195

dominate. In many respects, the creation of queues to which access can be bought is just the next logical extension of turning queue flow into cash flow.

We may still like to think of Britain as a nation that queues. And, yes, we still queue, perhaps increasingly so, but less and less do we do so under conditions of our own choosing.

CHAPTER FIVE

Toilets

Lavatory humour is rife in British culture, but the provision of public toilets is no laughing matter. (House of Commons Communities & Local Government Committee, 2007)

A s humans, there are a small number of things we have in common. Irrespective of wealth and privilege we will all, sooner or later, die. While we're on this earth we all need to urinate and defecate. For most of human history these latter basic functions have been dealt with in fairly simple ways. However, as wealth has increased and social expectations have changed, so the mores surrounding such functions have altered also. As we encountered earlier, and as the German sociologist Norbert Elias so wonderfully illustrated, it is only in the last few centuries that anything approaching 'shame' has attached to a variety of bodily functions, or indeed to the body. So successful has this process been that the consequence, broadly speaking, is that it is now assumed that matters such as urination and defecation are *private*, and should, wherever possible, be done away from the public gaze. Indeed, they are sufficiently private that they are rarely the subject of conversation.

As another means of exploring how our everyday lives have changed in the last seventy years or so our focus here is on *toilets* and behaviours related to them. These most quotidian of functions afford us another vantage point for looking at modern British society and thinking about the nature of our social order. What sorts of facilities are available, to whom are they available, and how they are used, managed and regulated? What has changed? And what do any of these things say about us?

First and most obviously, the indoor flushing toilet has become ubiquitous. In the twenty-first century no-one would seriously think that a house or a flat without one was habitable. This was far from the case in the 1940s and 1950s when outdoor privies were still relatively common. On the other hand, that old municipal staple – the public lavatory – has been in long-term, sustained decline or, as an industry professional put it, 'British public toilets have been in freefall'. So, we'll be exploring where we go, and why we go where we go. We'll also want to consider *how* we go. What expectations do we have about the nature of the facilities we use? First, and once again treading carefully, we'll take a step back in history.

Indoor facilities

Although flush toilets were invented in the late sixteenth century, the absence of a supply of running water meant that they remained absent from most houses well into the nineteenth century. Sanitary conditions in English cities in the eighteenth century were famously foul and it wasn't really until the arrival of cholera, smallpox and typhoid epidemics that significant improvements got seriously underway. In the poorest housing, conditions were particularly bad, with cesspools often unemptied, and even in more prosperous areas sometimes emptied directly into the road. Writing in 1842, the great reformer Edwin Chadwick wrote: '... in many of these places are to be seen privies in the most disgusting state of filth, open cesspools, obstructed drains, ditches full of stagnant water, dunghills, pigsties, &c. from which the most abominable odours are emitted. But dwellings perhaps are still more insalubrious in those cottages situated at the back of houses fronting the streets, the only entrance to which is through some nameless narrow passage, converted generally, as if by common consent, into a receptacle for ordure and the most offensive kinds of filth.'[1] Around the same time a report on conditions in Leeds noted that: '568 streets were taken for examination; 68 were paved; 96 were neither paved, drained nor cleaned; one of them, with 176 families, had not been touched for 15 years. Whole streets were floating with sewage.'[2]

The idea of private bathrooms as a necessity was slow to catch on, and even the George Gilbert Scott-designed Midland Hotel at St Pancras Station in London, intended as 'the most magnificent hotel in the world', had only four bathrooms for its six hundred bedrooms when it opened in 1873.[3] When it came, change was relatively swift, leading one historian – with a degree of hyperbole – to describe the late 1800s as 'the golden age of toilets'.[4] By mid-century estimates suggest that up to one half of middle-class homes had a 'water closet', usually involving some system of levels to operate a valve or pan system for disposing of the waste. A reliable source of water for flushing the waste was by no means usual and the accumulation of waste remained a common problem. In the mid-1880s, Thomas Crapper invented his 'Valveless Water-Waste Preventer', which reduced the amount of water lost from ill-constructed cisterns, and also included a side-valve to allow cisterns to refill. Although bath-rooms with running water became more common from around the 1870s – again for the middle classes – the working classes lagged far behind. Progress varied hugely city to city, town to town. Thus, while WCs for small houses were widespread in Liverpool by the end of the nineteenth century, Rochdale had only 750 WCs for ten thousand houses and nearby Manchester still operated the 'pail system' until the early 1900s – where casks were placed in front of houses for the collection of household waste from chamber pots. Where WCs were available for those in terraces and tenements they were often outside and were often shared between several households.

In the immediate post-war period, indoor facilities remained comparatively rare. The experience of Mass Observation diarist Herbert Brush, holidaying in Cornwall in July 1945, was not unusual: 'There is no WC in this cottage, and one has to go down to the Public Lavatory on the quay side, about fifty yards away and twenty feet down. No paper supplied.' As slum clearance gathered pace, gradually the proportion of houses without indoor toilet facilities began to decline. Nevertheless, in 1952, one in seven houses in Witney, Oxfordshire, were still using bucket lavatories. A 1958 housing survey of Morley, Yorkshire, found that one house in two had no bath and 30 per cent shared a lava-tory with another family. There were still at least one and a half million homes in the UK without a bathroom by the mid-sixties, and as late as 1970, half the houses in St Mary's, Oldham, still shared an outside toilet.

Focusing on the situation north of the border, one BBC report observed that 'By 1970 man had landed on the moon, yet one in four Scots still had to share an outside toilet.' In Govan, Glasgow, a campaign began in the early seventies to press for indoor loos.

When the first of the new facilities was finally installed in 1972, a senior local councillor arrived in a big black car, and made his way up to the third floor, in order to open what became known locally as 'Annie's loo'.[5] The official had the honour of ceremonially flushing the toilet for the first time. The next two decades saw the most dramatic changes in indoor provision. According to the census the proportion of houses without an indoor WC declined from just over one in ten in 1971 to less than one in two hundred by 1991.[6] Indoor loos may be assumed to be standard provision now but for a great many Britons this is a relatively recent development.

What have the Victorians ever done for us?

When eleven thousand doctors were asked by the *British Medical Journal* to vote on the greatest medical breakthrough since 1840, the number-one spot went to sanitation.[7] Fears of disease may have slowly begun to change household indoor amenities, but by far the most significant Victorian municipal reform was the massive sewer-construction efforts of the 1860s and 1870s. As we noted earlier, at the beginning of the nineteenth century the cesspool was 'the unchallenged mainstay of metropolitan sanitation'.[8] Legislation in the 1840s and 1850s placed new restrictions on the location of cesspools and made prosecutions of landlords who failed to maintain clean dwellings easier. Their eventual outlawing led local authorities to intervene with much greater regularity as well as placing much greater emphasis on the importance of working sewage systems. By the start of the twenty-first century the UK had 186,000 miles of sewers and over twenty-four million households were served.

It was in the 1880s – the so-called 'golden age' – that the other great Victorian municipal development properly emerged: the public lavatory. Such facilities had been promoted since the 1840s but a combination of forms of Nimbyism (Not In My Back Yard) – concern about increased traffic, attracting the 'wrong sort' of people, offending local female sensibilities – meant that it was close to the century's end before they appeared en masse. For much of the nineteenth century public urination had been commonplace, at least for men. The provision of toilet facilities, especially public lavatories, has continued to be a deeply gendered matter. The public lavatory was therefore the solution to twin problems of how to keep both filth and indecency out of sight – truly a form of *poor relief.* The first public toilets were urinals for men, initially linked to public houses but subsequently more generally provided by local municipalities. By 1850, there were over seventy such urinals in the City of London.

The Great Exhibition in 1851 brought a great many logistical and administrative problems, one of which was how to cope with the lavatorial needs of the millions of people that were expected to attend. The Victorians were uncomfortable discussing such matters publicly. Nevertheless, the Commissioners in charge eventually built WCs for male and female visitors, the use of which was to cost either a halfpenny or a penny. Convenient though it would be to assume so, sadly one historian has debunked the idea that this was the source of the phrase 'to spend a penny'.[9] The facilities at the Great Exhibition did set the trend for labelling the facilities 'Ladies' and 'Gents' however. The most significant outcome, though, was that the experience confirmed that, if supplied, the public would use such facilities – a total of one and a half million paying customers (women more than men because urinals were free) used the lavatories at

Crystal Palace. The Exhibition's Commissioners concluded that these numbers illustrated 'the sufferings which must be endured by all, but more especially females for the lack of somewhere to relieve themselves' and that if public lavatories were built there was little doubt they could be made 'perfectly remunerative'.[10] George Jennings, the person most closely associated with the design of the Crystal Palace, continued to campaign for installation of such facilities elsewhere, arguing that 'the Civilisation of a People can be measured by their Domestic and Sanitary appliances and although the proposition may be startling I am convinced the day will come when Halting Stations replete with every convenience will be constructed in all localities where numbers assemble.'[11]

This first flush of success was not to last. A number of experiments during the next decade failed dismally, with the numbers using facilities falling far short of those needed to make them pay for themselves. Urinals continued to be built and used, though a wide range of problems – from vandalism to indecency – meant that public resistance also remained quite strong. Pressure for change came from a variety of quarters. The Ladies' Sanitary Association (LSA), established in the 1850s, was particularly concerned about the absence of facilities for women workers, and in the early 1880s the City of London accepted a proposal for the building and running of two public conveniences. Sited at Ludgate Circus, there was to be one for men, with urinals and a single WC, and a second with separate facilities for men and women. The Ludgate Circus buildings also appear to have been the first time such facilities were officially labelled public 'lavatories', a euphemism allowing the word 'toilet' to be avoided. A new underground public convenience was opened in 1884 – though with no provision for women – and slowly the idea of municipally run conveniences began to take hold. In 1885, the Surveyor and Municipal and County Engineer declared that 'Public urinals ought to be erected by the urban authority as a matter of convenience to the peripatetic portion of any community, and also to prevent nuisances being committed in improper places.'[12] As Clara Greed, the leading historian in the field, points out, keeping men happy was always the aim of the city fathers and the provision of facilities for women was often, at best, an afterthought. In fact, it is likely better thought of as a deliberate choice by a male-dominated society that sought to restrict women's access to the city.[13] Men's place in the world of 'work' was well-established, and their 'capacity to pee on the streets and walls stands as a threat if alternative facilities are not at hand'. And to prove how effective a threat it was, the prompt for the provision of public facilities in Trafalgar Square, for example, was the erosion of the Portland-cement foundations of the National Gallery caused by men relieving themselves when waiting for night buses.[14]

The fact that women were forced to pay while men had access to free urinals reached the letters pages of *The Times*. Although the arrival of department stores meant that there were some public toilets for women, the general reluctance to accommodate women's needs continued.[15] As Caroline Criado Perez notes in her important book on gender inequality, the superficial egalitarianism of allocating equal amounts of floor space to facilities for men and women – which is the way it has been done historically and is even formalised in plumbing regulations – inevitably means greater access for men given that urinals take up much less room. As she rightly says, suddenly 'equal floor space isn't so equal'.[16]

Equality? Round and round we go

While the occasional pre-war public facility included purpose-built children's toilets, some with a drinking fountain outside to encourage family use (particularly in parks), the idea of baby-changing facilities was decades away. The Public Health Act 1936, which gave local authorities the right to build and run street 'public conveniences' also allowed them to charge fees as they felt appropriate. However, such fees continued to be applied to lavatories 'other than for urinals', in effect once again imposing charges on women but not necessarily on men. Payment was generally either via a turnstile or a penny slot at the entrance to the Ladies.

In the fifties, campaigns for reform centred around the use of turnstiles in women's lavatories. A mother juggling bags of shopping and children risked serious injury when she reached a six-foot-high toilet turnstile. On one occasion, with a hot and bothered holiday crowd in Cleethorpes, bent pennies put the ladies' conveniences out of action five times in one day. One woman in Sussex, badly injured when the iron bars of the turnstile jerked backwards and hammered her on the forehead, was reported to have died the following day.[17]

At their 1956 AGM, the National Federation of Women's Institutes voted for the abolition of turnstiles in favour of the more usual penny-in-the-slot admission to individual lavatories. Speaking for the resolution, Mrs Hedley of Loudwater WI, Buckinghamshire, said that she could see 'no possible use for turnstiles except as possible museum pieces dated 1955 for the enlightenment of future generations, who would view them with awe and horror as forms of ancient torture'. The National Council of Women passed a similar resolution at their 1959 conference and a group called The Chain Reaction joined the campaign against turnstiles. The 1961 Co-operative Party annual conference unanimously passed a resolution calling on the Government to prohibit the use of turnstiles in women's public lavatories.

The cause was taken up by the opposition Labour MP Barbara Castle who raised the matter in parliament in late 1961. She discovered that of twelve thousand public lavatories only 670 were now equipped with turnstiles. Of these, 525 were in women's lavatories with the remainder in men's lavatories. During the previous five years people had been trapped on at least 150 occasions, and twelve injured. During that same period turnstiles broke down over 2,200 times. Castle also described them as 'instruments of torture'.[18] A government spokesman estimated that the cost of replacement would be in the order of £150,000, leading also to an appreciable loss of revenue. Nevertheless, parliament agreed to a permanent ban on new turnstiles, and local authorities were asked to remove them as soon as possible.

A year later around two-thirds had been removed. Some councils still refused to act, despite protests from women's organisations. In response Patricia McLaughlin, the Ulster Unionist MP for Belfast West, introduced the Public Lavatories (Turnstiles) Act in 1963 which prevented local authorities from using turnstiles, though the new regulation did not apply to rail stations. Turnstiles may slowly have disappeared from most locations, but significant challenges still faced many women wanting to use public facilities. When Clara Greed visited the new Ladies toilet at Paddington Station in 1994, she was surprised to find that, despite an expenditure of millions of pounds, passengers still had to haul luggage down a flight of stairs. 'Worst of all,' wrote Greed, 'now one had to pay 20p to go through the turnstile, which is 15½ inches (40cm) across, hardly enough room for luggage, and the average pushchair is at least 18 inches (46cm) across.'[19]

Even when formal building regulations and national guidelines began to regulate the provision of lavatories, gender imbalances remained, and in some cases were effectively institutionalised. While early regulations required equal numbers of cubicles for men and women, men of course were also provided with urinals. Even when the codes were revised in 1996, Greed argued that it 'only marginally improved the situation for women'. Moreover, such provision took little or no account of how long men and women occupy lavatory space. According to Greed's figures, on average women spend more than twice as long in the loo as men. As Caroline Criado Perez points out, 'women make up the majority of the elderly and the disabled, two groups that will tend to need more time in the toilet. Women are also more likely to be accompanied by children, as well as disabled and older people. Then there's the 20–25% of women of childbearing age who may be on their period at any one time, and therefore needing to change a tampon or a sanitary pad.'[20] Studies as widely varying as those including all public conveniences in Wales to those solely in the British Museum all showed the same pattern – men were much better catered for than women.

Where women don't form a majority is among those making decisions about toilet provision. In terms of the planners, architects, designers, managers and policymakers involved in such decisions, women make up as little as 10 per cent of the total.[21] Despite the activities of a wide range of user groups campaigning for equality for women in provision, for greater accessibility, wider cubicles, lavatory attendants, and more baby-changing facilities, the pace of change has been slow. Sometimes the changes have been counterproductive, as in the example of the

Barbican's decision to turn both its male and female toilets gender neutral. The predictable outcome being that only men used the facilities that were gender neutral with urinals (i.e. 'the gents') and both men and women used the 'gender neutral with cubicles'![22]

In the background to all this, a further dramatic set of developments had been taking place – the long-term, staggering decline in the overall availability of public lavatories.

The decline of the public loo

From the late 1880s onward, the public lavatory had become a cornerstone of Victorian municipal architecture. By mid-twentieth century no respectable town centre would have been complete without its public conveniences. By the early twenty-first century public toilets were beginning to look a thing of the past. What happened? In part, cost has been an issue. In their Victorian and Edwardian municipal heyday, public conveniences were one of many ways in which localities illustrated civic pride. As the demands on local authorities grew, as belts tightened, and as municipal government itself faced an increasingly uncertain future, public lavatories were increasingly one of the casualties.

Sadly, for our purposes here hard data on the trends in public-toilet provision are difficult to find. Figures are not compiled with any regularity and are anyway tricky to interpret as numbers for individual facilities can mean anything from a huge construction (twenty WCs and fifty urinals) visited by thousands, to a basic urinal used by a few. Undoubtedly, though, the underlying trend has been a massive reduction in the number of public facilities provided. London's public toilets declined by 40 per cent between 1999 and 2006, and the capital was far from atypical. All over Britain public facilities have prepared to meet their Portaloo. The most frequently quoted figures suggest that more than half the public lavatories run by local authorities closed in the fifteen-year period from the late 1980s to early in the new century. Further culls have occurred since. In 2000, there were just over 6,600 public toilets in England. Five years later the Labour government, using registration figures for business rates, suggested that the number had declined to just over five thousand public conveniences for the whole of England and Wales.[23]

In 2006, it was calculated that there were four hundred public toilets serving England's capital city with its population of seven and a half million people (or one public toilet for close to nineteen thousand residents). This was not likely to be very 'convenient' as the Mayor's Office for London put it. They also reported that on the tube system only eighty-eight of 255 stations (just over a third) had public toilet provision. In January 2003, London Transport Users' Committee carried out research on forty transport interchanges and stations around London. They found that almost a quarter (22 per cent) had no public toilets, another quarter (25 per cent) had toilets that were out of use and that signage was often poor. Outside the capital, one report suggested that when the Department for Environment threatened to cap the spending of five local councils, two of them – Shepway and Torbay – shut down their public toilets overnight. A 2013 survey found that more than one in eight of all council-run toilets had closed in the previous three years and that eleven local authorities offered no public-toilet facilities at all.

The fate of the lavatory attendant is emblematic of the decline of this particular public service, and we should perhaps spend a moment with them before we move on.

Lavatory attendants

In their heyday no public lavatory was complete without an attendant. One such was Victoria Hughes who worked in Bristol's public loos from 1929 to 1962. In many ways she was the eyes and ears of Bristol's Durdham Downs community, especially on the 3.30 p.m. to 10.30 p.m. shift when local prostitutes were busiest. Their stories brought colour to Hughes' otherwise orderly strait-laced life. In her book *Ladies' Mile* she spoke about it being a great leveller:

> There's one thing about a lavatory, you know, she spans the class scale. There were the well-spoken tarts and the others. The clients who drove a Jag and the scruffy foreign seamen who had a few pounds of shore-leave pay and little else. The socialites who rode their horses across the Downs on Sunday mornings or took a stroll in their Sunday best – and those who slept fitfully with only bracken to their backs. I was on nodding terms with all of them.

A 1965 report proposed paying lavatory attendants more, calling them hygiene wardens and training them to tackle health issues. Concerns about disorder of various sorts were also prominent for it also suggested the introduction of an alarm system linking all conveniences with police headquarters. Nevertheless, the decline had already set in and by 1980 the wealthy City of London was one of the few municipalities still employing lavatory attendants. At the start of the year there were ninety-one plus one supervisor – a remarkably high number for the times – but by the end of the year even this had been slashed to sixty-one, and a number of loos had been closed. 'It is not only the traffic that makes getting around London a hazardous business,' wrote Alan Hamilton in *The Times*.

In 2013, a BBC documentary, *The Ladies and Gents*, focused on some of Scotland's remaining lavatory attendants. Robert Smith and Mo Gallagher dealt with the daily impact of drug-taking and prostitution in Glasgow's toilets. As Gallagher dryly remarked, 'Cleaning toilets is no the glamour that it's cracked up to be.' The debris confronting him ranged from used needles, which required safe disposal, to lost property such as umbrellas, walking-sticks and, amazingly, crutches. Many attendants said they found pride in their work and being their own boss. They had complaints but as one wag said, 'It's no good blaming the cistern.' At Uig, Isle of Lewis, Agnes Mclennan was still working as an attendant in her late seventies. The Uig toilets collected sand, dirt and water from the nearby beach and camping site. She cleaned them twice a day but felt it really needed three visits. Meanwhile, Flo Kenny had worked for twenty-six years as a full-time attendant with Angus Council: 'I bring in plants. I bring in loads of teddy-bears for the baby-changers, little ornament things, flowers on the sinks. That's what people want to see, instead of just a loo and a sink.'

As attendants from Victoria Hughes to Flo Kenny testified, as well as cleaning the work often involved counselling and care. They looked after children, dressed old ladies, and helped people with awkward bags. They provided safety pins, vending-machine change, and sold nappies, sanitary supplies, incontinence pads and condoms. They looked after people in distress and in numerous ways, large and small – they kept *order.* Although lavatory attendants haven't entirely disappeared, they now tend to be found in very specific premises, more often in private property like night-clubs where customers have already paid to get in, than in public lavatories where we might all benefit.

Attendants had a wide range of responsibilities though, at heart, their job was to manage and run a functional and clean service: to ensure the facilities were continuously usable and were as customers expected them to be. Though not necessarily recognised, and certainly not part of any formal job description, attendants also had a *social control* function. Memoirs, like Victoria Hughes', are full of stories of the activities of local prostitutes, the cottaging that was a regular feature of at least some toilets, and various forms of mischief – from quarrels and fights to vandalism. In their daily routine, the lavatory attendant might encounter any, or all, of these. Not just encounter but deal with. As Sidney Rogers wrote of his time as an attendant in Westminster in the 1960s, 'The police have been my friends. I worked with the police for years. The police have been very good to me. They've always treated me with respect. I was the first man on the Westminster City Council to ask for telephones, and in the end they fitted six night toilets with telephones so we could phone the police.' In his study of Welsh facilities, Chris Llewelyn observed that it 'is widely accepted that customers are reassured by the presence of an attendant in a public toilet and women especially favour the presence of female attendants in public toilets.' Llewelyn found that only 20 per cent of supervised toilets were affected by vandalism compared with 69 per cent of unsupervised facilities.[24] Now, in most cases no doubt there was no formal obligation to keep order but, just like bus conductors, park keepers ('watch out, parkie's coming!') and rail tickets inspectors, lavatory attendants kept a look out, and were the visible presence (what some social scientists would call the 'capable guardians') helping to keep order.[25]

The decline of the public lavatory was partly a consequence of deteriorating standards and rising expectations. Certainly, local authorities complained of a growing problem of criminal damage. In 1963, Midhurst Council even *appointed* a lavatory attendant in an attempt to stop vandalism. Concerns also grew around the problem of 'cottaging'. Homosexuality had been legalised (for those twenty-one or over, in private) in 1967, and in the immediate aftermath the number of prosecutions for what was referred to as 'public indecency' rose sharply, though precisely why was uncertain to researchers. It is possible that there was some increase in public sexual activity, but the new law certainly spurred on the police. By reaffirming the illegality of public sexual activity it reinforced police confidence in taking action. It also made prosecutions easier and they grew at an even faster rate than the number of offences being detected by the police.[26] What seemed to be at stake, at least so far as some observers were concerned, was once again civic reputation. As the *Stockport Express* noted in 1977: 'The recent spate of offences is not only making it unsafe for any male to walk into public buildings without fear of suspicion, but is also dragging down the town's good name. Chief Superintendent Hartley admits there is a purge on following complaints from the public.'[27] Looking back on the history of municipal provision, Clara Greed reported that a senior manager responsible for the fate of a whole city's lavatories had told her, 'the only good public toilet is the closed public toilet'. Attitudes were changing quickly.

Of course, the fate of the public lavatory was also affected by changes in private household life. Amenities within private homes had improved markedly and, gradually, indoor WCs became the norm. As they did so, public facilities, however well maintained, paled by comparison with the relative luxury, or certainly the privacy, of the domestic loo. Expectations about cleanliness, comfort and privacy were changing, and were doing so at a time when pressures on public facilities made it less and less likely that they would be able to meet such expectations.

But it was not just the lives of private citizens that were changing, so were governmental expectations. More particularly, in the latter decades of the twentieth century the regulations surrounding the provision of public toilets began to proliferate. We will say a little more about these later but, for now, it is enough to note that there was growing pressure on those providing public facilities to ensure that they included separate, carefully designed amenities for the disabled, formalised by the Equalities Act 2010, that there were baby-changing facilities, and that a wide variety of other, more technical specifications were met. Again, these shifting expectations arrived at a time when municipal government was ill-equipped, or increasingly unwilling, to meet them. This brings us full circle around to money once again. All this was occurring at a time in British political history when government was increasingly sceptical about the value of local authorities and was placing very considerable restriction on local expenditure. Given the wider circumstances it is perhaps little wonder that at least as far as the provision of public lavatories was concerned the Victorian era was coming to an end.

Aberdeenshire: from council facilities to comfort partnerships

The impact of the absence of a statutory duty on Councils to provide toilets and of tightening finances on the provision of public lavatories is well illustrated by the case of Aberdeenshire. In the aftermath of a review of its services in 2000, and with little warning, the County Council closed sixty-nine of its 107 public toilets (including one that famously – well for those in the know anyway – had appeared in the film *Local Hero*). At the same time neighbouring Aberdeen City Council planned to close eight traditional public lavatories and replace them with automatic toilets (without traditional lavatory attendants). As with the Burnley dog ban, the suddenness of the change, and the lack of explanation, left locals shocked and angry, and Aberdeenshire folk protested vehemently. Bus drivers complained about their local toilet being barricaded shut and long journeys caused especial concern. As one commentator observed in the press, 'drivers are worried – particularly those with prostate trouble, or piles'. In turn complaints about drivers' behaviour began to appear. As the local paper commented at the time, 'everyone remembers the incident last year when a … driver was disciplined because he was spotted urinating in the woods at Bridge of Don'.[28]

A wide range of other problems were preoccupying local officials, including both vandalism and various forms of sexual activity. As a representative of Aberdeenshire's environmental and consumer protection services observed, with no little naivety, 'Believe it or not, some people seem to get their kicks out of watching other people go to the toilet. We've found situations where men have bored holes in the walls with drills, presumably battery-powered.' In 2002, Aberdeen turned its attention to toilet facilities in its public parks. It did so after concerns were raised about 'unacceptable and overtly antisocial behaviour'.[29] The 'embarrassing and unsavoury' conduct that was the focus of most complaints it turned out was 'cottaging'.

Despite a government report on public toilets recommending that local authorities consult the local community if there was a threat of closures, the decision in Aberdeenshire felt peremptory. Some of the local loos were more than simply practical facilities – they were institutions with their own histories. Auchnagatt residents were angry about the closure of their public lavatory because it had been built with help from local people (with the council taking it over ten years later), and yet the toilet locks were now superglued and covered by a metal plate. When the toilet at Pennan, Aberdeenshire, closed it meant that the nearest public toilet was either twelve miles east (at Fraserburgh) or twelve miles west (at Banff); four of Banff's five toilets had also been closed. Perhaps not surprisingly, when government minister Sarah Boyack opened a new waste treatment plant near Banff she was barracked by local residents. Richard Lochhead, the Member of the Scottish Parliament (MSP) for North East Aberdeenshire, was quoted as saying, apparently without irony, 'It's clear that Scottish ministers have washed their hands of this issue.'

The reduction in public toilets caused serious worries about the fragile local economy – would fewer toilets mean fewer tourists? David Davidson, the Conservative deputy industry spokesperson, thought that the closure of public toilets directly affected Scotland's tourism industry, and Mike Roy, the town's co-ordinator for Banff and Macduff, said, 'A town centre without a public toilet is like a baby without a heart.' There were some reprieves. Seven of the closed facilities were soon reopened under the management of local community councils. In May 2001, a year after the original closure plan was enacted, the council financed the reopening of thirty toilets, though at least one of the originals had deteriorated so much that it wasn't viable.

Public toilets with attendants were each costing local councils over £40,000 a year, and those without an attendant between

£4,400 and £11,900 a year. 'Times had changed from when local authorities could be seen as the sole provider of public conveniences, with "publicly available" toilets, albeit with restricted access, now provided in many shops and other buildings,' said the authors of a 2007 Aberdeenshire report, *The Management of Public Toilets*. The future, as in so many areas of life, was to be a mixed economy. By counting facilities provided by tourist locations, public buildings, community-council toilets and 'comfort partnerships' (the council had begun to offer between £2,000 and £5,000 a year, depending on footfall, to businesses willing to let the general public use their toilets) it was claimed that the total number of toilets available to the public was almost back to pre-2000 levels. Indeed in 2012, the council even won the UK trophy for public toilets at the annual Loo of the Year award (known as the Toilet Oscars).

Community toilet schemes

By the early years of the twenty-first century, as the Aberdeenshire experience made clear, local council provision was, if not a busted flush, anything but the source of municipal pride it had been in earlier times. Public services were under huge pressure, with everything from quasi-markets to outright privatisation changing the landscape of British civic life. So far as toilet provision was concerned the early century 'invention' to deal with this new reality was the *community toilet scheme.*

The idea was very simple. Given local authorities no longer felt able to fund sufficient provision, they would work in partnership with local businesses to provide public access to what would otherwise be private facilities, or facilities restricted to paying customers. As Aberdeenshire had done, councils would offer remuneration to the owners of these facilities for their participation in the scheme. There is some dispute about the first of these community schemes to open. Some suggest that the 'comfort scheme' described earlier may have been the first. Brighton had also been operating a partnership scheme in the early 2000s.

However, it is the community toilet scheme operated by the London Borough of Richmond upon Thames that has gained most publicity and is often credited with starting what has become something of a trend. The scheme is part of the local Business Pride partnership between the council and businesses and means proprietors are paid a small amount each year in return for them making their toilets available to the public regardless of whether someone makes a purchase. Under the scheme, a business signs an agreement covering conditions of access to its toilet facilities by members of the general public during business opening hours, displays a sign showing membership of the scheme and undertakes to maintain toilet facilities in clean and hygienic conditions. The council, for its part, provides liability insurance, street signage and carries out 'occasional inspections of the toilets with the provider'.[30]

The Community Toilet Scheme was conceived in 2002, when Richmond decided to overhaul its local provision. Local residents were unhappy with the state of the borough's public lavatories, were concerned about proposals to close some of the facilities, and the council itself was trying to deal with issues of high costs, and a mixture of outdated facilities and unpopular and under-used Automatic Public Conveniences. The solution was the partnership scheme. A total of five automatic public lavatories were closed – saving over £80,000 a year – and were replaced by a series of local partnerships. There are currently around seventy participating partners, including pubs, restaurants, cafés, community centres, shops, council offices and supermarkets. Of these about half have facilities for disabled people and a little under a third have baby-changing facilities.

By 2011, there were thirteen London boroughs with community toilet schemes, with over 350 businesses in total participating. Richmond remained the largest, but others such as Merton, Southwark and Camden were tiny, with only two, five and six participants respectively. Many advantages are claimed for such schemes, not just financial. Richmond argues that incidents of anti-social behaviour are significantly lower than was experienced in public toilets in the borough. They also suggest that members of the public feel both safer and more comfortable using facilities in shops, pubs and restaurants than traditional public toilets. Equally, some others involved felt it was good for business – the British Toilet Association citing Tim Martin, chairman of J. D. Wetherspoon, who had linked increased profits to the chain having won the 2001 Loo of the Year trophy.

The schemes have critics too. There are doubts cast on both the motivations of the business partners and just how willing they are in practice to allow large numbers of non-paying visitors to use their facilities. Being private premises businesses retain the right to refuse entry. There is the question of hours of access – facilities are only open when the business is open and in many cases this means that beyond pubs and restaurants there is little availability in the evenings. Concerns were also expressed that women, families with young children and adults from particular ethnic and religious groups may feel very uncomfortable using pubs. At the very least then, critics have suggested, such community schemes should be backed up by public provision. Predictably, however, not all councils see this as the future – out of the thirteen London boroughs with community toilet schemes, four of them no longer maintain any public toilets directly. One way or another public lavatories are a declining presence in British civic life.

Bog standards

As you will be expecting of this book, given that our central concern has been with the everyday ways in which life is managed and maintained, we now need to turn our minds more directly to the issues of regulation and control. The provision of public toilets has been subject to regulation for over eighty years now. While the 1936 Public Health Act gave local authorities a power to provide public toilets it imposed no duty upon them to do so – it was, in effect, carry on at your convenience. Consequently, while the Act helped enable the proliferation of public lavatories in the first half of the century, it did nothing to impede their disappearance in the second half.

What began with the 1936 Act has now mushroomed into a huge array of requirements covering everything from building specifications, numbers of loos, size, hygiene, cleanliness, and access, all the way to the expectations on how the providers of services might deal with vandalism and antisocial behaviour.

Local authorities that do provide toilets are subject to many building regulations and British Standards controls. So far as publicly available lavatories are concerned British Standard BS 6465 simply says, 'The provision of sanitary appliances in public toilets should be determined according to local needs.' However, in relation to toilet provision within buildings, BS 6465, and an associated element in the Building Regulations, provide copious guideline standards for toilet provision. They cover the numbers of toilet facilities per type of building – affected by floor space and numbers of potential users – as well as the dimensions and plumbing requirements for the toilets. The Disability Discrimination Act 1995 requires public facilities to be accessible to disabled people. Part 3 of the Act states that reasonable steps must be taken to remove, alter or provide a means of avoiding a physical feature which makes it impossible or reasonably difficult for disabled people to use a particular service (e.g. public toilets). The relevant British Standards and building regulations associated with such provision cover such matters as the length and width of room in which the toilet is situated, the height at which the toilet seat should be placed and how far the pan should project, which side of the cistern the flushing lever should be placed, and to which part of the basin taps should be fitted among many other matters – though, perhaps surprisingly given all this, there is no special guidance covering the distribution and location of disabled toilets.[31]

Though the provision of public toilets remains largely voluntary, local authorities are able to require others to provide facilities at places of entertainment and other 'relevant places', such as venues hosting sports matches and other events where the public attend as spectators or where food or drink is sold to the public for consumption on the premises. Indeed, the requirement can be for these facilities to be made available free of charge. The British Standard is quite specific about the numbers of toilets places of entertainment and other venues should provide. For entertainment venues it is two for up to 250 males plus one for every additional 250 males, and two urinals for up to fifty males plus one for every 250 extra. For women it is two

WCs for up to twenty females plus one for every additional twenty. In shops and shopping centres it is one WC per five hundred males, plus one extra for every thousand more (plus urinals of course), and one WC per one hundred females up to five hundred, then one extra for every two hundred extra. Similar regulations cover primary and secondary schools, office washrooms, swimming pools, and pubs, bars and nightclubs. And this is just the numbers of toilets. We could go on (and on and on) covering regulations relating to the building of toilets (the Building Act 1984 for example), the requirements at motorway services (Department for Transport Circular 01/2008) and much more besides.

Beyond the basic regulations concerning the where, when and how much of toilet facilities, concerns about public behaviour in and around lavatories have resulted in a range of other legislative interventions. The Sexual Offences Act 2003 brought in a new offence, making it unlawful to conduct 'sexual activity in a public lavatory', attracting a maximum penalty of six months' imprisonment. Similarly, powers contained in the Anti-Social Behaviour Act 2003 and subsequent legislation enabled the police, local authority officers and Community Support Officers to issue Fixed Penalty Notices to anyone caught graffitiing or vandalising lavatory facilities. But in many ways legislative change is a rather outmoded form of regulation. There are now so many other, sometimes more subtle ways of managing and governing our behaviour. Technology is a favourite. Though there are generally limits to the use of CCTV where lavatories are concerned, many public facilities and those in places of work, now utilise a variety of means to monitor and control the amount of soap and water that is used when washing hands, and timing devices and motion sensors control how long warm air is blown as part of the hand-drying process. And, as in so many other parts of our lives, there are signs everywhere encouraging a range of behaviours. We are perhaps still some way off the example of a more recent development in one of Beijing's busiest public toilets. There, in an attempt to limit the usage – and apparently theft – of loo roll, automatic facial recognition has been introduced. The poor toilet user has to stand in front of a camera, removing hat, glasses and so on rather like going through immigration at an airport, before being given a full 60 cm of toilet paper. Seemingly there is a nine-minute wait for anyone who needs, for whatever reason, to use the machine a second time![32]

Prisons

While all around them there were improvements in sanitary conditions and raised expectations in relation to everything from toilet paper to handwashes, perhaps nothing captured the outsider status of prisoners more than their toilet facilities. The Victorians may have been keen on high standards when it came to municipal toilets, but the same was by no means true of prison building in the late nineteenth century. While some prisons had cells with integral sanitation, a great many did not. Indeed, at the end of the nineteenth century the majority of existing integral toilets were removed because of the scale of blockages and leaks.

Prisons were the exception to the general post-war improvements in sanitary conditions. In 1984, the chief inspector of prisons condemned sanitary arrangements as 'uncivilised, unhygienic and degrading'; only 11 per cent of inmates had access to in-cell sanitation. Indeed, it was only in the aftermath of the most serious prisons disturbances of the twentieth century, and in particular the Strangeways riot in 1990, that a radical overhaul of such prison conditions was proposed by an inquiry headed by Lord Justice Woolf. Reporting in 1991, Woolf said that the practice of 'slopping out' – the emptying of plastic buckets in which any human waste was collected overnight while prisoners were locked in the cells, and which he described as 'a symbol of the inhumanity which existed in prisons' – should be ended within five years.

An inquiry into British prison conditions by Human Rights Watch in 1992 had the following to say:

> The first thing those prisoners do each morning is line up to 'slop out.' Prisoners are typically locked in their cells at approximately 7 p.m. and let out of their cells briefly at 8 a.m. Therefore, prisoners are in their cells with their waste for 13 hours overnight. We were told the stench can be foul, particularly in triple occupancy cells. In deference to cellmates, prisoners try not to defecate in their slop pots during the night, but in desperation some will wrap their excreta in ripped sheets, socks or whatever is available to minimize the smell. In cells without mesh, these parcels are tossed out the window. In addition, we were told that at times during the morning slopping out session, the over-used toilets become clogged, resulting in an overflow of human waste.

As one ex-prisoner looking back at his time in Durham prison put it, 'I never thought using a toilet could ever be such a luxury, but it was at times like that, I realised just how much I had taken everything in life for granted.'

Although a major programme of prison refurbishment was put in train after the Woolf Inquiry, the pace of change was sometimes slow. Indeed, a freedom of information request to the Ministry of Justice discovered that toward the end of 2016, there remained over 1,200 cells in use that were without in-cell sanitation. In 2011, the High Court had ruled that the absence of such facilities did not breach prisoners' human rights.

As one group that monitors everyday life and conditions in prisons (the National Council for Independent Monitoring Boards) put it – with what is perhaps typically British understatement: 'It is difficult to come to any conclusion other than that all is not as it should be.'[33]

Great expectations

We have come a long way since the days when there was little shame attached to public urination and defecation, when open sewers were a widespread feature of our cities and human waste was disgorged straight into major rivers (though on the latter there seem to have been some backward steps recently). Victorian sensibilities led to the building of public lavatories and much greater emphasis on hygiene and cleanliness generally. The gradual disappearance of the shared outdoor privy and the near universal availability of indoor facilities has increased our expectations about the nature of toilet facilities. If one were to look around the standard toilet/bathroom in an ordinary British household what would one experience? Privacy almost certainly. Quite likely a lock on the door or some ability to ensure one wasn't disturbed. Toilet paper, not newspaper. Soap. Warm water. A towel. Our expectations of the toilet experience have changed and, no doubt, this has affected our attitudes toward public lavatories. Elizabeth Shove in her study of cleanliness suggests that the history of the bathroom has seen a succession of changing rationales. Initially, concerns about gentility and respectability were central with, subsequently as we have seen, a preoccupation with germs and disease becoming a core motivation for change. More recently, it has been luxury and convenience that have tended to dominate, affecting private and public facilities.[34]

According to the much-quoted observation from anthropologist Mary Douglas, dirt is an offence against order. Seeking to eliminate dirt, she said, is not a negative act but a positive one, the aim of which is organising our environment.[35] Indeed, much of our effort at creating order in industrial society has focused upon dealing with dirt – defining it (what is to count as *dirt*), managing it, organising it and, as often as possible, keeping as much of it out of sight as can be arranged. We dealt with dog dirt, so to speak, earlier in the book – a good example of something that was once very visible on public pavements and in public parks, but which is now the focus of concerted attempts at control. In short, we witnessed a process of change in which something that was once seen as a *nuisance* increasingly became defined as a *problem*. Much the same might be said of human waste. Clearly much of the concern in the nineteenth century in particular, but also well into the twentieth, grew out of very significant worries about public health. However, once typhoid, cholera and other major dangers were brought largely under control, matters of respectability, decency and decorum came to the fore once again. We mentioned the German sociologist Norbert Elias at the start of the chapter. In his theory of the 'civilising process', Elias charted long-term historical changes to manners and mores and argued that these were linked to shifts in increasing levels of social differentiation and integration – in effect they were a consequence of our increasingly complex societies. Changing standards of conduct, he argued, reflected greater social pressure toward self-control, initially among the rich and powerful and, subsequently, progressively throughout the social classes. Reflecting something similar, the architectural historian Adrian Forty has suggested the 'middle-class preoccupation with bodily, domestic and public cleanliness' in the early twentieth century was in part a consequence of 'the increasing political power of the working class'.[36] Middle-class 'refinements' were a means of distinguishing themselves from others.

Many of the twentieth-century changes have been to the experience of the toilet. We have learned to expect to have toilets in our own homes, which allow us to do our business in private wherever possible, and that these flush effectively, ensuring that we are confronted with the sight of human waste for as little time as possible. However, this no longer seems enough for modern sensibilities. Now, in part, it seems this is a question of changing attitudes and expectations. We are becoming less tolerant of a range of bodily odours. Both Sigmund Freud and Norbert Elias, in their different ways, charted long-term processes of growing intolerance of certain smells. As Freud observed, the 'incitement to cleanliness originates in an urge to get rid of ... excreta, which have become disagreeable to sense perceptions'.[37] Where once public space was the focus for concerns about bodily-related odours, the private bathroom has now become the frontline in the battle. This has consequences for personal responsibility for, as the academic Ruth Barcan has observed, where once odours might either have gone unnoticed or simply been associated with the mass of people, in our now private environments, smells are tied to the individual and we are increasingly obliged to manage them ourselves.[38]

Such 'olfactory management', as sociologists refer to it,[39] is of course closely tied to consumerism. Our new obligations where smell is concerned are a product – forgive the pun – of the growing commodification of everything that is involved in using the lavatory. Hygienic toiletries are a good example. The initial post-war market was mainly directed at females through the beauty industry (perfumes, face powder, etc) and the house-cleaning market (Jeyes Fluid, Dettol, etc). Then, in the fifties, the men's hygiene market opened up. It started at the top of the body with hair-creams (e.g. Brylcreem and Silvikrin) and worked its way to virtually every area of the male body. The UK market for men's deodorants and perfumes between 1993 and 2003 grew by 60 per cent. The male grooming market was estimated to be worth well over £40bn by 2017.[40]

So far as the lavatory is concerned, the pressure to conform to these ever-increasing commodified expectations was beautifully illustrated by an advert for something called Glade 'Touch n Fresh'. The advert began with a small child saying, 'Mum, I want to do a poo'. 'Come on then,' says Mum. So far, so good. But then the by-now jiggling child says 'but I want to do a poo at Paul's bathroom', indicating that he'd be much happier evacuating himself at his friend's house! He then announces, 'I'm going to do a poo at Paul's' and promptly leaves. The voiceover then helpfully tells us that 'Paul's bathroom has Glade Touch n Fresh. More discreet than an aerosol. It's no more bad smells, just a pleasant fragrance.'[41] So, yes, by 2009, mothers were being guilt-tripped into buying toilet products lest their small children be offended by the smell of their own poo. Indeed, we've now gone further still. Presumably with the saying 'prevention is better than cure' in mind, and just when you thought puns could sink no lower, the market was suddenly subjected to 'Poo-pourri'. Described as 'spray before you go', the theory is that the spray prevents nasty odours emerging from the loo; altogether better, we're invited to imagine, than simply masking them afterward (or even, heaven forbid, just not worrying about them). We have indeed come a long way from the outdoor privy.

In the last seventy years we've gone from pumice stones and carbolic soap, via Palmolive and Pears, to dead skin being chewed away by Garra Rufa and a Lush catalogue which includes soaps called Sexy Peel, Honey I Washed the Kids and 13 Soap: Unlucky for Dirt. According to one estimate, even by 1975 the average supermarket was already stocking nearly nine thousand products. By 2008, this had risen to forty-seven thousand, a small but nevertheless significant number of which will have been toiletries. As an illustration, when writing this we clicked on one leading supermarket's website. The next step was 'household goods', then 'air fresheners', then 'electrical plug-ins and refills'. No Glade Touch n Fresh (so I guess we're all off to Paul's house) but several other Glade items among the fifty-eight different possibilities on offer.

Now, presumably there are relatively few people that would consider a Thai Orchid plug-in air freshener an absolute essential bathroom item even if some are persuaded by buy such things. But one mundane essential we have all come to rely on is toilet paper – as the global pandemic, of which more later, illustrated only too well. An item that was seemingly available in perfumed, packaged form to Chinese royalty as early as the Ming Dynasty in the fifteenth century, toilet paper only became commercially available in the West in the late nineteenth century.

The first packaged toilet paper was invented by Joseph Gayetty in the US in the late 1850s. Described as 'unbleached pearl-coloured pure manila hemp paper', it was infused with aloe and sold as 'Gayetty's medicated paper for the water-closet'. By contrast with torn-up sheets of newspaper, this arrived in packs of five hundred sheets and sold originally for 50 cents. The next big breakthrough was rolled and perforated paper which, though patented in 1870s, was still unusual enough to win a gold medal at the Paris *Exposition Universelle* in 1899.

For much of the early twentieth century – and long beyond that in most British state schools – most toilet paper was of the somewhat challenging non-absorbent variety. Undoubtedly the best-known brand in the UK was Bronco (nicknamed 'John Wayne paper' because it was rough, tough and took shit from nobody); indeed, so unrefined was much toilet paper at this time that one company was still advertising its product as 'splinter free' as late as the 1930s. Something softer was on the horizon, however. A paper mill in east London started producing soft, two-ply toilet tissue in the early 1940s – manufactured for Andrex – and in the 1950s a number of companies began to launch coloured toilet tissues. They proved popular, though as late as the end of the 1960s, H.M. Stationery Office was still distributing the equivalent of twenty thousand rolls of Bronco a day for use by civil servants and other employees, all allegedly stamped with 'Government Property'.[42]

As with all commodities, variety is the key to economic success and toilet paper is no exception. For years bathrooms were filled with magnolia, pink, peach – even blue – toilet paper, often chosen to link in with the colour theme of the room itself. Intriguingly, recent years have seen white paper reassert itself. It has always dominated the market, but coloured toilet paper appears to be in dramatic decline. That same supermarket website we visited earlier only offers one shade of toilet paper in addition to white. So, tastes change, but you can't keep a modern capitalist industry at bay for long. Back to the website again and one finds that there is still plenty of variety, but now it's texture rather than colour that is on offer. From toilet paper infused with shea butter or aloe vera, to various forms of quilted extra softness and even 'lightly moistened toilet tissues', there is still plenty of choice. One estimate suggests that the UK market in toilet paper is now worth well over £600m a year,[43] though this is as nothing to the United States where the average American is estimated to use fifty-seven sheets a day (over twenty thousand a year since you ask), feeding an industry worth $8bn annually. So, our experience of using the toilet has changed markedly. Outdoor facilities are largely a thing of the (distant) past, and privacy is now very much the basic expectation, along with soft loo roll. Increasingly, we have been sold a variety of new requirements: soaps, creams, deodorisers and much besides. A once simple function is now overlaid with a wide range of generalised expectations concerning our conduct, up to and including any pungent leftovers that may linger.

Are you sitting comfortably?

Once again it is time to take stock. What do toilet facilities and our toilet practices have to tell us about modern British society? Well, it is clear that *general* standards and expectations have very significantly improved. Most domestic dwellings now have internal sanitation as standard. No more the cold, early morning walk to the outside privy with its torn-up sheets of old newspaper. Now the expectation at least is that there will be internal toilet facilities, connected to the mains sewers, with a flush that removes waste instantly and successfully. Hot and cold running water and soap with which to wash hands are next. In short, for the bulk of citizens, basic sanitation standards have improved markedly. These, in turn, have affected the way we view and we use public facilities. Again, it would seem we are less likely to be tolerant of what we now judge to be poor or inadequate facilities.

We are now clearly a much more 'private' people than we were seventy years ago when it comes to the toilet. It is not simply our rising personal expectations that are responsible for the decline of the public lavatory. A combination of financial pressures and moral concerns of one sort or another – vandalism, graffiti and public sex among them – all led, in their differing ways, to a growing sense that public lavatories were by no means always the most salubrious places. The post-war period was anyway one in which there was growing insecurity and more general concerns about rising crime. As local government budgets shrank, lavatory attendants – the front line of social control and order in public toilets – rapidly diminished in number, and no doubt this helped accelerate many people's sense of ill-ease at the prospect of using such facilities. Where municipal authorities were once the main provider of public lavatories that role is now increasingly taken on by private companies, either through formal community toilet schemes or simply informally as the place with the only available toilet.

One aspect of our social world that, in many respects, remains obstinately unchanged where lavatories are concerned is its highly gendered nature. The story of public facilities is one in which men's needs have generally been put first and where provision for women has almost always been a secondary concern, where it has been a concern at all. Though the general sexism underpinning provision is now acknowledged more readily than once it was, the general patterning of provision remains largely unaltered. One of the more recent trends has been toward greater desegregation of women's and men's toilets and the installation of an increasing number of 'gender neutral toilets'. Far from improving the situation, however, it has been argued that such developments, alongside the cuts to local provision that have continued in the twenty-first century, have combined 'to reshape the public toilet landscape in ways that continue to be detrimental to women'.[44]

Although the decline of the public lavatory and the rise of so-called comfort partnerships might superficially look like the retreat of the state in this aspect of our lives, such an assumption would be highly misleading. It is true that public lavatories remain something that is expected rather than formally required so far as local government is concerned, and the fact that legislation is permissive has facilitated the rapid decline in the numbers of public lavatories. There nevertheless continues to be pressure on local government to try to ensure that facilities are available to the public and, as importantly, the provision of toilets in almost every other area of society is extraordinarily tightly governed. From schools to workplaces, and sports arenas to motorway service stations, there is now a huge array of rules, regulations, standards and, indeed, laws, governing the building, provision, layout and maintenance of toilets. The day-to-day organisation and governance of the toilet in modern Britain is very substantially more complex, varied and detailed than in decades past. Our lives have changed greatly since the Second World War. Where toilets are concerned it will be clear to most people that social standards have altered significantly. If we add into this mix the growing impact of modern consumerism, then we see how what we anticipate in respect of comfort, privacy and availability has become substantially more varied and complex. If indeed we are sitting comfortably, then it is highly likely that we have more people to thank than we knew!

CHAPTER SIX

Parking

The absolutely key feature of the car is its mundane character, its significance for ordinary, everyday social life.[1]

'London streets are getting worse and worse with the increased traffic along them,' wrote the diarist Herbert Brush in April 1946. 'What will they be like in a few years' time when everybody has a car?'[2] Well, we have found out. Our roads are busy. Some are regularly close to standstill. In 2016, Transport for London said that the *average* traffic speed in the capital was under 8 mph – about two and half times average human walking pace. Motor vehicles are now all but ubiquitous and bring with them a host of challenges ranging from problems of speed – too fast or too slow – all the way through to the increasing problem of air pollution.

A 2017 report by Public Health England (PHE) on remedies for pollution found that 'illegal' pollution levels had been recorded in 90 per cent of urban areas, with significant potential impact on public health.[3] Much of this was a consequence of traffic and, in response, PHE and NICE (the National Institute for Health and Care Excellence) recommended restrictions on idling cars around schools, hospitals and other institutions where those most at risk – the young and the elderly – were likely to be concentrated, together with suggestions to plant more pollution-absorbing trees and hedges, and to train motorists to drive smoothly and to keep their tyres pumped up, together with greater support for cycling and electric vehicles.

Now, while none of these strictly concern the subject of this chapter, their importance is simply that they remind us just how significant the motor car is to modern life and how widespread its impact. Cars are the source of much of our mobility and they are what makes much of modern life possible. But they are very far from an unmitigated good. Indeed, because of the challenges they pose they are also a source of a huge amount of regulatory and control activity. A significant number of the laws and rules we are now subject to are a consequence of the proliferation of motor cars.

When we think of cars we tend to think about them on the move. They are regularly sold on the basis of their speed, as well as their looks, their comfort and their efficiency. They are viewed as mobile objects. And, yet, the reality is that cars rarely move. Private vehicles almost always stand still. According to the RAC, the average private car is parked at home about 80 per cent of the time and parked in other locations for a further 16 per cent.[4] The average car is therefore stationary for just over twenty-three hours per day and, given this is an average, a great many cars will therefore be stationary for considerably longer than that. Even when they are on the move, in many cases they will be being driven by someone who is looking for somewhere to park! As is regularly observed, parking is fundamentally about land use, and in a place as relatively crowded as Britain this is a significant concern. A rough calculation, based on the estimated space needed to park a car in a non-disabled bay multiplied by the number of registered cars, suggests that at least 350 square kilometres is needed to park all the cars in the country – a space the equivalent of one quarter of Greater London, and larger than Malta.[5]

It used to be a regular complaint among police officers that rather than being fixated on issues to do with drug use, violence or burglary, often all local residents appeared to want to talk about in community meetings was 'dog shit and double parking'. We dealt with the former in our opening chapter. Now it is the turn of the parked car. In the brief tour of the post-war history of parking that follows we will take in the birth of the car park, the arrival of traffic wardens, the rise of various forms of surveillance, and selections from the range of other options for parking regulation that have been used in the search for a sensible means of managing static vehicles. We'll divert briefly to rubber-neck at some crises, including gridlock in London and parking anarchy in Aberystwyth. But before we set off, a few words about the nature and scale of the problem.

The rise of the motor car

Of all the changes to the nature of our social worlds and to the physical nature of our environments since the Second World War, the impact of the motor car has to be among the most significant. At the beginning of the twentieth century, although there was a complex and widespread rail network, horse-drawn forms of transport were still dominant on the roads. Just in case we think that prior to the arrival of the motor car that the problems of urban transport were relatively minor, a study by the sociologist Nicola Spurling calculates that in 1900 there were an estimated fifty thousand horses in London powering eleven thousand carriages and hansom cabs,[6] omnibuses and moving freight. All this brought its own 'parking' issues and, reminding us of matters raised earlier in the book, this included the challenge of dealing with what would have been a minimum of six hundred tons of manure produced each day.[7] This began to change in the 1920s, and by the decade after the Second World War the motor car was well on its way to reshaping the landscape.

In the early 1950s there were around four million licensed motor vehicles. This had roughly doubled to eight million by 1960, doubled again to sixteen million by 1970, and was at almost thirty million by the new millennium. There are close to thirty-eight million licensed vehicles on Britain's roads at the time of writing – at least two for every three people of driving age.[8] Cars have come to dominate transport. Whereas six out of every seven households had no car in 1951, the figure was one in five by 2008, with over a third of households having more than one car. Or, finally, put it this way: there was one car for every twenty-two people in 1950, a figure which had grown to one for every six by 1964 and one per four people by 1972.[9] Not surprisingly, the distance travelled has increased also. Passengers travelled a total of 135 million miles in the early 1950s. This had trebled to over five hundred million miles by 2007, the bulk of which was accounted for by the motor car. Motor cycle numbers reached their peak in 1961, and then declined thereafter. Bus and coach travel was the most common form of transport in the early fifties, at over 40 per cent, but had declined to only 6 per cent by 2007. Where cars had accounted for about one quarter of passenger miles in the 1950s, this had increased to well over four-fifths by the early 2000s. The first thing we should note, therefore, is that this represents yet another way in which our lives in post-war Britain have become more private. In the immediate post-war period, approximately two-thirds of all journeys were undertaken on public transport. Now it is down to around 13 per cent.[10] We have become used to journeying largely alone.

As the number of cars increased so did the need to organise and manage them. And when we say 'them' what we really mean of course is 'us'. In much of the remainder of this chapter, although we will be considering the varied and growing means that are used to organise and manage parked cars, the real focus is the owner or driver of said cars. In reality, the management of motor vehicles is fundamentally the organisation of those citizens that use these vehicles. As drivers and passengers we, as citizens, are ordered, guided, channeled, directed and, yes, steered, via a host of techniques that centre around the management of the automobile. This is a matter therefore that is very profoundly about us and our everyday lives – lives, as we will see, that are increasingly enmeshed by laws, regulations, guidelines and conventions.

Signs of the times

Road signs were initially introduced by the AA and RAC in the early years of the twentieth century. As an indicator that some aspects of our national character are of longstanding, it is worth noting that Britain refused to comply with the emerging European standards for road signage, arguing that the conditions on British roads were unlike those on the Continent and that therefore it would go its own way. It was 1933 before 'Traffic Signs (Size, Colour and Type) Regulations' were issued by government and although a number of new controls and systems to encourage safety gradually emerged in the twenties and thirties, it was really only in the post-war years that these took off. The classification of roads into 'A' and 'B' began in the 1920s, as did the introduction of white lines, initially around bends and at junctions. The 1930s saw the first lines to divide carriageways, and 'Cat's Eye' reflective road markers were patented in 1934, though it was the blackout during the war that cemented their use. In 1930, the previously existing 20 mph speed limit for cars was removed, and under pressure from the Pedestrians' Association a 30 mph limit was introduced five years later in built-up areas. A speed limit of 20 mph applied to heavy goods vehicles until 1957, when it was raised to 30 mph.

Another 1930s innovation was the pedestrian crossing. 'Passages cloutés – the marked road crossing – originated in Paris in 1932, and almost immediately influenced the Ministry of Transport in London. It seems they considered both blue and yellow, or red and white stripes, before eventually settling on the black and white stripes that were introduced initially in the fifties in Slough and remain in use today. The term 'zebra crossing' is often credited to future prime minister James Callaghan (though not by his biographer). Consideration was given to 'jaywalking' legislation, fining pedestrians who didn't use the crossing, but this was thought too controversial and unlikely to be successful. In an attempt to inculcate good habits (what these days might be called a 'nudge' policy) footprints were painted close to the crossings to remind pedestrians where they were supposed to walk.

Crossings were marked by what became known as Belisha beacons: orange globes on black and white posts, named after

Leslie Hore-Belisha, then minister of transport. At the time the gaudy beacons were far from uncontroversial and attracted both criticism and vandalism. One report suggested that a fifth of the fifteen thousand beacons that had been erected in London were destroyed within their first four months.[11] Restrictions on vehicles were limited in part by the power of the motoring lobby and when the Highway Code was introduced in 1931, the minister of transport, Herbert Morrison, described it simply as 'a code of good manners to be observed by all courteous and considerate persons'.[12] In this context, the term 'all' meant both drivers and pedestrians. From 1934 onward, motorists were, however, expected to pass a driving test as an indicator that they were fully aware of the required 'good manners'. It is worth noting that in a country that has been notably sensitive to anything resembling an identity card that by the mid-1990s more than two-thirds of the adult population held a driving licence.

Understandably, for much of the twentieth century the dangers of moving vehicles prompted greatest concern. The number of fatalities rose steadily, reaching an annual peak of over nine thousand in 1941. It then began to drop quite rapidly until the huge expansion in motoring in the fifties, whereupon it rose again reaching another peak of around seven thousand fatalities every year from 1964 to 1973. Since the late 1970s, fatalities have reduced consistently, especially if one takes into account the continuing expansion in road traffic.[13] A wide range of measures, including speed limits, road signage, CCTV, seat belts, vastly increased car safety features and, as we saw earlier, drink-driving restrictions, have helped contribute to this state of affairs.

As we observed at the outset, however, it is not just moving vehicles that require ordering. Where static vehicles are concerned it is arguably street parking that is the greatest source of ongoing problems. Even in the early decades of the twentieth century, when cars were far from numerous, debates about how to manage non-residential parking were already underway. Official street parking, provided or managed by a local authority, arguably began in Birmingham in 1922, where twenty-two spaces were initially allocated. Liverpool followed in 1924, and the Public Health Act the following year officially granted powers to local municipalities to provide parking spaces. Blackpool subsequently introduced free parking in designated streets, all overseen by a uniformed attendant who issued tickets and collected gratuities. In London, however, there was considerable confusion as motorists were often unsure where cars could safely be left, and for how long. The publication of colour-coded maps in the 1930s clarified matters a little, and at this time the bulk of street parking was confined to public squares rather than main thoroughfares.

Post-war parking

The first parking restrictions were introduced in central London in the inter-war years, initially in Jermyn Street off Piccadilly, where parking was restricted to one side of the street on alternate days. But it was in the post-war period that regulations, restrictions and enforcement measures really started to proliferate. Indeed, this was true of road safety generally, something much more directly encouraged by government once the war was over. One of the most familiar road markings – yellow and double-yellow lines – came about as a result of a road safety promotional competition in 1947. It was won by a man named George Musgrave, an innovative chap who, not content with yellow lines, also came up with the idea of one-way systems and of limiting parking within a particular distance of pedestrian crossings. It was 1957, however, before yellow lines were eventually introduced, as were restrictions on waiting, loading and unloading. More road markings were introduced in the sixties, most obviously the yellow box junction which restricted traffic flow at busy road intersections. Fifty years after his competition win, George Musgrave once again made the national newspapers, this time having received a ticket for illegal parking outside a shop in his home town of Margate. Eighty-one-year old Mr Musgrave's phlegmatic response: 'The law is the law and I broke it.'[14]

'We need more car parks'

Currently still running, making it the world's oldest motoring event, the Emancipation Day Run from London to Brighton in 1896 may have featured the first official use of a car park, with cars being stored overnight in Central Hall in London's High Holborn. At the time cars could not generally be locked and it was also illegal to leave cars on the 'Queen's Highway', though there is plentiful evidence that the law was not much respected. A storage facility built a few years later at the turn of the twentieth century where visitors to the Crystal Palace could leave their cars may have been the first official occasion on which the term 'garage' was used.

The first multi-storey car park was opened in 1903, in London's Soho, and was big enough to house up to two hundred cars. By 1910, there were forty thousand registered cars in the capital and over 170 public garages, though only around ten had been purpose-built. Problems of car parking grew after the Great War, with cinemas and theatres, seaside promenades and transport hubs particularly affected. At this stage multi-storey car parks tended to have lifts and turntables to move the cars, though ramps began to appear in the 1920s. Most garages were still commercial enterprises and it was to be some time before municipal parking became a significant option.

In the years immediately after the war, even though car numbers had declined somewhat since the late 1930s, it was clear that existing parking provision in London was inadequate, certainly when the anticipated growth in car usage was factored in. One of the first studies of the London parking problem, in the early fifties, recommended that the government fund more new off-street car parks, particularly under London's squares. A few car parks were built, and a few bomb sites put into parking use, but the demand for more parking spaces far outstripped the supply. One technological response was to build up rather than across. The minister of town and country planning, Lewis Silkin, advocated making the inclusion of adequate parking space a condition of new planning consents, and also advocated mechanical parking as a solution. Floating parking decks on the Thames had even been proposed, though were never developed.

On a foggy, snowy day in January 1947, during a period of severe winter weather, a group of government officials and road engineers donned their overcoats and travelled down the Thames estuary to Erith. They were treated to a demonstration of Silkin's favoured solution to the car-parking conundrum: the Baldwin-Auger mechanical car parking system. 'The motorist drives straight in, brakes his car, locks his car, and leaves it,' said the publicity material. 'Then the floor moves around and parks the car entirely automatically, just as it reverses the procedure and delivers the car back ready to be driven straight off when the motorist returns.' Futuristic as it sounds, there were already three main types of automated car park at the time, though the Baldwin-Auger model was arguably the best known. Using power-driven rolling platforms, each the size of car-parking space, a car park with twenty spaces would have nineteen fitted, allowing the platforms to move around, cross over and slide sideways to leave space for the next to take its place. The parking capacity was argued to be double that of regular car parks, running costs were 50 per cent of normal car parks and installation costs only 10 per cent higher. There were lower risks of theft and fire, and it was relatively cheap parking. Although a few automated car parks caught on in Britain, the most popular of which were the 'pigeon-hole' variety in which cars were moved upward and stacked vertically in parking bays, such mechanical systems were never more than a minority solution, and had largely fallen into disuse by the 1970s.

Multi-storey car parks of the form we are used to today, with ramps and where drivers are responsible for parking their own cars, have proliferated. Indeed, by the 1960s, the vast majority of towns and cities had at least one such car park. However, the continuing widespread availability of on-street parking limited the spread and impact of the multi-storey, with one senior official commenting that 'nobody will risk their money in private enterprise ventures when there is the alternative of parking in the street for nothing'.[15] As a consequence, on-street car parking arguably continued to be the source of greatest continuing concern and conflict.

Residential parking

Before we move on, however, we should say a few words about residential parking. It is often observed that such has been the impact of the automobile that it has helped dramatically to reshape our social environment. From the scale of out-of-town shopping centres, to service stations that accompany the thousands of miles of motorways that bisect the country, evidence of the impact of the car, and of the need to park it, is everywhere. But the clearest example of the impact of the parked car in Britain is surely on the design and nature of houses. Though much of our housing stock, from beautiful Georgian townhouses to the more mundane urban terraces, was constructed before the arrival of the motor car, houses built in recent decades have generally always had a garage. The change really arrived in the late fifties and early sixties. In the early 1950s, as the pace of expansion of car ownership was nearing its height, many new houses were still being built without garages. The working-class estate in Essex famously studied by the sociologists Michael Young and Peter Wilmott in the fifties was largely without garages, the authors describing them as being about as rare 'as an indoor toilet was in nineteenth century Bethnal Green'.[16] A survey in the sixties suggested that only one quarter of households on council estates had access to a garage.

Nicola Spurling's study of the development of Stevenage New Town in the post-war years shows that when the first suburb was built in 1950, there was no planning for parking, partly because there was no national standard at that time and, reflecting the broader position, what she refers to as 'automobility' was not central to the imagined future of such communities, especially working-class communities. Indeed, planning at the time was based on the assumption that one parking space for every eight households was sufficient. Cycling, by contrast, was very much a feature, with the consequence that not only was a system of cycleways included in the planning, but it was clearly stated that garden sheds should be large enough to accommodate a bicycle.

The growing popularity of car ownership, and surveys found Stevenage to be above the average in terms of cars per household, meant parking quickly became an issue as the fifties progressed, not least as the absence of spaces meant the council faced a growing challenge in ensuring that parking on roads and verges was kept to a minimum. The local authority found that householders liked to have their vehicle close by and, as a consequence, local 'landscaped areas [were] being ruined'.[17] The District Council wrote to all residents reminding them of parking restrictions and saying it would use all its powers, including removal of vehicles, where necessary.

Not surprisingly, therefore, and in a very short period of time, a major about-turn occurred in Stevenage. Suburbs, newly built with little parking provision at the beginning of the fifties, were being 'retrofitted' by the end of the decade, and garages quickly became pretty much standard for all newly built houses. More widely, with provision for parking appearing in national housing standards, by the mid-sixties, as historian Simon Gunn reports, the built-in garage was increasingly seen as an 'integral part of the modern house by planners and private housebuilders alike'.[18] Despite this very fundamental reorientation, the sheer expansion of car numbers always outstripped the availability of off-street residential parking spaces. By 1966, there were already 1.2 million cars kept on-street (16 per cent of all cars), a figure that rose to 4.8 million (28 per cent of all cars) by the end of the eighties.[19]

Parking meters

Parking meters, you might think, are relatively uncontroversial (depending on how much is charged), representing a reasonably straightforward way of restricting and charging for parking. Far from it. Prior to their introduction to Britain in the late 1950s, and throughout the history of their use, they have been the subject of often heated debate. From the earliest days attempts to regulate parking have, at least in part, been presented as a stand-off between opposing interests: with regulators (government, councils, police etc) on the one hand and car owners or drivers and their representatives on the other. As early as 1947, Southend Corporation had sought government approval for the right to charge motorists to park cars in certain designated areas. However, the idea of such charging, with the consequent need to hire parking attendants, was fiercely resisted by motoring organisations. Indeed, in 1953, electors in Manchester rejected a proposal for the introduction of parking meters, with a spokesperson for the automobile associations describing the decision as a 'resounding victory for motorists'.[20]

As ever, it was traffic problems in London that were the source of much of the early proposals for new experiments. A plan for introducing parking meters in London had been hatched in the early 1950s, and one company, Venner Ltd, took up an American licence to manufacture meters for use in England. Such were the delays in introducing them, however, that they were initially forced to sell much of their stock for use in Commonwealth countries. By 1954, waiting restrictions were being imposed in Westminster and a range of other streets in the capital. At Christmas that year, the Metropolitan Police introduced 'no-waiting' experiments on seventy London streets in a bid to keep traffic flowing. The AA and RAC remained resolute in their opposition to meters and in 1956, two years before their eventual arrival in London, they voiced their concerns using such descriptions as 'highway robbery', 'a special taxation', and 'a means of collecting a fee'. That year Captain A.

W. Phillips, the general manager of the Royal Automobile Club (RAC), called a conference to warn the motoring public that unless something was done quickly they were about to be taken for 'a long and expensive ride and there will be no place to park at the end of it'.

Parking meters had been around for over twenty years in the USA before they finally arrived in Grosvenor Square, near the American embassy, in central London on 10 July 1958. New schemes had been agreed in both Westminster and Mayfair, and a delegation from the Birmingham Corporation visited London with a view to beginning their own experiment with meters. The London schemes were hardly extensive at this stage, with fewer than 650 spaces for the estimated 1,500 vehicles that were parked every day in the designated areas. *The Times* announced its support for meters in early 1958,[21] its leader arguing that some 'more moderate discouragement of parking' was required, and that this could be achieved by 'hitting the long-period parker with some severity'. It accepted the automobile associations' argument that motorists already considered themselves heavily taxed, but argued that the space occupied by parked cars, and the delays parked cars caused to traffic, made it 'by no means unfair that they should be made to pay for doing so'. Schemes continued to grow in London and Venner Ltd, who had successfully stayed in business while awaiting the green light, had installed close to five thousand of its Park-O-Meters by 1960.

The first summons resulting from the new meters was heard at Marlborough Street court, and was against a twenty-two-year old typist who didn't drive. She had been caught 'feeding' a meter (putting in additional money in order to get additional parking time – something specifically banned) on behalf of her boss who was delayed on a long-distance telephone call. The summons was dismissed, but the young woman was ordered to pay two shillings costs (twice what had been put in the meter). She was fortunate, for the nine others who followed her into court on similar charges were all fined at least £2.[22] As parking meter schemes increased the automobile associations continued their campaigns. Their most regularly voiced concern was that no alternative provision was being made for those wanting to park for longer than two hours. By the end of the decade the AA was asking government to consider an experiment with 'parking discs' as an alternative to meters.

Such were the continuing problems in central London that the minister of transport, the flamboyant and publicity-hungry Ernest Marples, described it as 'traffic thrombosis' and announced details of what he called his 'Pink Zone' for the West End of London over Christmas 1959. For the best part of a month, a general 'no waiting' restriction would be imposed, with the only parking allowed in metered spots or other bays marked with a 'P'. To encourage compliance, free car parks were set up on the edge of the zone at places like Elephant and Castle, Chelsea Barracks and on Waterloo Road. As Marples put it, 'If you park where there is no waiting, you do so at your peril.' It had been necessitated, he said, by the growing traffic jams visible in London and other cities: 'I honestly believe that people in this country are fed up to the back teeth with chaos and they want order. I believe this will be the beginning of a very interesting experiment.'[23]

Brighton and Bristol followed London's lead by introducing parking meters in 1961, but Leicester said no. By mid-1961, there were over six thousand meters in London, though its system was already showing signs of strain, with surveys finding that over a fifth of parkers stayed for longer than the permitted two hours and that meter feeding was extensively practised. The minister for transport said that whilst accidents had been reduced and traffic flow improved, the constant flow of cars looking for parking spaces was a hazard to safety and added to congestion. A complete overhaul, with increased charges, angled parking and ticket machines were all proposed.

Ratcheting up control

> Ask a Londoner – particularly a middle-class Londoner – how to raise standards of law and order in the city and they are likely to talk of putting more officers on the streets, upping the number of minorities in uniform and cracking down harder on minor quality-of-life offences. Which is odd, because parking attendants, who excel in all three respects, are almost universally detested.[24]

If one could point to a single thing that changed the way in which urban congestion, and consequently parking control, were seen and understood, it was a report, *Traffic in Towns*, published to much publicity in 1963. The report had been commissioned by Marples and was the product of an inquiry led by a civil servant, Colin Buchanan. At the time of his appointment in 1961, Buchanan had said in a public speech that the car was 'now threatening the civilized functioning of urban areas' and that 'the position to which we have now degenerated is that every day people in towns are being forced literally to run for their lives from traffic'.[25] The title of a BBC television documentary – *Our Strangled Cities* – broadcast to coincide with the report, captured the unease caused by the growth of the problem. The Report led to some fairly sensational, if largely supportive, reporting, with both the *Daily Telegraph* and the

Mail borrowing a phrase from the report for their headlines: 'Limit on the "Monster We Love" Urged'. At its core the Buchanan Report acknowledged that in future it might be necessary to consider focusing on the possibility of restricting the optional use of cars and, in achieving this, it pointed to parking control as the most useful measure. Henceforward, parking policy would be about more than parking. While it would, of course, continue to be about the practical challenges of accommodating cars, it would now also be traffic restraint or, more dramatically, about suppressing car usage. By 1967, official policy for on-street parking was described as being 'to prohibit parking wherever it would obstruct traffic movement and to ration other space wherever demand is high, usually by allocating it to short-term parking, with or without enforcement aids such as discs and parking meters'.

New auxiliaries

The formal responsibility for traffic control of course still fell upon the police, and as we saw earlier when discussing drink-driving, the fact that this often brought the police into contact with the middle classes – not the 'usual suspects' – had long been a source of considerable tension. A survey conducted by the Royal Commission on the Police in the early 1960s found that 10 per cent of the public and 36 per cent of police officers considered motorists to be especially critical or resentful of the police. In its final report, the Commission concluded that the evidence they had seen 'showed that an important – according to some witnesses *the* most important – factor affecting relations between the police and the public today is the problem of enforcing traffic laws. It is as motorists that ordinary men and women most often have dealings with the police.'[26] One major survey in the late 1960s found at least one fifth of all police time was taken up with traffic duties.

As traffic problems worsened calls for the introduction of traffic wardens began to grow. The chief constable of Nottinghamshire – the wonderfully named Captain Athelstan Popkess – was one of the first to push for traffic wardens as an integral part of the police organisation. In his city, he said, up to 44 per cent of police patrol strength was being taken up dealing with kerbside parking and other traffic issues. Rising crime rates meant that it was imperative, he felt, that police officers be freed to do other more pressing tasks. Popkess had always been an entrepreneurial figure, but in this case his views about traffic wardens were not shared by everyone within the police service. Many chief constables were unpersuaded, and the Police Federation (representing the rank and file) rejected the idea altogether, feeling that introducing less skilled auxiliaries was equivalent to setting up a sub-standard police force. Those involved in retail and other commercial enterprises were worried about the likely impact on businesses, and civil liberties organisations voiced concerns about the somewhat undefined powers this new force would carry.

It was the Road Traffic and Roads Improvement Act 1960 that eventually introduced traffic wardens and allowed them to handle a variety of parking offences as well as to patrol school crossings. In September that year, when they were first patrolled, Minister of Transport Ernest Marples said, 'I am here to do my best for the greatest number and stop the single, selfish motorist from destroying the rest of the motorists.' As he so accurately put it, what he was trying to instil was 'discipline and order' on the streets.[27] The brief for traffic wardens was to advise motorists about meter zones and enforce regulations in NO PARKING streets (where they could issue £2 tickets). The very first ticket was issued to Dr Thomas Creighton, who was answering an emergency call to help a heart attack victim at a West End hotel. The medic's Ford Popular, left outside as he tended the victim, was ticketed but there was such a public outcry that it was subsequently rescinded. Described in the press as a 'testing day for tact and tempers', thirty-nine police-employed uniformed wardens began their work in Westminster. Figures from the Metropolitan Police suggested that a total of 344 tickets were issued that first day in the Mayfair district of London. A spokesman for the AA said, 'The wardens have certainly shown that they mean business. We hope that their bag today can be put down to the first flush of enthusiasm, and that they are not going to try to hound drivers off the streets of London altogether. If that happens, we shall not be slow to step in.' How times have changed. In 2009, the London Borough of Westminster issued over half a million parking tickets, generating £69,301,000 and a surplus of £30,170,000. In all, in that year in London, well over four million tickets were issued worth almost £338m.

In Leicester in the early sixties some of the first traffic wardens in the country were paid £580 a year plus two pairs of boots. It was considered more important to restrict the number of vehicles illegally parked rather than chalk up prosecutions. In the first year the Leicester traffic wardens gave 6,255 warnings and only 2,908 fixed penalty tickets. Only 6 per cent of those ticketed went to court. By the second year the new service was deemed an unexpected success. Keeping the streets clear of vehicles had helped the city cope with extra traffic caused by the nearby new M1 motorway and a 50 per cent increase in registered vehicles in Leicestershire in the space of five years.

The first wardens were men, the assumption being that the challenges of the work required a sturdy male resilience. Before long, however, women over twenty-five were introduced to the job in London and by 1968, two-thirds of the five thousand traffic wardens employed by the police were women. Far from being a straightforward victory for equal opportunities, in part the hiring of women simply represented the triumph of a new form of stereotyping. As *The Times* reported in 1961, in Leicester where women wardens were among the first recruited, there was a considerable advantage to be gained because, 'A man feels a fool arguing with a woman. Nor can he suggest that she ought to be out catching burglars.'[28]

In addition to parking control, wardens directed traffic and undertook school crossing duty. Despite the two thousand plus traffic wardens in London by 1973, research found that motorists parked on a yellow line had a 90 per cent chance of evading the then £2 fixed penalty ticket. It was suggested that in Manchester some of the 'beats' walked by wardens were so large that they could only be covered twice in a day.[29] Indeed, across the country it was estimated that about one third of all penalty tickets issued were ineffective, mainly because the owner of the vehicle could not be traced. A study analysing on-street parking in London found that violation rates had risen from 25 per cent of parkers in 1967, to 61 per cent by 1981.[30] Indeed, by the early 1980s, the number of traffic wardens was in decline in many areas, and the level of fines was not keeping pace with inflation – still less acting as any sort of counter to the diminishing presence of wardens. It was, neverthless, a period in which the number and variety of parking controls increased dramatically[31] and, indeed, there were studies which found that a significant proportion of those questioned were in favour of stricter control and enforcement, with only a small minority against.[32]

By 1980, the average speed of traffic in London had fallen to 12 mph. Parking meters were no longer paying for themselves and parking compliance was close to collapse, leading some commentators to describe the situation in the capital as 'near anarchy'. A 1981 survey found that when parking-meter statistics were excluded, 86 per cent of parked vehicles with disability badges, 75 per cent of diplomats' cars and 66 per cent of doctors' cars were illegally parked.[33] In addition, about 30 per cent of cars parked at meters were illegally parked, and parking on single or double yellow lines was rampant – the researchers found that very few drivers even understood the distinction between single and double lines. And things had been getting worse for some time. Widespread violation of parking regulations was bringing the law into disrepute. Studies suggested that only 1 per cent of illegal parking acts resulted in some sort of penalty, and that half of all fixed penalty notices went unpaid.

In addition, the London traffic-warden force had dwindled to well below strength – from 2,079 wardens in 1973 to 1,100 in 1981. It had become increasingly difficult to recruit people to low-salary jobs, especially when they faced a heavy workload and often considerable abuse. Research suggested that the balance of costs and benefits in central London had shifted away from legal towards illegal parking. Parking enforcement was far from being a priority for the police, and although there were still significant resources devoted to it – still £40m a year at the end of the decade – it was clearly too little to ensure anything close to effective enforcement.

Wheel-clamping

Not surprisingly numerous new approaches to enforcement emerged in the early 1980s. By then the technology was available that would allow the fitting of detectors to vehicles that could pass information to some form of central authority, thus enabling remote surveillance of parking – and parking offences. Such measures were often considered overly intrusive and consequently tended to be confined to commercial fleets and other private business interests. In the eighties, traffic wardens, fines and, potentially, the towing of vehicles remained the main means of enforcement. It was at this point that government first permitted the use of wheel-clamping. It caused an outcry when it was introduced to central London on an experimental basis in May 1983, but it reduced illegal parking on yellow lines by up to 40 per cent in its first year and seemingly improved journey times also.[34] Six years later a road-traffic law review concluded that wheel-clamping had 'significantly reduced the illegal parking in central London'.[35] The AA predictably wished to see wheel-clamping used more selectively – perhaps by targeting only persistent offenders – but others, like Friends of the Earth, were all in favour of more extensive powers.

Between 1983 and 1986, the Metropolitan Police carried out about thirteen thousand wheel clamps a year. There were criticisms about indiscriminate clamping, and the level of fines didn't always cover the cost of removing the vehicle, but a Traffic and Parking Working Group report recommended that London councils should be able to charge for removing vehicles. The spread of wheel-clamping had a significant impact on police workloads and this and other demands led to a slow but steady decline in clamping numbers. The solution so far as a lot of councils were concerned was to contract out such enforcement and allow the private sector to take charge – privatisation anyway being increasingly popular in this period. In 1988, vehicle removals were also contracted out, and by the end of the decade both clamping and vehicle removals were at record levels, and the use of fixed-penalty notices had declined substantially.[36]

For a time there was little distinction between wheel-clamping on public land (e.g. streets) and wheel-clamping on private land (i.e. in privately owned car parks). Clamping on private land in Scotland ended in the early nineties, and in 2006 the House of Commons Transport Committee had urged greater restriction in England. A range of problems were identified among private operators, not least the excessive amounts being charged – £600 by one gang that was thought to have netted over £350,000 from a wheel-clamping operation[37] – and the aggressive and sometimes threatening behaviour often used by the less reputable operators. The seeming inability of the appropriate authorities to regulate private wheel-clampers eventually brought about the change in the law and in 2012, wheel-clamping on private land was finally halted (though it remains possible for the police and bodies such as the DVLA to use wheel clamps in places like airports, railway stations and car parks).

Two parking systems

Despite the proliferation of attempts to manage parking, dealing with stationary vehicles appeared to be an almost intractable problem. On the public highways the parallel systems of police and the traffic warden service continued to be responsible for enforcing parking regulations, and for issuing FPNs to deal with what still remained criminal offences. Gradually, however, there was a feeling this could not be allowed to continue. In 1990/91 alone, despite the Metropolitan Police and traffic warden service issuing nearly two million penalty notices, there was little sense that anyone had the capital's parking problems under control. The challenges in the provinces weren't as great, but were often still very significant. The next change was a very important one, and it was to decriminalise parking offences and to shift responsibility for enforcement away from the police and toward local authorities. In 1991, the Road Traffic Act passed responsibility for the enforcement of on-street parking controls to London boroughs, and made similar changes possible, though voluntary, outside London (the Traffic Management Act 2004 eventually made it compulsory outside London). In the first decade or so over 150 authorities opted to adopt what was known as decriminalised parking enforcement (DPE).

On one level, the shift toward localised, non-criminal enforcement was a success, with enforcement levels increasing significantly. In London, the number of Penalty Charge Notices (PCNs) issued annually jumped from about two million to six million following decriminalisation. The change was a radical one, the RAC saying the 'transition from the benign or laissez-faire police enforcement and the much more efficient to enthusiastic enforcement by, or on behalf of London boroughs has been predictably controversial and even confrontational, as both motorists, parking attendants and the London Boroughs embarked on a steep learning curve'. In 2003, local authority parking attendants issued over seven million penalty notices for obstruction, waiting and parking offences in seventy-five authorities in England and Wales, plus thirty-three London boroughs, compared to only one million issued in the other 313 authorities where parking enforcement remained under their control. In part, the assiduousness of local authorities reflected the fact that under the new provisions such parking enforcement had to be self-funding, with operating costs underwritten by the revenue from fines. In practice, the scale of fines tended to vary quite considerably, reflecting the differing nature of parking offences and a continuing public resistance to parking enforcement.[38]

Although the reform was in some ways viewed positively there were also continuing problems and resentment. Some resulted from the considerably reduced discretion the new parking attendants had compared with police-employed traffic wardens: they could not, for example, cancel a PCN once it had been issued. Further, the continued existence of two systems of enforcement was, at best, confusing. Parking was enforced under different rules. The penalties imposed in the two systems tended to differ: in the early 2000s the standard penalty under criminal enforcement was £30; under civil enforcement it tended to vary anywhere from £40 to £100. As the wonderfully titled chief parking adjudicator for England and Wales noted: 'it is totally inappropriate in this country that on one side of the road you are treated as a criminal, you go through the courts and obviously the sanction for not paying is imprisonment, and yet if you do exactly the same thing on the other side of the road it is a civil contravention'. Furthermore, public suspicion that much parking enforcement was simply an income-generating device was hardly helped by the fact that the published surplus made by local authorities from enforcement in 2005 was over £400m. By 2019, English councils made a combined profit of £930m from their parking activities. This was far from evenly distributed and Westminster City Council, operating one of the largest parking and enforcement services, generated over £69m a year from its parking activity, nearly twice as much as the next most profitable borough: Kensington and Chelsea.[39]

'Carmageddon' in Aberystwyth

As should be clear, much of the story of the regulation of parking is one of proliferating formal control – with, it must be said, only partial success. Unlike many things we've considered in this book, carefully organised and regulated parking is not something that we appear to be capable of managing informally. Indeed, not only do we parkers need to be subjected to very careful oversight, but many of us seemingly continue to resent the fact that there are so many restrictions on where we can leave our cars. But, is all this regulation really necessary? Wouldn't we manage if some or all of it were removed? Well, thanks to some plucky folk in the mid-Wales university town of Aberystwyth we know the answer to these questions. And the answer appears to be a resounding 'no'!

In June 2011, following the general trend, parking in Ceredigion, Wales, was decriminalised. The police issued redundancy notices to the traffic wardens who had served Aberystwyth, Cardigan, Lampeter, Aberaeron and New Quay, but because of an administrative glitch it was another year before Ceredigion County Council could formally take over civil parking control. In short, no-one was in charge and the outcome was a year of inconsiderate parking, traffic jams and occasional punch-ups. 'As predicted, parking chaos erupted in the centre of Aberystwyth at the weekend, just days after traffic wardens were taken off the streets,' wrote the *Cambrian News*. 'Cars were parked in disabled bays, on zigzag lines, in loading bays, on top of junctions, on double yellow lines and a fight even broke out between two drivers as road rage erupted.'

At the time, Ceredigion had a population of roughly eighty thousand people, 90 per cent of whom had access to a car. It also had close to three million visitors each year. The local newspaper was full of stories of parking-related problems, with drivers complaining of the search for a space taking over half an hour. The *Cambrian News* opted to shame selfish motorists. Going against the modern trend of pixilating number plates in photographs, the newspaper ran a regular feature with pictures of badly parked vehicles with their number plates clearly visible. 'The little back streets got clogged up with double parking, small shops couldn't get their deliveries, wheelchairs and prams were blocked from using the pavements safely,' said one Aberystwyth resident. 'Cars and 4 x 4s were selfishly parked on yellow lines causing misery to all.' The chairman of the local chamber of commerce commented that the 'degree of selfishness, laziness and rudeness is just terrible'. Speaking to the *Sunday Telegraph*, the councillor said: 'Community cohesion is a fragile thing. I suppose you don't realise how much you need order until it isn't there. If you went around asking people about their pet hates, they'd probably all say "traffic wardens", but here we are with a chance to show that we could get by without them, and we seem to have failed.'

The *Cambrian News* summed up matters at the end of Aberystwyth's year of parking dangerously, saying that 'if nothing else it had proved that laws need to be in place, and enforced, to ensure a free flow and safety in our streets'. Seemingly, delivery drivers had found their jobs almost impossible, and large vehicles such as buses and lorries had huge trouble negotiating all the parked cars. For those who just had a quick errand to run, it became almost more trouble than it was worth. The newspaper described the year as 'an interesting "experiment", if only because it has shown the majority of residents that wardens are in fact a "necessary evil". Without people to enforce the laws, it has become clear that anarchy will rule.' As the *Guardian* newspaper observed, 'Thomas Hobbes never had to find a parking space in

Malmesbury, but he would have understood the wider lessons from wild west Wales.'[40]

Many agreed. The car park operator, NCP, described Aberystwyth as 'the worst place in the country to find a parking space'. In its evidence to the House of Commons Transport Committee, the Local Government Association quoted a local motorist, Kevin Evans: 'The situation has gone from everyone celebrating the end of traffic wardens to incidents of road rage, huge traffic jams and residents not being able to move their vehicles from their driveways. It seems strange to say but a growing number of people will be happy to have the wardens back.'

In June 2012, a new civil parking enforcement team, comprising a supervisor and six full-time enforcement officers, came into operation. Their enforcement duties covered the whole of the county of Ceredigion, with the team working seven days a week, including evenings and bank holidays. In the week in the run up to the formal launch of the new scheme, 178 warning PCNs were issued, followed by fifty for proper on the first day of operation of the new scheme and 252 in the first week. At the end of the first three months of the scheme over 2,200 cases had been registered and over 1,800 PCNs had been paid, with revenues from the new scheme at £57,000. As the town's Mayor anticipated, 'The return of traffic wardens in early June will bring back some much needed order to the town.'

Complexity in Kensington and Chelsea

Given the proliferation of parking schemes and regulations perhaps not surprisingly one of the complaints regularly made by drivers about parking is just how confusing it can often be. Where and when can one park? Are the signs clear? The juxtaposition of ever-greater pressure on parking spaces, and the increasing number of rules, has led to an extraordinarily complex patchwork of parking possibilities (or, quite likely, non-possibilities). Though atypical in many respects, the London Borough of Kensington and Chelsea nevertheless offers a very good illustration both of some of the intricacies confronting the modern motorist and of the nature of modern parking regulation. An inner-London borough, it has a huge number of residents living in a relatively confined geographical area. And a great many of the houses and flats in the borough were built at a time when city planners and architects were more concerned with horses and carriages than motor cars.

Kensington and Chelsea has over sixty-eight thousand households and issues over thirty-five thousand parking permits. There are, however, significantly under thirty thousand residents parking bays in the borough so, in effect, the whole borough is a controlled parking zone, and one in which even the possession of a permit doesn't guarantee a space. But talking of bays and permits hardly captures the complexity of parking regulation in the borough. To cope with the array of needs and demands that exist, the borough had the following among its parking provisions in 2019: Accessible Permit Holder Bays (20); Antique Dealer Bays (Saturdays only) (103); Blue Badge Disabled Bays (192); Car Club (in effect 'pay as you go') Bays (212); Diplomatic Bays (127); Doctors' Parking Bays (18); Electric Vehicle Charging Bays (43); Loading Spaces (60); Pay and Display Bay (4,673); Residents' Permit Bays (approximately 29,400); Residents' Motorcycle Permit Bays (97); Personalised Disabled Bays (163); Police Bays (22); Visitor Solo Motorcycle Bays (217); Spaces for Taxis (141); Housing Estate Resident Permit Bays (187); Housing Estate Visitor

Permit Bays (31); Housing Estate Disabled Permit Bays (14). In addition, it has what it describes as a range of 'off-street bays', including: Housing Estate Resident Permit Bays (823); Housing Estate Visitor Permit Bays (70); Housing Estate Disabled Permit Bays (75); and Kensington Leisure Centre Disabled Bays (7), together with one off-street car park in Holland Park that has 57 regular spaces, 6 reserved for a restraurant, 3 disabled bays and a motorcycle bay.

Just to complicate matters further, Kensington and Chelsea – along with three other boroughs in the centre of London – is exempt from the national blue badge scheme which allows disabled drivers particular dispensations. It operates its own scheme which offers more limited concessions operated under different rules from the blue badge system elsewhere.[41] The consequence is that disabled drivers are unable, for example, to park on double yellow lines and must look for a dedicated 'blue badge' parking space. There are fewer than nine hundred such bays in the whole of central London. Additionally, however, Kensington and Chelsea operates a separate 'purple badge scheme' for disabled residents and for others working or studying in the borough. The criteria for eligibility are otherwise the same as for the blue badge but, of course, it must be applied for separately. The borough's scheme is enforced by a team that investigate and prosecute violations, leading to sixty-five prosecutions in 2018 and fines totalling over £15,000.

Instilling order so far as parking in Kensington and Chelsea is concerned is far from effortless. In 2019, the cost of providing what the council describes as its 'on-street service' was almost £12m. Fortunately, at least so far as the council is concerned, such is the demand for such services that the income derived by it is over four times that, at £49m. The more than twenty different categories of parking bay in the borough collectively construct a complex web of categories of driver/parker, all organised to keep traffic going, access to shops, restaurants and bars flowing, and enabling at least a proportion of the local residents to park near their flats or houses. Citizens are carefully demarcated into different groups, their rights of access denoted by licences and badges, parking spaces identified by road markings and street signage, and control carefully monitored by inspectors and cameras. In this particular context, order is something that comes anything but naturally.

The moral world of parking

Writing over half a century ago, the American journalist and campaigner Jane Jacobs said, 'Today, everyone who values cities is disturbed by automobiles.'[42] In fact, her concern was less cars in themselves than the ways we had gone about trying to accommodate them, not least via road building, and the drastic effects this had on urban life. Our focus here has been what to do with cars when they are stationary – what we should now be thinking of as their standard state. From at least the 1950s, parking control has been a serious matter for government. What began as a practical problem of how and where to locate parked vehicles has increasingly become an attempt to reduce our use of, and dependency on, the motor car. In short, it has become another example of governmental attempts to modify social behaviour. Controlling parking means controlling drivers. Indirectly, therefore, it is another avenue via which citizens' everyday lives are managed and organised. And from fairly simple beginnings, this is now a field of activity as one historian of parking has observed, which 'is heavily legislated, regulated, commodified and policed'.[43] Anyone who has or uses a car or other vehicle is used to thinking about the law of the road – by which we generally mean laws governing moving vehicles – covering everything from licences and taxes, to speed limits, safety belts and alcohol consumption. Add parking into the mix and one quickly gets a sense of just how minutely governed drivers are. And, given that three-quarters of the population now has a driving licence this is, in effect, a means of observing just how minutely governed most of us are when it comes to this area of our lives.

In our brief excursion through the recent history of parking controls we have seen something of the widely ranging attempts that have been made to manage this particular problem. These have included everything from ever more sophisticated, and larger, car parks – multi-storey, underground and rooftop – to out-of-town shopping malls with dedicated parking, and yet demand still regularly seems to outstrip supply. This is an area of activity where formal regulation has been key – and seemingly much more so than in many other areas of life we have considered. The post-war period has seen regulations mushroom, placing limits on where and when cars can park. We've moved from single and double yellow lines, to residents' parking zones, controlled parking zones, metered bays, pay and display areas, and a huge variety of other restrictions, now increasingly enforced by closed-circuit television and automatic number plate recognition, as well as a variety of folk in uniform. It is complex, and the complexity is often frustrating. Consequently, and not surprisingly, there are now a variety of companies – ParkMe, JustPark, and Confused.com – which offer guides to the cheapest and easiest places to park straight to the driver's mobile phone.

The House of Commons Transport Committee gave
these examples of poor signage[44]

But it is clear also that it is not simply the complexity that we find annoying. For all that it appears that significant formal regulation is necessary for a degree of rationality, predictability and order to be maintained so far as parking is concerned, we seem to remain resolutely unhappy about it, and many of us appear to continue to be unwilling to comply. The authors of a 2006 House of Commons Transport Committee report suggested that 'Parking policy and enforcement is at root about encouraging mutual respect and tolerance on the streets of every city, town and village in the country.' Well, if so, the evidence we have so far is not desperately encouraging. Levels of non-compliance continue to be high, significant numbers of drivers remain resentful of the fact that there are stringent controls in many places, and appear unhappy with the penalties that are applied for rule-breaking. Compared with matters ranging from drink-driving to the wearing of seatbelts, parking remains a significant issue of contestation. The RAC Foundation estimated that over eight million parking tickets would be issued in 2018, the equivalent of around twenty-three thousand tickets every day, and edging close to one ticket for every four cars over the course of the year. These are not exactly occasional infractions. The penalties are not exactly minor either. The lowest tend to be £50–70 (at 2020 prices) rising to at least £130 in parts of London. There is ordinarily an incentive for early payment – generally 50 per cent reduction – but, nevertheless, such a fine is hardly inconsequential.

If the Aberystwyth experience proved anything it was that without formal management and enforcement, a certain level of parking chaos seems likely to ensue. And, yet, it's important not to get carried away here. In the effort to restore orderliness it was not that Ceredigion was flooded with enforcement personnel. Seven officers, covering a population of seventy-eight thousand people, and working in shifts to cover every day of the year, hardly constitutes blanket surveillance. Nevertheless, the symbolic, or potential, presence of people with power to hand out parking fines appears to be sufficient to affect the behaviour of enough people for a greater degree of orderliness to reappear. A degree of formal social control is required, so far as parking is concerned at least, to provoke a sufficient input of self-control. And of all the matters we have considered in this book it is parking regulation that appears to need the greatest level of formal input. We are anything but entirely self-regulating where parking is concerned.

The moral world of parking is a complex one. People don't like congestion. They recognise the need for some form of system to organise parking and they are often unhappy when they see people parking in the wrong place. But it takes a range of highly complex regulations, together with a system of surveillance and punishment, to instil a sufficient degree of compliance. Even then many simply won't conform. And, of the many more that do, at least a proportion will often do so reluctantly and with quite a significant degree of resentment.

It is not that informal sources of control are absent where parking is concerned – many people exercise a large amount of self-control over where they park and, no doubt also seek to influence others. Shaming and a variety of other techniques are regularly used where people are found to be breaking the rules – when drivers without blue badges are found to be occupying spaces provided for the disabled for example. But formal rules and regulations, and the presence of a system of enforcement, are required to keep us in our legitimate parking place. What marks parking out from many of the other issues we have considered is just how unwelcome regulation appears to be, however necessary it is to orderly towns and cities. Despite the continuing high levels of non-compliance we know that without the main weapons of the frontline of the parking battleground – road markings, wardens, meters, tickets, automatic number plate recognition and, albeit occasionally, clamping – we would likely slowly slide into some equivalent of Aberystwyth's 'carmageddon'.

CHAPTER SEVEN

Order, Order . . .

I t is time to draw a few tentative conclusions. We have been
exploring a number of questions in this book. At a very
general level, our focus has been on the shape and nature of
British social order. At heart, as we've said, this is simply a way
of looking at how aspects of our lives are organised, what our
daily routines and practices are, how such matters are arranged
and how they might have changed. From one angle, therefore,
this is a volume about post-war social history. As we said at the
outset, the focus has not been on those things you would find
at the heart of a standard social history: changes in family and
working lives, political and economic shifts, developments in
religion and culture. Or, at least, it has only been concerned
with such things very indirectly. Rather, our attention has been
on a small number of everyday matters: drinking, smoking,
queuing and toilets among them. What, we wanted to know, is
how have our habits, practices and customs in these areas of
our lives changed? Why have they done so? And what are the
implications?

One consistent focus has been on the issue of regulation. In
broad terms we have been concerned to examine the question of

271

the extent to which everyday lives are increasingly surrounded and permeated by regulations and regulatory activity. More particularly this raises questions about the forms that regulation takes and the role that regulation plays among the various ways our conduct is governed. One might easily assume that when matters of order and regulation are considered, the fundamental underlying issues are with restrictions, limitations, constraints and restraints. And, in part, of course, they are. But this is only one element in how regulation works, for as well as being restrictive, regulation is also productive. Rules, guidelines, protocols and procedures are also forces that help to create, mould and pattern what we do. In organising social worlds, they also animate them and shape them. By *ordering*, therefore, we have been concerned not just with boundaries and limitations, but with the broader means by which our society is created and sustained, and therefore with how it looks, feels and is experienced. So, yes, in part this book has been about regulation in its more restrictive sense of direction, control, and even coercion. But it has also been about how things are constituted, organised, classified, generated, enacted, shaped and accomplished. Where regulation and control are a focus one must acknowledge that the things that indicate what we are not supposed to do simultaneously signify what we are free to do – perhaps even supposed to do.

A further observation. As we have encountered regularly throughout this book, while many of the regulatory systems we focus on are formal in nature, at least as much of what we have been considering has concerned informal sources of regulation, not least the social norms and expectations that surround and infuse conduct. Such customs and mores constitute social expectations about everyday behaviour, about how we will conduct ourselves and what we expect of others. Again, such expectations imply both restriction and freedom. Indeed, the spectre of Thomas Hobbes is frequently invoked where regulation is concerned: we are sold the idea that freedom is something to be valued but is something which comes at a price.

Though we've used the word regulation above, in large part this book is about changes in the nature of what sociologists refer to as 'social control' – whether formal or informal. The term, which is as old as sociology itself, at its simplest refers to all those processes that are involved in ensuring that individuals conform to social rules and expectations – in essence, those things that go to make up the capacity of a social group to regulate itself.[1] Classical sociology, born out of the changes accompanying the emergence of industrial and urban societies in the nineteenth century, was centrally concerned with the problem of social order and therefore of social control. Over time the term social control gradually came to encompass everything from the work of formal institutions such as the police and criminal justice system all the way through to the socialisation of children and the social psychological processes that help to ensure conformity. The consequence was that it was not a term that tended to be used with any great precision.[2] Despite its inherent vagueness it is useful for us here as it helps focus on the wide range of means by which behaviour is influenced or managed and the ways in which order is defined and maintained.

Despite this focus we have deliberately not asked the question of whether we are more or less *orderly*? That has not been our concern and, in many respects, is not easily answerable anyway. Of course, there are indicators. We have a range of markers we could consider – ranging from crime levels to a number of other behavioural indicators to do with drug use, drunkenness, neighbourhood cleanliness, vandalism, graffiti, noise and much else.

But even here, and perhaps not surprisingly, the picture that would emerge would not be straightforward and would not invite easy conclusion. Nevertheless, and reflecting our core interest here, we do think it is possible to make a general claim. In all the areas of our lives examined in this book it seems clear that we are more *ordered*. Broadly speaking it appears we are subject to greater regulation and oversight, to new styles of surveillance and management, and to forms of ordering that are more extensive, and often more intensive.

Take the dog shit story. While not a simple one overall, it is nevertheless a fairly clear example of an area of increased regulation – indeed *vastly* increased regulation. The existence of dog faeces in public places, once generally unregulated, is now surrounded by central government legislation, local by-laws, on the spot fines and a wide range of forms of guidance encouraging us to do the decent thing. Little of this existed in the early post-war decades.[3] The bulk have emerged in the past forty years. Some similar patterns can be identified in relation to drinking, smoking and parking. In none of these cases would it ever have been true to say that they were unfettered activities. Nevertheless, the general trend in the past half-century or more has been toward significantly increased use of a variety of instruments to outline what can be done, by whom, where and when. Now, increased regulation shouldn't straightforwardly be assumed to mean greater restriction. Take alcohol. Overall, there can be no doubt that this is a field in which there is greatly increased monitoring and where there has been a proliferation of rules. However, within it – in relation to licensing for instance – there are examples of generally more liberal or permissive practice, albeit involving a greater array of guidelines than were previously present.

Increased regulation may take many forms and have differing consequences. In broad terms, for example, the growing numbers of controls over the sale and consumption of tobacco have been aimed at restricting and reducing use. By contrast, this has not been the general aim where alcohol is concerned. Yes, new rules and laws have been introduced which seek to restrict consumption at particular times, in particular places, or by particular people. But the overall objective has not generally been to reduce the amount of alcohol sold – indeed, some of the time alcohol has only indirectly been the source of concern. This forces us to recognise that the aims of regulation may vary and may also change over time. In the case of parking, for example, where systems of control initially sought to instil some sort of order on congested roads and busy towns and cities, this objective has more recently been joined, and sometimes overtaken, by the desire to restrict the use of motor vehicles.

This leads us more directly to the question of the rationales for intervention. How are changes to laws and other regulations explained and justified? On what basis do we want citizens' actions in relation to their pets, their consumption of tobacco and alcohol, their use of cars to change? Again, such matters vary depending on the area of conduct under consideration. Health concerns have been a significant impetus for promoting new forms of regulation or intervention in several areas we have considered in this book. Concern about health dangers to children played a significant role in the early local authority campaigns to limit dog faeces, increasing knowledge of the carcinogenic consequences of smoking were a crucial driving force in increasing controls over smoking, and danger on the roads was the core impetus in growing restrictions over drinking and driving. But if health concerns remained central to campaigns around smoking this was less the case where both dog muck and drinking were concerned. And as the case of alcohol so neatly illustrates, a concern with health has never been the only issue. Most obviously, and for some time, a preoccupation with crime and disorder has been the primary motivating force behind alcohol regulation for some time. Health concerns initially played an important role in turning dog excreta into a public problem, but subsequently change has been at least as much a consequence of shifting sensibilities as it has been fear of disease. We are less tolerant of muck. Our social expectations have changed and our behaviour has also.

One consistent theme has concerned what might be termed the 'moral ordering' of the matters under consideration: changing social expectations about what is considered appropriate where. This can be seen very clearly in relation to drinking. Where we drink has changed, as has who we drink with. Concerns ranging from health effects to problems of disorder surround drinking, with the language of risk increasingly infusing talk about alcohol consumption. The decline of drinking at work is partly a consequence of formal regulation but is arguably, just as we observed in relation to dog muck, also a reflection of changing attitudes and sensibilities. In this connection, perhaps the greatest shift has been seen in relation to smoking. At the beginning of the period covered by this book smoking was considered both desirable and fashionable. Roll forward just over half a century and it is a 'habit' that is increasingly viewed as dirty, dangerous and deviant. On film and television smoking has become a key signifier. The easiest way to establish that a scene is set at some point prior to the 1970s is for the director simply to ensure that all their main characters light up a fag wherever possible.

Change in relation to some of the themes we have considered – dogs, parking, and aspects of drinking and smoking, even toilets – has been at least partly about the management of public space. In a fascinating article on how local councils and other bodies have responded to what appears to be a growing problem associated with gulls in seaside towns, Sarah Trotter observes that the birds are 'transgressive of the socio-spatial order which is created and policed around them by human beings'.[4] Her point, put simply, is that the regulatory frameworks that have grown in response to the apparent nuisance caused by gulls have at least as much to do with how we manage public space as it does these 'divebombers', 'attackers', 'invaders' and 'terrorisers' themselves. The actions taken locally are, more than anything else, designed to try to get 'gulls out of "our" urban spaces'. Rather like the training of dog owners to pick up after their pets, an important strategy has been to try to educate local citizens not to feed the birds, or to leave food unattended in a manner that might attract birds. In the case of both seagulls and dogs, the language of antisocial behaviour has been utilised to capture a sense that public space is being used inappropriately. As Trotter notes, this vision of public space combines ideas of protection (public health, safety), civility (in the case of dogs the prosocial behaviour of cleaning up after pets), and responsibility (it is those who fail to comply who create wider problems).

If in the case of dogs (and gulls), regulation, at least in part, is undertaken as a means of establishing a particular form of orderly public space, the example of changes in queuing arguably partly reflects shifts in the organisation and management of commercial enterprises. This is an area of activity that in some circumstances has become increasingly formalised. While there are arguably areas of civic life where queuing is now less common, or where social expectations of queuing no longer seem to apply or appear to have broken down, there are many others where the management of queuing has been turned into something approximating a science. Queuing is one very good illustration, therefore, of how from one perspective regulatory systems are the basis for governing and restricting behaviour, whereas from another they are also productive systems by which certain styles of conduct are created and defined. How to buy, shop, and consume – and what this means for our identity and sense of self – is something where guidance and instruction is ever plentiful. And in terms of the shopping experience, the queue is now one of the most heavily managed and patrolled parts of the activity. It is now carefully analysed and then managed and manipulated in order to reduce the running costs in shops, to maximise sales and to reduce customer frustration. From self-scanning, to self-service, to customer signalling systems, we are now all subject to the rigours of 'queue discipline'. But in some contexts this 'we' is a contingent rather than a universal one. If we're wealthy enough, impatient enough or both, there are many areas where we can now pay to jump from one queue to another, quicker one.

If we do find ourselves standing in a queue, these days one will almost certainly find that there is signage pointing out how to queue, where to queue and perhaps when to move forward. The proliferation of symbolic messaging is a feature of contemporary life that is central to the new regulatory landscape, indicating preferred forms of behaviour, encouraging adherence to rules and expectations, and sometimes threatening penalties for failure to do so. So abundant are such signs that there are more types than we could possibly list, even if we stuck to just one of the themes in this book. Indeed, if we were just to select one (it could be any) we would find a proliferation of signs and notices indicating which behaviours are allowed, approved and encouraged, and which are not. As we say, these signs take several forms. There are the more straightforward *instructional* ones. There are two types, the more common of which simply states that something must not happen or should not be done:

No Parking.
No Fouling.
No Smoking.
Do not flush sanitary products or wet wipes down the toilet

Its partner is the *instructional* sign that indicates what you should do:

Please queue here
Please queue this way ⇨
Please queue here for speedy shop till
Maintain social distance – 2m apart

A variant, which doesn't go so far as to tell one what to do, is the *declaratory* sign that simply indicates that certain things don't happen in this particular place:

Alcohol Free Zone.
Poop free zone.
No smoking area.
This is a smoke free site

Then there are a range of signs – the *threatening* variety – that not only indicate the impermissible, but also warn of sanctions of various sorts for those that fail to comply:

Alcohol Free Zone
If you consume alcohol
in a public place in this area
you could be fined up to £500

No Smoking
It is against the law
to smoke in these
premises

This is a Public Space Protection Order area
Dogs must be kept under control at all times
You may commit an offence if you:
1. Fail to remove your dog's faeces
2. Fail to put your dog on a lead when
   requested by an authorised officer
3. Walk more than four dogs at once

Offenders may be prosecuted or fined

Below the range of instructional, declaratory and threatening signs, there are those that are more exhortatory and encouraging, though a degree of passive-aggressiveness is often involved. These signs often play on guilt and assumed social pressure. Some simply spell out what might be thought to be general social mores, but now apparently need to be detailed:

Polite notice
Please clean up after your pets

Toilets
Did you wash your hands?
Please flush the toilet after use with the lid closed

Priority seat
for people who are disabled, pregnant or less able to stand

Signage appears ubiquitous in modern Britain and these various styles of communication illustrate something important about our contemporary social order. Although, as we've noted, some of the messaging is quite firm and, indeed, some is even threatening, at heart the approach of the bulk of this material is to remind, prompt, encourage, persuade, coax and cajole. They represent a constant encouragement to behave in particular ways. They are an ever-present reminder of expectations – so ubiquitous that some social scientists have described them as 'the official graffiti of the everyday'.[5] We are told we must remember to pick up after our dogs, not smoke indoors, park only in the places and at the times allowed, queue in a particular direction and wait for our number to be called, wash our hands, give up our seats to those more needy and so on . . . and on. At heart this is part of a wider process that the French philosopher Michel Foucault would have referred to as the 'disciplining of the self' and the German sociologist Norbert Elias would have seen as evidence of the intensifying social constraint towards self-constraint. Both scholars were making an observation about a broad historical trend in which forms of external constraint and control gradually gave way to subtler, internalised forms of self-restraint. For Foucault, surveillance was central to the new form of discipline. Rather than a threatening presence, external surveillance is both something that becomes a source of protection and an instrument that encourages and inculcates self-control. As the signs on London's buses that announce that CCTV is in operation say: 'For your safety and security you may be being recorded'. It is fairly easy to imagine how this type of sign, and the technology it refers to, help produce the kind of self-managing citizens that Michel Foucault suggests we have increasingly become. What scholars such as Foucault and Elias remind us is that formal systems of punishment, while important, are far from being *the* crucial element in the maintenance of social order and, very possibly, may be of declining importance.

Elements of such a shift can be seen in various aspects of everyday life covered in this book. Now, we must not overstate this argument, for we have certainly not suggested that formal mechanisms of regulation are withering. Quite the reverse. As we have illustrated, if anything they appear to be proliferating. But observing that formal controls appear to have expanded rapidly is not the same as suggesting that these are the primary reason that behaviour has changed. Let's begin with cleaning up after dogs. Here, self-evidently, new formal rules have multiplied. However, although there has been a lot of formal activity the bulk of this has involved the creation of new instruments of regulation, rather than enforcement action. It seems there is little evidence, apart from one or two exceptional cases, that official enforcement has played much of a role in backing up these formal measures. Few prosecutions have been brought; few fines have been imposed. Enforcement generally seems to be threatened rather than implemented. The major function of such formal regulations appears to be symbolic. This is confirmed in the case of seagulls that we briefly discussed earlier, another focus of plentiful regulatory activity but relatively little formal enforcement, certainly so far as things like fixed penalty notices and fines are concerned. That this is the case doesn't make such measures unimportant. Far from it, for their symbolism is very significant and central to their utility – instilling greater discipline in dog owners and other citizens – without the need for much in the way of formal enforcement. Most of the time most of us readily comply. We've learned the rules, internalised them and now we self-police.

Now here again let's not get carried away for there are other examples in this book that potentially tell a slightly different story. The ban on smoking in pubs and places of work, for example, undoubtedly required legislation to establish the new boundaries for behaviour. Drinking and driving laws had to be passed, and enforced, for new social practices to take hold. But even in areas such as these it is clear that most of the time it is not the threat of being caught and punished that is the primary constraining factor. Rather, it is that, over time, social attitudes and expectations have changed – often much influenced by changes in formal regulations – and these act as a brake on conduct. Again, we have internalised new standards. The one most obvious partial exception is parking. Here, for no doubt a complex set of reasons, it seems that some level of surveillance and enforcement activity is vital in maintaining order. Without it, as the Aberystwyth experience indicated, systems start to fail. The parking example is different for a second reason. Not only does compliance appear to be lower in this case but many car drivers express extreme unhappiness about the enforcement of the rules and are so dismissive of them that they become serial offenders. Unlike many other areas considered in this book, we appear to be more doubtful about the legitimacy of parking rules and certainly to be more willing to break them. If drivers were as well behaved as dog owners, we would need fewer traffic wardens.

Our concerns have largely been about how we organise ourselves and what underpins this organisation. However, when using terms like 'organisation' it is important that this is not taken to imply some sort of overall design, some hidden hand responsible for the shape of the everyday social world. The reality, rather, is that notwithstanding the impact of governments, corporations and other institutions, there is always something serendipitous, unanticipated or accidental about social order. The consequence is that although it is generally quite predictable, it is also constantly under construction, constantly emerging, and in some sort of flux. Stable but also changing. As the American criminologist Otwin Marenin once observed, order here doesn't imply some absence of change but, rather, it points to 'regularity, an irreducible minimum of confidence in the future which allows groups and individuals to engage in routine activities, including the promotion of change'.[6] Or as the philosopher David Hume put it in the mid-eighteenth century, 'custom, then, is the great guide to human life. It ... makes us expect, for the future, a similar train of events with those that have appeared in the past.'[7]

There are, however, some contemporary observers who feel that the period in which we are living is less stable, and more changeable, than the periods that preceded it. It is possible that this feeling of instability is simply a reflection of an inescapable part of the human condition – the sense that we are beset by forces that our ancestors did not have to contend with. Nevertheless, and perhaps with good reason, many commentators in recent decades have argued that we live in quickly changing times. A range of terms, from postmodernism to globalisation, have been conjured to capture aspects of what are taken to be the significantly shifting sands on which we stand. Such terminology implies that the degree to which the character of the modern world has changed is sufficient to signify a qualitative shift with the past. In an attempt to capture our contemporary social order, one that is less predictable and more mutable than those that preceded it, the sociologist Zygmunt Bauman, for example, has described modern times as *liquid*. But, even in this case, it is not that the world is unpredictable; more that we have to work harder to ensure there is predictability. As Bauman puts it, 'keeping fluids in shape requires a lot of attention, constant vigilance and perpetual effort – and even then, the success of the effort is anything but a foregone conclusion'.[8]

So, what is happening? Either our contemporary times are liquid despite the proliferation of regulations we have noted or, possibly, the explosion of rules, directions and instructions has occurred precisely because our world seems so changeable. Whatever the relationship, what seems undeniable to us is that, at heart, across the majority of the spheres of activity we have considered in this book, levels of regulation and oversight have increased markedly. In short we are, as we suggested earlier, much more *ordered*. Indeed, we think there is a further broad generalisation we can make. Not only do we appear to be surrounded by increasingly wide-ranging and often quite fine-graded systems of regulation and changing social expectation but, by and large, we seem to display generally high levels of compliance. New social norms are established, occasionally quite quickly, internalised and generally adhered to. From our increased willingness to pick up after our pets, the limitations on our smoking, our drinking at work, to our standing in line, and with the partial exception of parking our cars, we appear to be a generally acquiescent lot. Faced with rapidly changing restrictions on our conduct, most people most of the time abide by the rules.

One question that might be raised against the tentative

conclusions we have outlined thus far concerns whether they might need to be amended if the subjects under discussion were different. For example, would the broad claim about being increasingly *ordered* still hold if we chose matters other than drinking, smoking, parking and so on? Different spheres of civic life, as we have seen, appear to be subject to different forms of regulation, and appear to display different patterns when it comes to the processes of change in evidence in the post-war period. Consequently, it is entirely conceivable that a different selection of subjects would tell a different story, not just add differences of detail to the general observations made here. However, in terms of the broad sweep of what we have wanted to argue, we feel fairly confident that it would remain relatively undisturbed even when the subjects are changed. Let us finish by very briefly considering a couple of examples.

First, swearing or so-called 'bad language'. Surely that is something that has become more evident, more permissible and, consequently, is less subject to close regulation? Well, yes and no. If we take language that is used on television as a proxy for the wider issue – it is actually very difficult to reach any general judgements about broader social usage – it seems clear that there are many words that would not previously have been uttered but which can now be heard regularly on television. Certain forms of swearing are by now quite routine, particularly after the watershed. But mention of the watershed should immediately alert us to the fact that there are limits to what is permissible – in this case the regulation dictating that material considered unsuitable for children should not, as a general rule, be broadcast before 9 p.m. or after 5.30 a.m. 'Material unsuitable for children' is defined by the regulator, Ofcom, as something that can 'include everything from sexual content to violence, graphic or distressing imagery and swearing'. On the latter it says, 'the most offensive language must not be broadcast before the watershed on TV or, on radio, when children are particularly likely to be listening. Frequent use of offensive language must be avoided before the watershed and must always be justified by its context'.[9] It is one of the reasons why you might hear sports commentators apologising when microphones pick up swearing on a football or rugby pitch. Yes, there is undoubtedly much more swearing on television than was once the case. When Kenneth Tynan used the word 'fuck' on television in November 1965, it caused a sensation. It would be sensational now if, post-watershed, Gordon Ramsay uttered a sentence without using it. The reality, however, is that despite what on the surface appears to be increasing freedom, the language used on television is very carefully monitored and regulated. Channel 4, for example, offers a careful breakdown on the circumstances in which different (potentially offensive) words can reasonably be used, and when 'bleeping' or 'dipping' the sound to mask or disguise the word should be considered.[10]

But let's turn our attention away from traditional understandings of 'swearing' and toward wider questions of what it is considered inappropriate to say. Doing so offers a variety of examples of ways in which our attitudes toward, and the rules and regulations surrounding, language have changed over the past half-century. One of the more obvious is in connection with what is now widely referred to as 'hate speech'. Ever since the Public Order Act 1986, which criminalised expressions of racial hatred, the legal net has been widened to make it impermissible to express hatred against anyone on the basis of their colour, race, disability, nationality (including citizenship), ethnic or national origin, religion, gender identity, sexual orientation, transgender orientation or perceived transgender orientation. The perceived impermissibility of certain words has led to a backlash in some quarters and to accusations of so-called 'political correctness'. In recent times, certain forms of expression have become sufficiently controversial for 'trigger warnings' to be considered necessary where potentially controversial views, or controversial language might be used, and for 'no-platforming' to become something of a trend – involving the denial or attempted denial of a stage for people expressing views felt to be deeply unpleasant or potentially inflammatory. We need not dive too deep here. The point, simply, is that while there appears to be a certain permissiveness in some quarters, there is anything but in others. Language is another field where regulation is arguably increasingly extensive and, certainly, social attitudes toward what is permissible are far more complex.

As a second example, and one which was arguably at the heart of concerns in what became known as 'permissive Britain' back in the sixties, there is sex. Surely, we are now less prudish, more open, and generally freer to follow our desires and predilections? This is surely an area where we are less rule-bound and regulated? Well, in some respects, of course, that is true. Sex before marriage is commonplace, as is cohabitation by unmarried couples. Same-sex relationships are now legally recognised and social disapproval has largely disappeared. There appears generally to be much greater freedom both to talk about sex and to engage in sexual activity. Moreover, sexual imagery has become extraordinarily widespread, and the internet has made such imagery – and pornography most obviously – routinely accessible and has consigned shady sex shops largely to the dustbin of British history. But – by this stage you knew there was going to be *but* – this is only part of the story. While of course these developments can, from one perspective, be presented as a form of liberation, it is also the case that an increasingly complex array of rules and regulations has been brought into being, covering a range of matters from access to birth control; abortion/termination of pregnancy; laws around sex work; same-sex marriage; reproductive rights; sex education in schools; adult conduct and contact with children; and, rules governing sexual imagery, to name but a few. Though in one sense there are now many apparent freedoms that were previously denied, there are also multiplying means by which we and our behaviours are defined, categorised, understood, discussed and judged and, yes, regulated.

We may return to these and other subjects at a later time. For now, taking in matters that range from dog shit to double parking, we feel we can safely conclude that the Britain we live in is generally very orderly, and certainly increasingly *ordered*. Moreover, in a range of important ways our orderliness must be understood as a social achievement rather than a consequence of surveillance or official control. Yes, laws and regulations are important and, indeed, they too have proliferated. They signal social expectations and standards, and offer the potential for official intervention and for the imposition of penalties. But in all the areas we have considered – with the notable exception of parking – compliance is generally high and penalties and punishment are few and far between. For all that formal regulation has proliferated, and has surrounded and permeated our lives, self-control is generally strong, thanks to our willingness to internalise social norms and abide by them. We are, indeed, *orderly Britons*.

But what about sudden disruption. Would we appear so orderly when a crisis hits, when our social routines are suddenly thrown out of kilter by some massive and unexpected change?

How would we cope then? Well, for good or ill we have recent experience that helps us begin to answer this question. We have been living through just such a natural experiment. Outside of wartime, the COVID-19 pandemic offered one of the most dramatic sets of challenges to everyday order that any will have experienced in their lifetimes. Before we leave, therefore, it is worth considering what the experience of the pandemic has to teach us about social order.

The Pandemic and Orderliness

Late in 2019, news stories from China talked of a new strain of coronavirus. There was much speculation as to the likely dangers but, at first, no especial sense of what was to come. Indeed, how could there have been? The global pandemic that followed in the early months of 2020 was unlike anything anyone still alive had experienced before. Requiring massive lockdowns of citizens, closures of schools, universities and businesses, and leading to huge economic disruption and unprecedented upturns in unemployment levels, it was something that had long been anticipated, and feared, but to which perhaps only the so-called 'Spanish flu' in the aftermath of the First World War was in any way comparable in modern times.

This brief postscript, written as things were still unfolding in 2021, takes the opportunity to consider elements of what has occurred during these unprecedented times and to relate them to some of the themes and issues raised in the preceding chapters. Early days still in some ways, but enough has happened, it feels, to allow for a few reflections on the underlying theme of this book: orderliness. Like other nations, the citizens of the UK were faced with extraordinary changes to their lives, not the least

291

of which for many was being asked to 'stay at home', not to see family and friends, to wear masks, and keep a safe 'social distance' – judged to be two metres in Britain – and to work online rather than face-to-face. How would we adapt? What were the rules? Would we obey them? What would happen if we didn't? Who would enforce distancing and other matters? Would chaos reign, some new form of order be quickly and easily established, or would something more complicated emerge?

Of course, as we say, this story is far from over, and any observations are general and tentative. Nevertheless, and cutting to the chase, our overwhelming conclusion at this stage is a positive one (though we also have some less than positive things to say too). Yes, there have been failures of governance, some of them arguably very significant indeed. There have also been any number of examples of problems and breakdowns in – or at least challenges to – order. And as weeks turned into months, and confusion and frustration grew with both the restrictions that people were expected to live under, and confusion as to what the rules *actually* were, there was anger and resentment in many quarters at what was taking place. But those things are not the main story. The truth of the matter is, faced with the most extraordinary changes and challenges, order during the pandemic was generally sustained, albeit in a new form. Indeed, order was not just sustained, but was transformed, and quickly. Moreover, as readers might by now expect, it was created and sustained primarily by citizens themselves, rather than by the state, the police or by minute surveillance. Yes, government have been vital in setting the general parameters for new ways of behaving – and some of the main failures have occurred when those parameters have appeared unclear, unfair or inconsistent. Yes, the police did get involved, and new forms of surveillance gradually emerged.

But, by and large these were not particularly central to what was achieved.

The most extraordinary and sudden change took place: what we quickly learned to call 'lockdown'. A new way of life, staying at home, not travelling to work and not interacting with others outside one's own home became a daily reality. As Joe Moran put it, this lockdown 'laid bare the strangeness of the everyday. It ... severed us from many of our routines and coated those that survive with a deep glaze of oddness.'[1] And indeed there was something extremely odd about life in the pandemic. Equally profound, however, was how quickly normalised so much of it became. New styles of social organisation came into being, did so quickly and, by and large, became deeply embedded. There was broad social acceptance and widespread acquiescence with the new ways of being. It offered a straightforward yet rather profound insight into the everyday and reminded anyone who needed it that this is precisely how order is created and sustained. As sociologists have long observed, order and predictability in everyday life is our most fundamental and greatest social achievement. So, with this very necessary good news at hand, let's look a little closer at what has happened.

In and out of lockdown[2]

The World Health Organization was first informed by China of cases of pneumonia of unknown origin in Wuhan in late 2019, and by the third week of January 2020, cases were confirmed in Japan, Thailand and the Republic of Korea. To this point the 'risk level' in Britain was officially determined to be 'very low'. This was upgraded to 'low' in late January as the fast-growing number of cases in Wuhan, and the spread to other countries became clear. At this time anyone returning to the UK from Wuhan was told to 'self-isolate' for fourteen days. One week later the first two cases of COVID-19 were identified in the UK, both Chinese nationals staying in York, one of whom was studying at the university. There was a third case a week later, this one being dubbed a 'super-spreader' having been linked with nearly a dozen other cases, some in the UK, some elsewhere. New Health Protection (Coronavirus) Regulations were put in place, imposing restrictions on any individual considered by health professionals to be at risk of spreading the virus, and in particular advising those Britons who had been in northern Italy, where a major outbreak had occurred, also to 'self-isolate'. The health secretary described this as a 'belt and braces' approach to protecting the public.

By late February 2020, there were still only a dozen or so identified cases in the UK, but at the end of the month the first death of a Briton from the virus occurred – a passenger on a cruise ship moored off the coast of Japan. By early March, it was clear that a worldwide pandemic was underway. In Europe, cases were escalating quickly, and Italy, which seemed especially badly hit, took the decision to close schools and universities. On 2 March, the government's emergency COBR committee discussed the pandemic, and was chaired for the first time by the prime minister. The following day the government published its action plan. This had four phases: contain, delay, research, mitigate – with 'contain' being the governmental priority at that point.

The first death from the virus in Britain, a woman in her seventies, occurred on 5 March 2020. Within a further week more than a hundred new cases were emerging every day, the Chancellor of the Exchequer was announcing emergency economic measures, and it seemed clear that the terrible scenes that were by now coming from Italy might well be only weeks away in the UK. Mid-March saw the first signs of 'panic buying' in the supermarkets, and the first announcements that shoppers should try to be more considerate of others' needs. The week of 16 March was a turning point. Two new measures were introduced: self-isolation of households containing anyone with two key symptoms; with everyone else to stop non-essential contact with others and all non-essential travel. Having urged everyone at the beginning of the week to work from home where possible and to avoid restaurants and pubs, by the Friday the prime minister told cafés, pubs, bars, restaurants, as well as nightclubs, theatres, cinemas, gyms and leisure centres that they had to close by the end of the day. By this point fifty-five people had been officially identified as having died from the virus. The chief scientific adviser suggested that it would be a 'good outcome' if the total number of eventual deaths remained under twenty thousand. By the end of the week it was announced that all schools were to close.

Continuing problems with shortages of some goods in shops led the environment secretary the following day, 21 March, to ask everyone to 'be responsible', to think of others and to remember that shortages made life very difficult for front-line workers. In a newspaper article the PM wrote that the best gift that Mother's Day was 'staying away'. Rather '... the best thing is to ring her, video call her, ... And why? Because if your mother is elderly or vulnerable, then I am afraid all the statistics show that she is much more likely to die from coronavirus, or COVID-19. We cannot disguise or sugar coat the threat.' A variety of measures were put in place to ease pressure on the supply chain. On Monday 23 March, the PM officially announced the beginning of the first 'lockdown'. The new advice about social distancing included avoiding contact with anyone displaying COVID symptoms; avoiding non-essential use of public transport; working from home, where possible; and avoiding large and small gatherings in public spaces, and gatherings with friends and family. Everyone, it was said, should be trying to follow these measures as much as is practicable. On 25 March the Coronavirus Act 2020 received Royal Assent and became law. Passing through parliament with only four days of scrutiny, the legislation extended governmental reach in three main ways: increasing powers to detain 'potentially infectious persons'; giving greater power to prevent mass gatherings; and, extending the forms of surveillance available.

To underline the seriousness of the threat, within a week the prime minister, Boris Johnson, the health secretary, Matt Hancock, and the chief medical officer, Sir Patrick Vallance, had all tested positive for the virus. On 5 April, the Queen addressed the nation. In a widely praised speech, in addition to thanking everyone on the front line and carrying out essential roles 'who selflessly continue their day-to-day duties outside the home in support of us all', she said, 'I also want to thank those of you who are staying at home, thereby helping to protect the vulnerable and sparing many families the pain already felt by those who have lost loved ones. Together we are tackling this disease, and I want to reassure you that if we remain united and resolute, then we will overcome it.' In a government daily briefing in the middle of April, the Foreign Secretary announced that the current distancing measures that were in place would need to be adhered to well into May.

Indeed, it was 10 May before the prime minister announced a conditional plan for ending lockdown. In a statement in the

House of Commons, he began by noting the scale of what had occurred in terms of everyday behaviour, saying 'We have together observed the toughest restrictions on our freedoms in memory, changing our way of life on a scale unimaginable only months ago.' The challenge was now charting a way out of the restrictions while minimising risk. The result was a complex set of instructions, including: anyone who cannot work from home was to be actively encouraged to go to work; sectors that are allowed to be open should indeed be open, but subject to social distancing; anyone with COVID symptoms – or in a household where someone else has symptoms – should self-isolate; people should continue to avoid public transport wherever possible; and, limits placed on walking and taking exercise would be lifted.[3] If the changes helped keep the infection rate down, the public were told that from the beginning of June it would be possible to move to the 'second phase'. This would involve the phased reopening of shops and the return of some children to nurseries, childminders and primary schools. It might also allow for cultural and sporting events to be held behind closed doors for broadcast.

But the big date was 4 July 2020 – referred to in some quarters as 'independence day', and what the prime minister described as a 'significant return to normality' – when pubs, restaurants, galleries and museums reopened, though again under the proviso that care was taken to socially distance and limit contact – with the two-metre rule reduced to 'one metre plus'. People from two households were now allowed to meet up in any setting but, again, were advised to continue physical distancing. For the people of Leicester, however, it was anything but independence day. A week earlier the first 'local lockdown' had been announced, closing schools and shops in the area and limiting social contact and travel.

The Leicester experience was in some respects an augur of things to come. Further local lockdowns followed. Initially, Blackburn and Luton were told that new measures that were being introduced to ease the lockdown would not apply to them because of relatively high infection rates, and at the end of July increased restrictions were placed on Greater Manchester and on parts of Lancashire and Yorkshire as a consequence of increased transmission rates. Early August saw lockdown measures reintroduced in Preston, and in early September, Birmingham and some neighbouring districts were subject to increased restriction on social mixing. By mid-September, large parts of the north-east of England, Lancashire, Yorkshire, Merseyside and Leicester were also under local lockdowns. As students started to reassemble in university towns and cities, and infection rates started to rise markedly, it appeared only a matter of time before greater national restrictions reappeared.

In early October, a three-tier system (medium, high and very high) of alerts was announced, ranging from the lower level where the restrictions already in place at that time ('rule of six' – indoor and outdoor social gatherings above six banned in England – and pubs closing at 10 p.m.) would be maintained; a higher level with no household mixing indoors, and contact outdoors limited to 'bubbles'; and the highest level where no household mixing was allowed, the 'rule of six' applied outdoors, and pubs could only remain open if they served full meals, i.e. effectively operated like a restaurant.[4] Asked whether the measures would be sufficient the chief medical officer said that he was not confident that this would be enough to 'get on top' of the problem, implying that further measures might have to be taken. Indeed, leaked documents from the government's scientific advisers suggested that they had called for a short national lockdown – a so-called 'circuit breaker' – some weeks earlier. Indeed, in addition to restricting all contact inside homes with members of other households, the scientists had called for the closing of all bars, restaurants, cafés, gyms and hairdressers, and had suggested that all university and college teaching should take place online. Initially only Merseyside was placed into the highest tier three category, though it was clear that other areas might have joined sooner rather than later. Within a week it was being suggested that Lancashire, Greater Manchester and large parts of the North East might have to be placed in tier three. There was growing frustration, even anger in some quarters, at what was felt to be the unfair treatment of some regions, and research suggested that public trust in government handling of the health crisis had shrunk markedly by this point.[5]

A second national lockdown in England was introduced on 5 November 2020, with the country being told it was to last four weeks. Consequently, the country returned to the three-tier system beginning on 2 December, with the hope that this would enable businesses to take advantage of pre-Christmas shopping demand. With the COVID situation worsening by this stage, very few areas were placed in the lowest tier, with the majority being placed in tiers two or three. The initially announced intention was that three households would be able to meet, indoors, through the five-day period in which the rules were to be relaxed over Christmas. To many this never seemed realistic, and with little warning, under a week before Christmas, all such plans were scrapped and were replaced with a new four-tier system of restrictions. In the new tier four, which covered London and much of the South East, only one household could meet. In the other tiers, three households could meet, but only on Christmas

Day itself. In Scotland, similar rules applied with three house-holds being allowed to meet on Christmas Day whereas in Wales it was two households only.

The response to the pandemic in the UK had generally been fragmented. The broad outline above offers a rough description of what occurred in England during 2020 but, from early on, political leaders outside England departed from the Westminster model in the controls imposed in Scotland, Wales and Northern Ireland. In particular, as restrictions were eased in England, governments in Scotland and Wales showed greater caution, lessening restrictions at a generally slower pace. All three first ministers – Nicola Sturgeon, Arlene Foster and Mark Drakeford – decided that their countries would retain the 'Stay at Home' message and not adopt England's new 'Stay Alert' slogan when it was introduced, and both Scotland and Wales extended the lockdown for longer than was the case in England. From the end of the first lockdown in England onward the UK had different regulations in place in each of its four constituent nations.

The winter brought a significant worsening of the pandemic in the UK with both infection rates and numbers of deaths from COVID quickly on the rise and with hospital facilities coming close to being overwhelmed. In early January 2021, England entered its third national lockdown, schools were closed – many children having returned for one day only – and restrictions along the lines of those operating in the first lockdown were implemented. With mass vaccination underway the prospect of an end to lockdown was discussed regularly, with government eventually announcing that it planned to have schools reopen from early March, to allow groups of six to meet outdoors and limited travel from the end of the month, together with the reopening of non-essential shops from mid-April. Indoor mixing was likely to be permissible from mid-May with the full ending of lockdown anticipated toward the end of June.

With over a year passing between the imposition of the first lockdown and the announcement of the potential ending of the third, huge changes had taken place. The number of people who had died (defined as 'people who had had a positive test result for COVID-19 and died within twenty-eight days of the first positive test) was approaching 130,000, several vaccines had been developed, tested and approved, and over half the UK population had had at least one jab. The recession caused by the pandemic was described as 'unprecedented in modern times', the drop in GDP in 2020 being the steepest since records were first kept in the aftermath of the Second World War.[6] The cost of the measures taken by government to support businesses and households was estimated to be around £250 billion. And, as outlined above, the restrictions placed on citizens' everyday lives were extraordinary, restricting entry to private homes, stopping families seeing each other, limiting weddings, funerals, leisure activities, and radically changing the working landscape for many. As one commentator put it, were it not for the pandemic 'no liberal democracy would contemplate the measures used by government'.[7] Let us turn now to some of the features of British social order – and orderliness – during these extraordinary times.

Early days: 'panic buying'

One of the memories most people in Britain will have of the pandemic, certainly in its early weeks, is shortages of certain items in the shops. Empty shelves where toilet rolls used to be became normal for a while. Seemingly there was a rush to stock up on a variety of 'necessities'. That dry goods would run dry was all too predictable. That demand for yeast would rise so quickly was perhaps rather less so. All of a sudden discussion of rationing once again entered national consciousness. Of course, many had been here before. Those who had lived through the Second World War and its aftermath had clear memories of food restrictions and, as we noted earlier, of the lengthy queuing that went with it. Some no doubt also remembered those who broke the rules, the black market for hard to find items, with the figure of the 'spiv' becoming a common trope in the war years and their aftermath.

Although reports of a new virus spread in early 2020, for many it seemed the fact that something very unusual was taking place only really hit home when they heard the stories of panic buying in supermarkets, of fights breaking out, and occasional examples of people profiteering from the shortages that were developing. The run on various goods in Britain seemed in part to have been provoked by the news of panic buying in Hong Kong, Australia and elsewhere. In mid-February, toilet roll shortages were reported in Hong Kong, as were stories of mass buying, and even a claim that an armed gang had stolen six hundred rolls from a store. By the beginning of March, when the number of COVID cases in Britain was still only in the dozens, Australian supermarkets began to report that a range of products such as rice, sugar and cat litter were beginning to run low. These shortages, however, seemingly paled into insignificance compared with the run on toilet rolls. These 'conditioned symbols of safety', as one psychologist called them,[8] became so scarce that Woolworths and other major stores quickly began to impose a limit on sales. One Australian newspaper, the *Northern Territory News*, even printed an edition with an extra blank eight-page insert, its front page saying, 'Get your limited edition one-ply toilet paper newspaper sheets'. In the aftermath of one supermarket fight in New South Wales, a senior police officer said, 'we just ask that people don't panic like this when they go out shopping. There is no need for it. It isn't the Thunderdome, it isn't Mad Max, we don't need to do that.'[9]

During the early weeks of the pandemic in Britain it became clear that the shortages that were identified were found primarily in supermarkets. Many shoppers, if they were fortunate enough to live near to small, independent stores, often found them to be reasonably well stocked with items that had seemingly run out elsewhere. Indeed, what the pandemic shortages quite quickly revealed was that it was not a supply problem, but a supply chain problem. Supermarkets, where the bulk of modern shopping takes place, have systems which carefully monitor stock and organise themselves to be able to order 'just-in-time', minimising unused stock in both warehouses and on shelves. Small changes in demand can have a large impact. Yes, supermarkets ran out of particular goods but not because such goods didn't exist. In the main it was a consequence of being unable to get them on the shelves in sufficient quantity with sufficient speed.

In Britain, on 15 March 2020, the four major supermarkets – Asda, Morrisons, Sainsbury's and Tesco – who collectively controlled about two-thirds of the grocery market, decided they needed to intervene. In a letter headed 'Working to Feed the Nation', they asked shoppers to behave responsibly, and sought to reassure them that supplies would not run short if customers exercised control: 'We would ask everyone to be considerate in the way they shop. We understand your concerns but buying more than is needed can sometimes mean that others will be left without. There is enough for everyone if we all work together.'[10] The first major government comment came on 20 March, when the health secretary, Matt Hancock, said people should buy only 'what they need and not more than what they need'. In part, it seems, Hancock's intervention was prompted by a viral video that featured a nurse who, having just finished a lengthy shift, spoke of her despair at finding her local supermarket stripped of fruit, veg and other essentials. 'Just stop it,' she said, 'because it's people like me that are going to be looking after you when you're at your lowest, so just stop it. Please.'

But what actually went on? How disorderly were we? Not very is the answer. First of all, the increase in shopping, and any stockpiling of goods, appears to have been quite shortlived. Sales figures from Tesco pointed to quite a steep increase in supermarket sales around the time that the first UK domestic transmission of the virus was reported, with the increased sales lasting for around three weeks. It then declined quickly thereafter, before picking up again a little around the time the government issued its 'stay at home' guidance. This was confirmed by the market research company Kantar Worldpanel, which suggested that it was the week beginning 16 March that saw the big spike in grocery shopping, with nearly nine in ten households visiting a grocer in the first four days of that week – adding an equivalent of forty-two million extra shopping trips in that period.[11]

Second, much of the serious over-buying seems to have been confined to a small minority in the population. Figures from Tesco again suggested that around 10 per cent of shoppers were driving about 30 per cent of sales volume. More importantly, Kantar suggested that its data showed that no more than 3 per cent of the population engaged in what might seriously be described as 'panic buying' (we'll come back to this phrase shortly). The huge increase in sales was seemingly accounted for, they felt, by the very large increase in consumers who were 'adding just a few extra purchases ... and were shopping more regularly than usual'.[12] In late March/early April, the Office of National Statistics' Opinions and Lifestyle Survey found that 74 per cent of people said that they had struggled to get groceries and toiletries in the previous seven days. Twenty-four per cent said they had bought extra supplies of groceries and toiletries, and almost everyone (97 per cent) said they thought others were doing so. The same survey found that over 37 per cent said that 'access to groceries, medication and essentials' was a source of concern. By late May this was down to 28 per cent.[13] A large survey of the UK population suggested that around three-quarters of people engaged in little or no 'over-shopping' during the pandemic.[14]

Such findings undermine some of the assumptions widely touted in the early weeks of the pandemic and lockdown. Any change in shopping behaviour was generally one of degree. Basically what it meant was that lots of people went to the shops *slightly* more frequently and/or bought *slightly* more goods. Yes, there were some supplies that ran short but, in the main that was because these incremental increases led to temporary shortages on the shelves. Those who engaged in more egregious forms of 'over-buying' were very much in a minority, indeed a very small minority. Crucially, there's really no evidence of 'panic'. To the extent that shoppers changed their habits, these changes reflected altered circumstances: in the main that they were working from home and that, increasingly, they were being asked to limit their visits to the shops. That shoppers sought to get hold of goods like toilet rolls when they heard that there were or were likely to be shortages was therefore perfectly rational. There's nothing quite like an empty shelf to make you feel like you might be missing out. And, as you can't predict how long things will remain the way they are, it makes sense to buy something while one can. All very understandable, all very far from anarchic and, by and large, all quite quickly solved. We adapted and did so swiftly.

Law and regulation

One of the consistent themes throughout this book has been the proliferation of formal rules and regulations that now seem to surround so many areas of our lives. The same general trend could be seen in the course of the pandemic, with the passage of major new legislation together with a vast array of new forms of regulatory advice. Though there is no need to dive into detail here, a brief outline will give some sense of the scale of what happened.

As we noted earlier, with a minimum of parliamentary discussion, government passed the Coronavirus Act 2020. This made a range of changes, removing barriers to hiring recently retired NHS and social care workers, strengthening the quarantine powers of police and immigration officers, significantly increasing the ability of government to restrict or prevent public events, and postponing elections. In addition to this Act there were also a range of 'lockdown laws' – in essence secondary legislation made using public health powers. With public health being a devolved responsibility in the UK, these coronavirus regulations were often different in England, Scotland, Wales and Northern Ireland. In the main, the restriction covered four main areas: those relating directly to the 'lockdown' and restricting movement, gatherings and business operations; rules requiring the wearing of face coverings; restrictions and requirements relating to international travel and quarantine; and, rules covering the necessity of self-isolation. On top of these a series of other instruments were used to create local lockdowns, including closing local businesses.[15] All this, of course, was intricate enough but was given added complexity by the fact that it was also an unstable landscape, being amended regularly as the nature of pandemic changed.

Accompanying the intricate legislative backcloth were a bewildering array of guidelines and other forms of governmental advice. The publication of such guidelines added at least three potential sources of confusion. They, like the legislation, were temporary and oft-changing. It was difficult therefore for any other than the most assiduous to keep up. The distinction between what was a regulation – and therefore advisory – and what was law – and therefore compulsory – was far from always clear, even it seems to the police. Finally, but most basically, the regulations were themselves complex and far-reaching. Again, without bothering with detail, take one iteration of England's '(COVID-19) Coronavirus restrictions: what you can and cannot do'. Just at the level of the subjects included within it, its extent is clear, covering: meeting family and friends indoors/outdoors; support and childcare bubbles; going to work, school or college; universities and higher education; childcare; parent and child groups; providing care or assistance; support groups; exercise, sport and physical activity; funerals and commemorative events; weddings and civil partnership ceremonies; and, places of worship. We'll stop there – that's the first half of the list – and move on to consider what all this meant for policing Britain's citizens.

Policing the lockdown

When it was announced in late March 2020, the first lockdown was put in place for three weeks. It was clear to most from the outset that that was very much an initial period while assessments were made, and there was little surprise when the restrictions were extended for a further three-week period. There was little sense at that stage of just how long restrictions would last, or how often they would be reintroduced and reconfigured. Initially, the basic requirements were that people should: stay at home; work from home where possible; and, leave home no more than once a day for exercise, to shop for essential items, or to fulfil any medical or care needs. It was said that parks would remain open for exercise, but people should not gather in groups. The reaction was predictably mixed. Not everyone was happy, and there was a certain amount of confusion as people worked out what was allowed or reasonable, and what was not. There were some well-publicised cases of clear breaches of the rules and consequently much talk of how such measures were to be policed. Indeed, especially in the early days, there was controversy.

In the first week of the lockdown, policing headlines were largely dominated by Derbyshire Constabulary. The force deployed drones in the Peak District and subsequently published filmed footage of walkers who had travelled to a local beauty spot to take their exercise. In a tweet accompanying the footage, the police said, 'Despite posts yesterday highlighting issues of people still visiting #PeakDistrict despite government guidance, the message is still not getting through. @DerPolDroneUnit have been out at beauty spots across the county, and this footage was captured at #CurbarEdge last night.' The critical reaction was both fairly immediate and very strong. A former Supreme Court Judge, Lord Sumption, rather hyperbolically, said, 'This is what a police state is like. It's a state in which the government can issue orders or express preferences with no legal authority and the police will enforce ministers' wishes.'[16] To be fair to him he did go on to say that he felt most police forces had been thoroughly sensible and moderate. Derbyshire though, he felt, 'have shamed our policing traditions'. The former justice secretary, David Gauke, said that he felt the police actions were 'badly misjudged', pointing out that the walkers in the police footage were maintaining social distance.

Derbyshire almost certainly did both get it wrong and rather badly overstep the mark. What the episode also illustrated, however, was the difficult position the police found themselves in. They were being asked to enforce regulations that were far from entirely clear and posed quite a challenge for people to interpret. Getting it wrong some of the time in such circumstances was almost inevitable. The legal underpinning for enforcement had also changed markedly, with new legislation having dramatically expanded police powers. But, as is well established and as the police well know, public trust and consent is required for the police to be able to do their jobs successfully. This new situation, which was unprecedented, necessitated great care and it was Derbyshire's heavy-handedness that seemed to upset people most. Government came to the Constabulary's aid, within a few days 'clarifying' its advice to suggest to people that they should stay local and not travel unnecessarily for exercise.[17] The force was not out of the water, as it were, for further controversy ensued when it was revealed that, in response to breaches of lockdown regulations at another local beauty spot – the 'blue lagoon' at Harpur Hill – they had dyed the water black to discourage swimmers.[18] Among the critics was the former chancellor, George Osborne, who suggested the force had 'lost all common sense'.[19] However, as the force quickly pointed out, the dyeing of the water was a tactic that had been regularly used in the past to discourage people entering what were known literally to be dangerous waters. The decision to do so during lockdown was simply to discourage those who were visiting the lagoon from swimming.

One of the main problems of policing was inconsistency. In the early weeks of lockdown forces responded to the situation in markedly different ways. In a four-day period at the end of the first week of the new regulations it was reported that police in Lancashire had issued 123 enforcement notices against people breaking the new rules whereas Bedfordshire had issued none. New guidance issued by police leaders advised forces to 'apply the law in a system that is flexible, discretionary and pragmatic. This will enable officers to make sensible decisions and employ their judgement. Enforcement should be a last resort.' Even a cursory skim of the instructions, however, showed just how tricky the landscape would be for the police to navigate. Officers were told that if they saw someone outside the place they lived without a 'reasonable excuse', then they could: direct that person to return to the place where they are living; give the person concerned any reasonable instructions you consider to be necessary; and, use reasonable force in the exercise of the power to remove the person to the place where they are living. Those in breach of the regulations could be issued with a fine of £60. A second offence would bring a penalty of £120, with a cap at £960 overall. In a tale that turned out not to be apocryphal, the government was forced to make a public statement letting people know that they were able to buy anything from shops that were open after stories emerged of the police patrolling supermarket aisles, telling people to stick to 'essential' items only. In one of the more ham-fisted public interventions a Midlands chief constable said that his force would consider roadblocks and searching people's shopping trolleys if the public didn't follow the rules.[20] Happily, such daftness was generally the exception rather than the rule.

Research published after the end of the second week of lock-down showed that only 6 per cent of the public thought the police had been too heavy-handed in general and 14 per cent thought they had been insufficiently tough. Most thought they'd got it about right. The survey offered a real insight into public attitudes toward the police role in maintaining social order and where the limits of action were felt to be. The public were gener-ally comfortable with the use of standard police powers such as, where appropriate, stop and account, arrests and on-the-spot fines. Much greater scepticism was aimed at tactics such as the use of drones, naming and shaming of rule-breakers on social media, facial recognition technology, or with people being asked to report others who had breached the rules.[21] In this latter regard it was perhaps not surprising that Cambridgeshire Constabulary's publicising of an online form to report people who had broken COVID-restrictions was the focus of some-thing of a backlash in the press and online.[22]

As the pandemic unfolded, the official line emanating from forces in England and Wales was that they were adopting what they called the 'Four Es' approach: primarily involving engaging, explaining and encouraging, with enforcement as a last resort. Problems certainly arose, not least out of the profusion of regula-tions that were introduced by government, something the police service found difficult to keep up with.[23] Continued examples of the police overstepping the mark were often a consequence of failures to distinguish clearly enough between what was required by law, and what was merely indicated by government guidance. Further, it seemed messages from government to the police were by no means always clear, with the Chair of the National Police Chiefs' Council describing the relationship with Downing Street as occasionally 'tense and difficult'. Looking back over the first year of the pandemic the Police Inspectorate concluded that the difficulties caused by occasional failures of communication between government and police were exacerbated by 'widespread confusion in relation to the status of government announcements and statements by ministers'. In short, the proliferation of new regulations, their differing statuses, and the sometimes inconsistent messaging from those in charge, all complicated what the police felt they were being asked to do.

By and large most forces eventually managed to adhere to the general advice that they keep formal enforcement activities in reserve. Over the course of roughly the first year of the pandemic, the police issued almost sixty-nine thousand fines for various lockdown-related breaches. Those included a small number (under three hundred) of large fines for offences linked to parties, protests and other public gatherings, slightly under 2,500 for failure to wear a face covering, and close to six hundred against businesses for failure to comply with rules linked to opening hours, table service, face coverings and similar. The largest category, nearly twelve thousand, related to failure to adhere to rules on restriction of movement.[24] There was wide variation between forces. Dyfed-Powys and Northumbria issued by far the most fixed penalty notices, the former issuing at about twenty times the rate of the force that used them the least: Humberside. More significant was the unequal impact of aspects of pandemic policing. Regular reports in the press noted very sizeable disparities in the use of particular police powers – stop and search most obviously. One suggested that young black men had been stopped and searched more than 20,000 times in London during the first lockdown – equivalent to more than a quarter of all black 15- to 24-year-olds in the city.[25] As Deborah Coles of the pressure group Inquest put it, 'Emergency powers have only exacerbated unfair, excessive, and discriminatory policing, especially against racialised communities.'[26]

Notwithstanding some significant missteps, day-to-day policing during the pandemic was managed without significant, ongoing controversy. The same was broadly true of public order policing, often the site of greatest controversy. There were major challenges, not least in mid-2020 in the aftermath of the murder of George Floyd in Minneapolis. Protests associated with the Black Lives Matter movement spread across a huge number of cities in the US, and subsequently well beyond, including across the UK. The protests had a number of interesting features. They were multi-racial, well-organised and generally peaceful. Though there were criticisms of some of the policing, in the main a facilitative, de-escalatory approach was dominant, and the political reaction was less divided than some had expected, even if it was far from uniformly positive. The most significant exception occurred in early 2021 in connection with a vigil held on Clapham Common after the abduction and murder of Sarah Everard. What began as a peaceful event broke up in scenes of women being arrested and manhandled by police officers, and led to widespread condemnation and ongoing anger. Even then, however, the official investigation into the events argued that the Metropolitan Police acted neither inappropriately nor in a heavy-handed manner,[27] and there was evidence that, if only by a small margin, a majority of the public were of the same view.[28]

Research in the early months of the pandemic found generally high levels of compliance. A study by academics from London universities found almost nine in ten people said that they had neither socialised with people they didn't live with nor travelled for leisure. Why were people complying? The researchers found no evidence that the new legal rules were a particular source of deterrence. Rather, and as you might expect if you've followed the various stories in this book, it appeared that the laws were widely seen as giving expression to values that people agreed with. The belief that 'we are all in it together' really did seem to be crucial.[29] In the early weeks of the first lockdown research suggested that around 90 per cent of the population said that they were trying to abide by the government's regulations, a relatively small proportion (15 per cent) said they were finding it very difficult and 14 per cent said that they felt they would be unable to cope for another month. Only 1 per cent said they had ignored the advice, and while some may have been reluctant to admit doing so, it did suggest a very high level of compliance overall.[30] Orderly Britain indeed. We will return briefly to the evidence on compliance throughout the various lockdowns but, first, we need to take a brief diversion via Barnard Castle to consider one of the more egregious examples of rule-breaking during the first lockdown.

The Cummings effect

It became clear quite early on that the virus was affecting a wide range of people within government. Among those going into self-isolation were the chief medical officer, the health secretary and a junior minister in the Department of Health and, at one time it was said, up to one third of the cabinet. Most famously, of course, the first to test positive, and most severely affected, was the prime minister. Boris Johnson would eventually end up in St Thomas' Hospital for seven days, including three in intensive care. In late March, just after it was acknowledged that the prime minister had tested positive, television cameras captured his chief adviser, Dominic Cummings, running along Downing Street, and a couple of days later it was announced that he was experiencing coronavirus symptoms and was self-isolating.

In late May a news story broke in the *Guardian* and *Daily Mirror*, saying that earlier in the month Cummings had travelled to Durham during the lockdown. The official government statement on the matter said that the travel had been essential to ensure Cummings' young child could be cared for. 'His actions were in line with coronavirus guidelines.' Given that most of the public were staying at home, the story quickly took on all the characteristics of a public scandal and threatened to overwhelm government messaging on the virus. Further details soon emerged which only appeared to make the scandal grow. Not only had Cummings and his family travelled north, but while there his wife and son had made an emergency visit to hospital. Moreover, on the day before they all returned to London they had been spotted at a local beauty spot, Barnard Castle, about a half-hour drive from where they had been staying.

Two days after the story first emerged the PM addressed the subject directly, beginning a speech saying he wished to answer 'the big question that people have been asking in the last 48 hours ... is this government asking you – the people, the public, to do one thing while senior people here in government do something else?' No, was his answer, and that all Cummings had done was to follow 'the instincts of every father and every parent. And I do not mark him down for that.' Indeed, having spoken to him at great length about the matter, Johnson concluded that Cummings 'has acted responsibly, and legally, and with integrity, and with the overwhelming aim of stopping the spread of the virus and saving lives'. Later, in answer to questions, the PM admitted that he understood why people might feel confused or offended, but thought that once they were aware of Cummings' intentions, 'people will understand'.

The reaction to the PM's speech suggested he was wrong about anticipated public understanding. They included the normally loyal *Daily Mail*, whose front page editorial on the Monday morning, under the headline, 'What planet are they on?', said Cummings' behaviour was a clear violation of 'the spirit and the letter' of the rules governing the lockdown, that would have the consequence of giving 'every selfish person a licence to play fast and loose with public health'. Later that day, Cummings appeared in the Rose Garden at 10 Downing Street to give a lengthy account of his actions and to take questions from journalists, including a subsequently widely derided claim that the reason for his family's trip to Barnard Castle was so that he could test his eyesight – which had been giving him trouble – before the long drive back to London.

Beyond the fact that Cummings neither apologised for his actions, nor resigned, what did happen? The answer, intriguingly, is once again order largely prevailed. There was no large-scale breakdown, no mass failure to comply. Research undertaken in the aftermath by three universities found that almost everyone had heard of the Cummings story and the vast majority (84 per cent) felt his actions were unjustified, with over two-thirds saying that it had made them angry. On the surface, then, there appeared to be strong potential for some sort of reaction. Interestingly, when asked, although again the vast majority of people (84 per cent) said they felt people in power bent the rules when they needed to, only a small minority (16 per cent) admitted to doing so themselves.[31] Subsequent research in May 2020 found only 1 per cent of people suggested that the likelihood of their sticking to the rules was 'not very much'. Moreover, while the sense that others were breaking the rules might have influenced others to do so, there appeared to be some evidence that the anger over Cummings' also reinforced in others the need to continue to comply. As the researchers put it, 'the story seems to have produced a sense of cynicism regarding public health rules that could prove difficult to "put back into the box". Yet, at the same time, Mr Cummings may also have provided a role model of how *not* to behave.'[32]

Mutuality and ritual

In the preceding pages we've sketched out a broad timeline of the first year of the pandemic, the restrictions that were introduced and the huge changes this made to everyday lives. If one of the strongest messages that emerges from this book is that everyday social order is something that is generally sustained by informal social norms and forms of mutual engagement, then it should also be clear by now that this applied just as strongly to life during the pandemic as it does at any other time. Our lives changed – we hoped temporarily – as we were asked to stay at home, work from home, refrain from visiting friends and family, and keep socially distanced when out and about. New laws were introduced and new regulations proliferated. While such formal ordering was necessary – important even – laws, policing and enforcement were far from sufficient in ensuring general compliance. Rather, we internalised the new social rules, governing ourselves, restricting and limiting our own behaviour. We were *guided* by the guidelines but, in the main, surveillance by authorities was not what kept us in line. We developed and learned new social routines, new rituals of everyday life. As observed over a century ago by the French sociologist Émile Durkheim, routinised social practices, and rituals, rites and ceremonies are a central part of the performance of creating and reproducing social order. Such rituals and ceremonies are often deeply symbolic, capturing messages about ourselves, our beliefs and our expectations. Rituals, Durkheim felt, are central in sustaining social solidarity, and to nourishing those things that glue us together. Our shared ways of talking and behaving are a core means by which we establish a sense of community, of shared involvement in a social life. Ritual, like all social conduct, is not static, and while much ritual may appear long-standing and semi-permanent, new forms emerge – especially in times of major social change it might be thought. Again, the pandemic was no exception.

While, very understandably, the negative consequences of COVID-19 were often uppermost in people's minds, and in the news bulletins, the crisis also revealed many positive elements of social solidarity. Within just a few weeks of the first lockdown, numerous positive community consequences of the new reality were being revealed. Sixty per cent of people said that they had offered to help a neighbour and almost half of people surveyed said that they had received assistance from the local community.[33] One of the clearest illustrations of the desire to do something for others was found in the response to the call for volunteers to support the National Health Service in providing support to the elderly, to those who were self-isolating and to medical staff and others on the front line who needed deliveries. It was originally suggested that up to 250,000 volunteers might be needed, and within weeks closer to one million had signed up.

One of the most positive stories that emerged in the early days of the pandemic was the rise of support groups – mutual aid groups – that responded to the fact that vulnerable people would need to be shielded and would thus be cut off. Within a week of the initial official announcement of the practice of 'shielding' the elderly, it was estimated that over one thousand mutual aid groups had been established. A website sprang up (www.covid-mutualaid.org) to map these groups, with over four thousand eventually coming into being, much of their work being organised via social media. These were truly community initiatives. In the vast majority of cases they had no official links and no support beyond what their volunteers offered. As the website put it, mutual aid 'is where a group of people organise to meet their own needs, outside of the formal frameworks of charities, NGOs and government. It is, by definition, a horizontal mode of organising, in which all individuals are equally powerful. There are no "leaders" or unelected "steering committees" in mutual aid projects; there is only a group of people who work together as equals.'

In the early days of the pandemic one practice that emerged and was widely adopted was the 'clap for (our) carers' that took place at 8 p.m. on Thursdays for a period of two months. The origins of the ritual are not entirely clear, but it appears that so far as Europe is concerned something along these lines first took place in Italy – perhaps not surprisingly given it was one of the first in lockdown. Italy had seen a variety of public events, many of them musical, where people had come out on their balconies or in front of their houses to celebrate various successes. It was in this context that a Facebook group (Applaudiamo l'Italia) promoted a round of applause in mid-March 2020. Within a week France had followed suit, with applause initially occurring at 8 p.m. each day. Although the phenomenon decreased over time, ritualistic applause was still to be found in France two months later as the country entered the second phase of lockdown.

In Britain, reports suggested that the 'clap for carers' was the brainchild of a Dutch woman, Anne-Marie Plas, who was living in Britain and who said she was inspired by similar events in the Netherlands and elsewhere in Europe. It had originally been planned as a one-off event, on 26 March, as a show of support for NHS staff three days after lockdown had begun. From these beginnings it became a weekly event, an 8 p.m. Thursday engagement when neighbours would meet remotely while clapping or bashing pots and pans in support of all key workers. In the event it was a time-limited ritual, lasting ten weeks in all, and by the end it was clear that for a variety of reasons a degree of fatigue had set it. Anne-Marie Plas was quoted as saying, 'To have the most impact, I think it is good to stop it at its peak ... I think the narrative is starting to change, and I don't want the clap to be negative.' Whatever the reason or, more likely, reasons, it was becoming increasingly clear that this new ritual had served its original purpose – which clearly for most involved was to show solidarity with those on what was being referred to as the 'front line' – and was now in danger of becoming mixed up with a range of other concerns. The ritualised clapping ended, but the rainbows and other messages of support that had been put up in windows, and chalked on walls and pavements, remained as symbols of what had been a brief but successful expression of togetherness in difficult times.

© Tim Newburn, April 2020

Beyond the headline consequences of the pandemic such as working from home, home-schooling and various forms of social isolation, everyday lives were altered in numerous small ways. What the celebrated American sociologist Erving Goffman called 'interaction rituals' – in essence, our standardised routines – were disrupted and altered, often very markedly. Most obviously, for a long time we were advised to keep at least two metres distance between us and anyone not in our household. To maintain this, we began using pavements in different ways. What previously might have looked impolite, now looked like thoughtful action as we gave others ('social') distance. We began walking in roads more frequently, stepping away from others in a new 'COVID dance', and using parks and other open spaces in ways many had tended not to do previously, or had done so far less frequently. Usual forms of physical greeting such as kissing and hugging were abandoned, to be replaced initially by elbow touching and then distanced greeting; perhaps we would learn to bow

321

slightly like the Japanese many suggested. Although in Britain bowing has not yet caught on, readers will be aware of a range of modifications that they and others made in order to signal some form of greeting during the absence of their normal repertoire.

As we discussed earlier, the British were once famed for their queuing. Something that was an everyday staple in the post-war years is an activity that, in recent times, has arguably become both more complex – different types of queue in different places – as well as more fragile. On the one hand, in some places queuing became something that was increasingly analysed and managed, largely in pursuit of profit. On the other, there were circumstances where it appeared to be breaking down, now occurring with less predictability and being received with less tolerance. The pandemic, however, put the queue back front and square in British public life, but did so in entirely new ways. The snaked crush of people was now replaced by the, roughly, two-metre socially distanced queue. Stay in line, keep your distance, wait for the person in front to move, and occasionally check what the people behind you are doing – the new norms of shopping were quickly established. Supermarkets introduced signage in various forms to indicate these two-metre spaces and smaller shops sometimes followed suit. Arrows were stuck to the floor to indicate directions of travel, and signs, tape and other markers were introduced to manage queuing to check out. Sometimes it was monitored, but most of the time it was self-policed. Though sometimes such lines broke down and people failed to abide by the 'new normal', more often than not queue discipline prevailed.

In contrast with their alleged ability to queue, Britons' reputation for cleanliness has not always been so great. As Andrew Marr put it when looking back on the immediate post-war years, 'To put it bluntly, many British people in the forties would, by our [now] sensitive standards, have smelt a little.' International research a decade ago into standards of hygiene found the British to be particularly poor at handwashing, many lying, claiming they had washed their hands when they hadn't, especially after going to the toilet.[34] This was potentially a major challenge given that washing hands regularly and thoroughly was, of course, one of the key bits of advice in the pandemic. Here, once again, there was evidence of widespread social compliance, with one study suggesting that this was among the forms of behaviour that had changed most markedly.[35] Something similar can be said about mask-wearing. The British government was fairly slow to recommend mask-wearing, citing insufficient evidence. One consequence was the British public was also somewhat slow to take up mask-wearing. In the event, however, there was little public resistance, with 87 per cent of people saying they were 'very' or 'quite willing' to wear a mask, and only 3 per cent 'very unwilling'. Moreover, and unlike the United States, for example, there was no partisan divide – mask-wearing didn't become linked with a particular political stance, except in the House of Commons and among a very small minority of the public.[36]

Final thoughts

At this stage we should return to the general messages emerging from the pandemic and, indeed, from the book as a whole. As we noted earlier, levels of public compliance during the first major lockdown were generally high and, despite the widespread criticism of Dominic Cummings' behaviour, generally remained high. Over the course of two lockdowns research did detect some general decline in average compliance but, on investigation, found that this was explained by the behaviour of a minority of people. Sticking to the rules remained the choice of the majority. Some behavioural psychologists speculated early on that there would be 'behavioural fatigue' – people getting fed up with the changes – but evidence for this was at best mixed. A further possibility was what was slightly clumsily referred to as 'alert fatigue', in effect confusion caused by mixed messaging. Though evidence for its impact again is not strong, confusion among both politicians and the police from time to time certainly illustrated the complexity of official messaging in the pandemic,[37] and it is perfectly plausible that this may have contributed to some apparent breaking of the rules (though much less plausible where those who had set the rules were concerned). In many of the areas we have studied change has been slow and resistance has often been great. In Britain, the pandemic, by contrast, brought about seismic changes with great rapidity, and without significant resistance. Amenability and acquiescence were much more evident than opposition or defiance.

What research on the pandemic also reaffirmed was that it was neither changes in the law, nor the actions of the police, that were crucial in ensuring such acquiescence. Legislation was important, but it was more symbolic than substantive. Put straightforwardly, changing the law signalled to the population that behaviour needed to change. Meat was put on the bones via various forms of regulation. Such regulatory change occurred often, indeed often with bewildering frequency. On receiving such signals, generally through messaging which explained what the new expectations were, and notwithstanding some confusion, the majority changed their behaviour. Importantly though, people continued to comply, in the main, not because of some threat of enforcement but because new social norms, new expectations, had been established, learned and instilled.[38] By and large people understood and agreed with the new expectations. Opinion poll after opinion poll showed the public to be largely supportive of the lockdown, with the anti-lockdown protests remaining very marginal events – despite rather disproportionate media coverage. Indeed a poll by Ipsos Mori in spring 2020 found that support for lockdown was higher in the UK than in many other countries, with such support crossing party political boundaries.[39] The high level of compliance must, of course, partly reflect the level of perceived risk induced by the pandemic. In addition, however, it seems clear that the broad sweep of COVID-related regulations were perceived to be appropriate and legitimate with, as a consequence, strong social pressure to conform.

Across the areas we have considered in this book, and as the pandemic reaffirms, our post-war world is one in which rules, instructions, guidelines, directions, regulations and commands have proliferated. The pandemic brought forth a vast array of new rules and regulations together with some sweeping legislative changes. Major restrictions on individual liberty were justified in the name of a public health emergency. How lasting they will be only time will tell. But, as the pandemic also vividly illustrated – confirming what we have seen in a variety of other areas – rarely is it the case that the threat or actual enforcement of these laws and regulations plays more than a symbolic role in the maintenance of our social order. We may be surrounded, perhaps increasingly surrounded, by formal rules and regulations, but we continue to be largely self-policing. We are capable of swiftly internalising new social expectations, and learning new ways of behaving. Despite the 'declinism', the doom-mongering and the catastrophising of some commentators, the reality is that even under the most extraordinary of social conditions we continue to be *orderly Britons*.

Endnotes

Introduction

1 https://www.bsa.natcen.ac.uk/latest-report/british-social-attitudes-38/new-values-new-divides.aspx

2 See for example, Hitchens, P. (2018) *The Abolition of Britain: From Winston Churchill to Theresa May*, London: Bloomsbury; Liddle, R. (2015) *Selfish Whining Monkeys: How We Ended Up Greedy, Narcissistic and Unhappy*, London: HarperCollins. Much more thoughtful analyses can be found in: Edgerton, D. (2018) *The Rise and Fall of the British Nation: A 20th Century History*, London: Allen Lane; Hamilton-Paterson, J. (2018) *What We Have Lost: The Dismantling of Great Britain*, London: Head of Zeus

3 Pinker, S. (2019) *Enlightenment Now: The Case for Reason, Science, Humanism, and Progress*, London: Penguin

4 Tomlinson, J. (2009) 'Thrice denied: "Declinism" as a recurrent theme in British history in the long twentieth century', *Twentieth Century British History*, 20. 2, pp. 227–251

5 Truss, L. (2007) *Talk to the Hand: The Utter Bloody Rudeness of Everyday Life*, London: Fourth Estate

6 Vulliamy, E. (2016) 'Bill Bryson: "The British have become more greedy and selfish" like the US', *Independent*, 25 June 2016

7 Bryson, B. (1995) *Notes from a Small Island*, London: Doubleday; (2015) *The Road to Little Dribbling: More Notes on a Small Island*, London: Doubleday

8 Appleton, J. (2016) *Officious: Rise of the Busybody State*, London: Zed Books; 'Signs of stupidity', *Daily Express*, 2 July 2009

9 Perec, G. (1997) *Species of Spaces and Other Pieces*, London: Penguin

10 Sumner, W. G. (1907) *Folkways: A Study of the Sociological Importance of Usages, Manners, Customs, Mores, and Morals*, Boston: Ginn and Company

11 Westgarth, C., Christley, R. M., Marvin, G. & Perkins, E. (2020) 'Functional and recreational dog walking practices in the UK', *Health Promotion International*, pp. 1–11

12 Westgarth, C., Christley, R. M., Marvin, G. & Perkins, E. (2019) 'The responsible dog owner: The construction of responsibility', *Anthrozoös*, 32, 5, pp. 631–646

13 Geertz, C. (1973) *The Interpretation of Cultures*, New York: Basic Books, p. 43

14 Gusfield, J. R. (1981) *The Culture of Public Problems*, Chicago: University of Chicago Press

15 As the American criminologist Charles Tittle noted many years ago, 'social control as a general process seems to be rooted almost completely in informal sanctioning'. Tittle, C. R. (1980) *Sanctions and Social Deviance: The Question of Deterrence*, New York, NY: Praeger, p. 241

Dog Shit

1 This was a social achievement that gradually emerged in the nineteenth century. This 'model of Western human-canine relations' is referred to by Chris Pearson as 'Dogopolis'. Pearson, C. (2021) *Dogopolis: How Dogs and Humans made Modern New York, London and Paris*, Chicago: University of Chicago Press

2 This was a rise of one third from pre-pandemic levels of around nine million.

3 Ackerley, J. R. (1956) *My Dog Tulip*, London: Secker & Warburg

4 Walton, J. K. (1979) 'Mad Dogs and Englishmen: The conflict over rabies in late Victorian England', *Journal of Social History*, 13, No. 2, pp. 219–239

5 Walton (1979)

6 https://journals.sagepub.com/doi/abs/10.1177/146642405307300209

7 Though for a more rounded view see: Hood, C., Baldwin, R. & Rothstein, H. (2000) 'Assessing the Dangerous Dogs Act: When does a regulatory law fail?' *Public Law*, Summer 2000: pp. 282–305

8 McCarthy, D. (2016) 'Dangerous dogs, dangerous owners and the waste management of an "irredeemable species"', *Sociology*, 50, 3, pp. 560–575

9 Pemberton, N. (2017) 'The Burnley Dog War: The politics of dog-walking and the battle over public parks in post-industrial Britain', *Twentieth Century British History*, 28, 2, pp. 239–267

10 'Dog fight for the parks', *Guardian*, 15 August 1977

11 Law Report, *The Times*, 14 July 1978

12 'Dog owners lose parks ban test case', *The Times*, 15 July 1978

13 'Dog lovers' leader obeys ultimatum by Judge', *The Times*, 28 July 1978

14 'Man jailed for not paying dog-walking fines', *The Times*, 31 October 1978

15 Pemberton (2017)

16 'Defiant dog walker in jail', *Guardian*, 10 March 1979

17 'Dog owners face £23,500 bill', *The Times*, 27 December 1979

18 'Dog cleanup law begins today', *New York Times*, 1 August 1978

19 'To scoop or not to scoop', *New York Times*, 20 August 1972

20 'Dog cleanup law praised after a year', *New York Times*, 2 August 1979

21 Brandow, M. (2008) *New York's Poop Scoop Law: Dogs, the dirt and due process*, West Lafayette, IA: Purdue University Press

22 Pearson, C. (2017) 'Combating canine "visiting cards": Public hygiene and the management of dog mess in Paris since the 1920s', *Social History of Medicine*, 32, 1

23 This Act was superseded by the Clean Neighbourhoods and Environment Act 2005 (with regulations introduced in 2006)

24 https://www.bbc.co.uk/news/uk-33064119 (accessed 5 August 2019)

25 Webley, P. & Siviter, C. (2000) 'Why do some owners allow their dogs to foul the pavement? The social psychology of a minor rule infraction', *Journal of Applied Social Psychology*, 30, 7, pp. 1371–1380

26 Lowe, C. N., Williams, K. S., Jenkinson, S. & Toogood, M. (2014) 'Environmental and social impacts of domestic dog waste in the UK: investigating barriers to behaviour change in dog walkers', *International Journal of Environment and Waste Management*, 13, 4

27 'Operation poop: Council wardens using night vision goggles target owners who let their dogs foul public land', *Daily Mail*, 31 January 2012

28 https://www.lancs.live/news/local-news/new-dog-warden-appointed-help-9828618

29 Atenstaedt, R. L. & Jones, S. (2011) 'Interventions to prevent dog fouling: A systematic review of the evidence', *Public Health*, 125

30 It still boasts a number of items of dog excrement removal equipment http://www.trafalgarcleaningequipment.co.uk/dog-excrement-removal

31 Levitt, S. D. & Dubner, S. J. (2007) *Freakonomics: A rogue economist explores the hidden side of everything*, London: Penguin

32 'DNA testing for dogs', *Wired*, 9 April 1998

33 'England's DNA doggies', *Newsweek*, 3 March 1996

34 'Pooper-snooper', *Daily Mail*, 17 March 2012

35 Details of the company and its technology can be found at: https://www.pooprints.com/

36 'It's a dirty business: great outdoors suffers side-effect of Britain's lockdown dog boom', *Guardian*, 30 January 2021

37 Pemberton, N. (2017), at p. 20, emphasis added

38 Westgarth, C., Christley, R. M., Marvin, R. & Perkins, E. (2019) 'The responsible dog owner: The construction of responsibility', *Anthrozoös*, 32:5, pp. 631–646

39 https://www.thekennelclub.org.uk/about-us/about-the-kennel-club/the-kennel-club-codes/the-kennel-club-canine-code/

40 Elias, N. (1978) *The Civilizing Process: The history of manners*, Oxford: Basil Blackwell

41 Linklater, A. & Mennell, S. (2010) 'Norbert Elias, The Civilizing Process: Sociogenetic and psychogenetic investigations – An overview and assessment', *History and Theory*, 49, 3, pp. 384–411

Smoking

1 A huge cache of hitherto secret documents from seven cigarette manufacturers and two affiliated organisations doing business in the US became available to the public as a result of legal action in 1998. Anyone wishing to see just how far the tobacco industry was willing to go can access these documents. A useful guide to them can be found at: https://www.who.int/tobacco/communications/TI_manual_content.pdf

2 Pugh, M. (2009) *We Danced All Night*, London: Vintage

3 Pugh (2009)

4 Broom, J. (2018) *A History of Cigarette and Trade Cards*, Pen and Sword History

5 https://www.ncbi.nlm.nih.gov/pmc/articles/PMC2844275/

6 Jackson, M. (2010) 'Divine Stramonium', *Medical History*, 54, pp. 171–194

7 Kynaston, D. (2010) *Family Britain*, Bloomsbury

8 Abrams, M. (1959) *The Teenage Consumer*, London Exchange Press

9 Tinkler, P. (2003) 'Refinement and respectable consumption: The acceptable face of women's smoking in Britain, 1918–1970', *Gender and History*, 15, 2, pp. 342–360

10 Amos, A. & Haglund, M. (2000) 'From social taboo to "torch of freedom": the marketing of cigarettes to women', *Tobacco Control*, 9, pp. 3–8

11 Conversation with Sir Richard Doll, *British Journal of Addiction*, 1991

12 Kynaston, D. (2008) *Austerity Britain*, Bloomsbury, at p. 578

13 Berridge, V. (2003) 'Post-war smoking policy', Twentieth Century British History, 14, 1, pp. 61–83

14 Berridge, V. (2006) 'The policy response to smoking and lung cancer', *The Historical Journal*, 49, 4, pp. 1185–1209

15 Berridge (2006)

16 Berridge (2006)

17 Berridge (2006)

18 Kynaston (2010)

19 Kynaston (2010)

20 Kynaston, D. (2015) *Modernity Britain*, Bloomsbury Paperbacks

21 Wald, N. & Nicolaides-Bouman, A. (1991) *UK Smoking Statistics*, 2nd ed., Oxford University Press

22 Kynaston (2015)

23 Kynaston (2015)

24 Conversaton with Sir Richard Doll, *British Journal of Addiction*, 1991

25 Berridge, V. (2005) 'Smoking and the new health education in Britain', *American Joournal of Public Health*, 95, 6, pp. 956–966

26 Wald, N. & Nicolaides-Bouman, A. *UK Smoking Statistics*, 2nd ed.

27 Berridge (2005)

28 Berridge (2003)

29 The use of this phrase in connection with the 1960s is Virginia Berridge's in 'The policy response to smoking and lung cancer'

30 Daube, M. (1979) 'The politics of smoking: thoughts on the Labour record', *Community Medicine*, 1, pp. 306–314

31 Froggatt, P. (1989) 'Determinants of policy on smoking', *International Journal of Epidemiology*, 18, 1, pp. 1–9

32 Hughes, J. (2003) *Learning to Smoke*, Chicago: University of Chicago Press

33 Berridge, V. (1999) 'Passive smoking and its pre-history', *Social Science and Medicine*, 49, 9, pp. 1183–1195

34 The idea was popularised by Malcolm Gladwell (2002) in *The Tipping Point*, New York: Abacus

35 Milov, S. (2019) *The Cigarette: A political history*, Cambridge, MA: Harvard University Press

36 Mekemson, C. & Glanz, G. (2002) 'How the tobacco industry built its relationship with Hollywood', *Tobacco Control*, 11, 1

37 http://news.bbc.co.uk/1/hi/uk/72813.stm
38 Public Health England (2015) *Reducing Smoking in Prisons*
39 Parry, O., Platt, S. & Thomson, C. (2000) 'Out of sight, out of mind: workplace smoking bans and the relocation of smoking at work', *Health Promotion International*, 15, 2
40 Berman, M., Crane, R., Seiber, E. et al. (2014) 'Estimating the costs of a smoking employee', *Tobacco Control*, 23, pp. 428–433
41 Conversation with Sir Richard Doll, *British Journal of Addiction*, 1991
42 https://ash.org.uk/media-and-news/press-releases-media-and-news/voluntary-pubs-smoking-scheme-useless-public-health-campaigners-warn/
43 Freeth, S. (1998) *Smoking-related behaviour and attitudes*, London: Office for National Statistics
44 https://www.london.gov.uk/sites/default/files/gla_migrate_files_destination/archives/assembly-reports-health-smoking_report.pdf
45 https://www.bbc.co.uk/news/health-40444460
46 https://www.bbc.co.uk/news/health-40444460
47 Nutt, D. (2020) *Drugs Without the Hot Air*, Cambridge: UIT Press
48 Wilson, A. N. (2009) *Our Times*, Arrow
49 https://ash.org.uk/media-and-news/press-releases-media-and-news/england-a-decade-after-the-smoking-ban-heading-for-a-smokefree-future/
50 https://www.ons.gov.uk/peoplepopulationandcommunity/healthandsocialcare/healthandlifeexpectancies/bulletins/adultsmokinghabitsingreatbritain/2018
51 Hughes, J. (2003) *Learning to Smoke*, Chicago: University of Chicago Press
52 Hughes (2003)
53 Brandt, A. (1990) 'The cigarette, risk and American culture', *Daedalus*, pp. 155–176
54 Nutt (2020)
55 London Health Commission (2014) *Better Health for London*, October
56 https://www.theguardian.com/society/2020/jul/18/english-councils-call-for-smoking-ban-outside-pubs-and-cafes

Drinking

1 https://onlinelibrary.wiley.com/doi/abs/10.1111/j.1360-0443.2008.02438.x
2 Cabinet Office (2004) *Alcohol Harm Reduction Strategy for England and Wales 2004*, London: Cabinet Office

3 Bhattacharya, A. (2016) *Youthful Abandon: Why Are Young People Drinking Less?*, London: Institute of Alcohol Studies

4 Mass Observation (1987) [1943], *The Pub and the People: A Worktown Study*, London: The Cresset Library

5 Institute of Alcohol Studies (2017) *Pubs Quizzed*

6 Foster, J. & Ferguson, C. (2012) 'Home drinking in the UK', *Alcohol and Alcoholism*

7 Institute of Alcohol Studies (2017)

8 'What has influenced the evolution of pub food?' *Morning Advertiser*, 20 February 2019

9 UK Hospitality Christie and Co Benchmarking Report 2018

10 Jennings, P. (2007) *The Local: A History of the English Pub*, The History Press

11 Allied, Bass Charrington, Courage, Scottish and Newcastle, Watney Mann and Whitbread

12 IPPR (2012) *Pubs and Places: The social value of community pubs*, London: IPPR

13 Alcohol Concern (undated) *Making Sense of Alcohol*

14 Angus, C. et al. (2017) 'Mapping patterns and trends in the spatial availability of alcohol using low-level geographic data: A case study in England 2003–2013', *International Journal of Environmental Research and Public Health*, 14, 406

15 This refers to sales by volume. Institute of Alcohol Studies: http://www.ias.org.uk/uploads/pdf/Factsheets/FS%20industry%20012018.pdf

16 Foster, J. & Ferguson, C. (2012)

17 IPPR (2012) *Pubs and Places*

18 Valentine, G., Holloway, S. L., Jayne, M. & Knell, C. (2007) *Drinking Places: Where People Drink and Why*, York: Joseph Rowntree Foundation

19 Yeomans, H. (2018) 'Taxation, state formation, and governmentality: The historical development of alcohol excise duties in England and Wales', *Social Science History*

20 Institute for Fiscal Studies (2016) *Green Budget*

21 The equivalent in 2020 would have been around £90m

22 Nicholls, J. (2009) *The Politics of Alcohol*, pp. 191–192

23 Greenaway, J. (2008) 'Agendas, venues and alliances: New opportunities for the alcohol control movement in England', *Drugs: Education, Prevention and Policy*, 15: 5, pp. 487–501

24 Thom, B. (1999) *Dealing with Drink: Alcohol and Social Policy in Contemporary England*, Free Association Books

25 Academics sometimes refer to this governmental strategy using the horrible term 'responsibilisation'

26 'Drink limits useless', *The Times*, 20 October 2007

27 Department of Health (1995) *Sensible Drinking: Report of an Inter-Departmental Working Group* (details taken from: Alcohol Harm Reduction Strategy, 2004)

28 *Hansard*, 10 February 1966, vol. 724, col. 655

29 Willett, T. C. (1964) *Criminal on the Road: A Study of Serious Road Offences and Those That Commit Them*, London: Routledge and Kegan Paul

30 'The breathalyser: 10 years on', *New Scientist*, 27 October 1977

31 Via the Transport Act 1981

32 Lerner, B. H. (2012) 'Drunk driving across the globe: Let's learn from one another', *The Lancet*, 19 May

33 Parliamentary Advisory Committee for Transport Safety (2017) *Fifty Years of the Breathalyser: Where Now for Drink Driving?*

34 https://assets.publishing.service.gov.uk/government/uploads/system/uploads/attachment_data/file/810908/national-travel-attitudes-study-2019-wave-1.pdf

35 Institute of Alcohol Studies (2017) *Running on Empty: Drink-Driving Law Enforcement in England*, London: IAS

36 Nicholls (2009), p. 220

37 Nicholls (2009), p. 223

38 Ramsay, M. (1989) *Downtown Drinkers*, London: Home Office

39 Home Office circular 88/1990

40 https://londonist.com/2012/09/mapped-londons-banned-zones

41 Measham, F. (2006) 'The new policy mix: Alcohol, harm minimisation and determined drunkenness in contemporary society', *International Journal of Drug Policy*, 17, pp. 258–268

42 Broadcast on Radio 4 show 'Does the team drink?', 6 August 2019 https://www.bbc.co.uk/sounds/play/m0007bdq

43 https://yougov.co.uk/topics/lifestyle/articles-reports/2016/10/31/fancy-pint-lunch-even-meal-its-unacceptable-says-p#targetText=The%20overwhelming%20majority%20of%20the,to%20start%20drinking%20by%206pm&targetText=Men%20are%20much%20more%20likely,to%20a%20quarter%20of%20women.

44 https://www.telegraph.co.uk/news/2017/02/15/city-workers-lloyds-london-banned-daytime-drinking/

45 The jobs where career success means drinking at work, BBC 25 April 2017 https://www.bbc.com/worklife/article/20170425-the-jobs-where-career-success-means-drinking-at-work

46 https://www.petebrown.net/2017/02/20/remembering-lunchtime-drinking/

47 https://www.independent.co.uk/voices/lloyds-of-london-lunch-time-drinking-banks-right-to-ban-it-a7586031.html © Janet Street Porter/The Independent

48 Adams, T. (2018) *Sober: Football. My Story. My Life*, London: Simon & Schuster

49 https://www.thetimes.co.uk/article/david-bumble-lloyd-id-have-a-pint-of -lager-at-lunchtime-then-go-out-to-bat-f5qlw06zs#

50 White, M. 'Lunchtime tipple in the house of spies', *Guardian*, 24 July 1982

51 https://www.telegraph.co.uk/foodanddrink/10210966/What-became-of-the-drunken-sailor.html

52 http://news.bbc.co.uk/1/hi/magazine/4758941.stm

53 Longrigg, C. 'Drinking is out as bosses get tough', *Guardian*, 16 November 1996

54 'Currie urges company chiefs to check their drinking', *The Times*, 30 September 1987

55 http://www.ias.org.uk/uploads/pdf/In%20the%20Workplace/indg240.pdf

56 'Most firms back drinks ban at work', *Guardian*, 19 November 1991

57 http://news.bbc.co.uk/1/hi/magazine/4758941.stm

58 https://www.drinkaware.co.uk/research/data/comparisons/

59 Karlsson, T., Lindeman, M. & Österberg, E. (2012) 'Does alcohol policy make any difference? Scales and consumption', *Alcohol Policy in Europe: Evidence from AMPHORA*

60 For an extensive discussion of the issues see: Nutt, D. (2020) *Drugs Without the Hot Air*, Cambridge: UIT Press

Queuing

1 Mikes, G. (1946) *How to Be an Alien*, London: Andre Deutsch

2 McKibbin, R. 'Mass-observation in the Mall', *London Review of Books*, 2 October 1997

3 Bogdanov, K. (2013) 'The queue as narrative: A Soviet case study', in Baiburin, A. et al. (eds) *Soviet Cultural Anthropology after the collapse of Communism*, London: Routledge

4 Gandhi, A. (2013) 'Standing still and cutting in line: The culture of the queue in India, *South Asia Multidisciplinary Academic Journal*, https://doi.org/10.4000/samaj.3519

5 https://www.nytimes.com/2011/07/20/world/americas/20venezuela.html

6 Mann, L. (1969) 'Queue culture: The waiting line as a social system', *American Journal of Sociology*

7 Wexler, M. (2015) 'Re-thinking queue culture: The commodification of thick time', *International Journal of Sociology and Social Policy*, 35, 3/4, pp. 165–181

8 Bailey, A. R., Alexander, A. & Shaw, G. (2019) 'Queuing as a changing shopper experience: The case of grocery shopping in Britain, 1945–1975', *Enterprise and Society*, 2, 3, pp. 652–683

9 Cooley, C. H. (1922) *Human Nature and the Social Order*, revised edition, New York: Charles Scribner

10 Milgram, S. (1963) 'Behavioral study of obedience', *Journal of Abnormal and Social Psychology*, 67, pp. 371–378

11 Milgram, S., Liberty, H. J., Toledo, R. & Wackenhut, J. (1986) 'Response to intrusion into waiting lines', *Journal of Personality and Social Psychology*, 51(4), pp. 683–689

12 Goffman, E. (1983) 'The interaction order', *American Sociological Review*, 48, 1, pp. 1–17

13 Larson, R. C. (1987) 'OR Forum—Perspectives on queues: Social justice and the psychology of queueing', *Operations Research*, 35, 6, pp. 895–905

14 Candappa, R. (2018) *Rules Britannia*, London: Ebury Press

15 https://www.debretts.com/everyday-etiquette/how-to-queue/

16 'Please queue', *The Times*, 1 January 1939

17 Hennessy, P. (2006) *Never Again*, Penguin, p. 50

18 Quoted in Kynaston, D. (2008) *Austerity Britain*, Bloomsbury, at p. 71

19 Hennessy (2006)

20 Bailey et al. (2019)

21 Zweiniger-Bargielowska, I. (1994) 'Rationing, austerity and the Conservative Party recovery after 1945', *The Historical Journal*, 37, 1, pp. 173–197

22 Zweiniger-Bargielowska (1994)

23 Moran, J. (2005) 'Queuing up in post-war Britain', *Twentieth Century British History*, 16, 3, pp. 283–305

24 Quoted in Garfield, S. (2005) *Our Hidden Lives: The Remarkable Diaries of Postwar Britain*, Ebury Press, at p. 138

25 'Queues', *The Times*, 20 November 1922

26 'Please queue', *The Times*, 31 December 1938

27 Moran, 'Queuing up in post-war Britain', p. 288

28 'Have you a reservation?', *The Times*, 28 November 1957

29 Liffen, J. (1999) 'The development of cash handling systems for shops and department stores', *Transactions of the Newcomen Society*, 71:1, pp. 79–101

30 Shaw, G. & Alexander, A. (2008) 'British co-operative societies as retail innovators: Interpreting the early stages of the self-service revolution', *Business History*, 50:1, pp. 62–78

31 Alexander, A., Phillips, S. & Shaw, G. (2008) 'Retail innovation and shopping practices: Consumers' reactions to self-service retailing', *Environment and Planning*, 40, 9, pp. 2204–2221

32 'Piggly Wiggly' Stores, in which shoppers 'wiggled' round short, narrow aisles, selecting pre-packaged goods all of which had already been advertised and 'pre-sold'. The first such store was opened in Memphis in 1916 and by 1923 there were over 2,500

33 Liffen (1999)

34 Shaw, G., Curth, L. & Alexander, A. (2004) 'Selling self-service and the supermarket: The Americanisation of food retailing in Britain, 1945–60', *Business History*, 46:4, pp. 568–582

35 Bowlby, R. (2000) *Carried Away: The Invention of Modern Shopping*, London: Faber and Faber

36 Bailey et al. (2019)

37 du Gay, P. (2004) 'Self-service: Retail, shopping and personhood', *Consumption Markets & Culture*, 7:2, pp. 149–163

38 Powell, *Counter Revolution: The Tesco Story*, quoted in Bowlby

39 Bailey et al. (2019)

40 Mass-Observation Archive: TC 78/3/B. Entry recorded as female, aged thirty-nine, working class

41 Bowlby (2000)

42 Bailey et al. (2019)

43 'Waits at Supermarkets', *The Times*, 27 May 1964

44 'Speeding the process', *The Times*, 5 February 1968

45 'Technique for a quick exit', *The Times*, 25 April 1969

46 Sheard, S. (2018) 'Space, place and (waiting) time: Reflections on health policy and politics', *Health Economics, Policy and Law*, 13, pp. 226–250

47 Sheard (2018)

48 http://news.bbc.co.uk/1/hi/uk_politics/770994.stm

49 *The Times*, 7 August 1946

50 *The Times*, 30 September 1968

51 *The Times*, 5 December 1975

52 *The Times*, 10 December 1975

53 *The Times*, 10 May 1984

54 Monopolies and Mergers Commission (1988) *Post Office Counters Services*, London: HMSO, CM 398

55 *The Times*, 4 April 1987

56 Piaget, J. (1979) Relations between psychology and other sciences, *Annual Review of Psychology*, 30, pp. 1–8

57 Sharr, A. (2014) 'The cultural politics of queuing tape', *Cultural Politics*, 10, 3, pp. 389–403

58 *The Times*, 23 August 1991

59 Woolgar, S. & Neyland, D. (2013) *Mundane Governance: Ontology and Accountability*, Oxford: OUP, p. 190

60 Sandel, M. J. (2012) *What Money Can't Buy: The Moral Limits of Markets*, London: Penguin

61 Alexander, M. et al. (2012) 'Priority queues: where social justice and equity collide', *Tourism Management*, 33

Toilets

1 Jackson, L. (2014) *Dirty Old London: The Victorian Fight Against Filth*, New Haven, CT: Yale University Press

2 Wright, L. (1960) *Clean and Decent: The Fascinating History of the Bathroom and the Water Closet*, London: Routledge and Kegan Paul

3 Bryson, B. (2010) *At Home: A Short History of Private Life*, London: Black Swan

4 Horan, J. L. (1996) *The Porcelain God: A Social History of Toilets*, London: Robson Books, p. 78

5 Young, R. (2013) *Annie's Loo: The Govan Origins of Scotland's Community Based Housing Associations*, Argyle Publishing

6 Accessed through the UK Data Service

7 https://www.bmj.com/content/suppl/2007/11/16/334.suppl_1.DC4

8 Jackson (2014)

9 Jackson (2014)

10 Jackson (2014), p. 165

11 Wright (1960)

12 Quoted in Flanagan, M. (2014) 'Private needs, public space: Public toilets provision in the Anglo-Atlantic patriarchal city: London, Dublin, Toronto and Chicago', *Urban History*, 41, 2, pp. 265–290, at p. 271

13 Walkowitz, J. (1992) *City of Dreadful Delight: Narratives of Sexual Danger in Late-Victorian London*, Chicago: University of Chicago Press

14 Greed, C. (2010) 'Creating a non-sexist restroom', in Molotch and Noren (eds) *Toilet*, New York: NYU Press

15 'Stores lack toilet facilities', *The Times*, 1 December 1965

16 Criado Perez, C. (2019) *Invisible Women: Exposing Data Bias in a World Designed for Men*, London: Chatto & Windus

17 Hansard, House of Commons, 28 July 1961, vol. 645, col. 794

18 'M.P. says turnstiles are torture', *The Times*, 20 June 1963

19 Greed, C. (1995) 'Public toilet provision for women in Britain: An investigation of discrimination against urination', *Women's Studies International Forum*, 18, pp. 573–584

20 Criado Perez (2019)

21 Greed (2010)

22 'Barbican to review its gender-neutral toilets after furious row breaks out', *Evening Standard*, 6 April 2017

23 House of Commons Standard Note, SN/SC/976 Public conveniences

24 Llewelyn, C. (1996) *Toilet Issues: A Survey of the Provision and Adequacy of Public Toilets in 18 Towns and Cities*, Welsh Consumer Council

25 Hollis, M. E., Felson, M. & Welsh, B. C. (2013) 'The capable guardian in routine activities theory: A theoretical and conceptual appraisal', *Crime Prevention and Community Safety*, 15, pp. 65–79

26 Walmsley, R, (1978) 'Indecency between Males and the Sexual Offences Act', *Criminal Law Review*, July, pp. 400–407

27 Quoted in Smith, C. (2014) 'The evolution of the gay male public sphere in England and Wales, 1967–1983', Unpublished PhD thesis, Loughborough University

28 'Pees and queues of driving NE buses: Drivers hit by toilet closures', *Aberdeen Evening Express*, 1 May 2000

29 'Police in bid to clean up park toilets: Notice warns gays to beware', *Aberdeen Evening Express*, 24 June 2002

30 https://www.richmond.gov.uk/services/roads_and_transport/public_conveniences/community_toilet_scheme

31 This is mainly drawn from Greed, C. (2004) 'Public toilets: The need for compulsory provision', *Proceedings of the ICE – Municipal Engineer*, 157, 2, pp. 77–85

32 https://www.theguardian.com/world/2017/mar/20/face-scanners-public-toilet-tackle-loo-roll-theft-china-beijing

33 The ex-prisoner quote is taken from: Honeywell, D. (2016) 'Returning to HMP Durham prison 30 Years on', *Prison Service Journal*, 224 at p. 16; The Human Rights Watch quote is taken from: https://www.hrw.org/sites/

default/files/reports/UK926.PDF; the Ministry of Justice response to the FOI request is at: https://www.whatdotheyknow.com/request/363599/response/1003511/attach/3/108001%20Mick%20Geen.pdf. The IMB report is at: http://www.justice.gov.uk/downloads/prison-probation-inspection-monitoring/In-Cell_Sanitation_Report_V2_Aug_10.pdf Thanks are due to the British Society of Criminology; Dr Kate Herrity and Professor David Wilson for guidance on this subject

34 Shove, E. (2003) *Comfort, Cleanliness and Convenience: The Social Organization of Normality*, London: Berg

35 Douglas, M. (2002) [1966] *Purity and Danger*, London: Routledge, p. 5

36 Forty, A. (1986) *Objects of Desire: Design and Society Since 1750*, London: Thames & Hudson, quoted in Shove (2003)

37 Freud, S. (1985) *Civilization and its Discontents*, in *Civilization, Society and Religion*, London: Penguin Freud Library, 12, pp. 288–289

38 Barcan, R. (2010) 'Dirty spaces: separation, concealment and shame in the public toilet', in Molotch and Noren (eds) *Toilet*, New York: NYU Press

39 For example: Classen, C., Howes, D. & Synnott, A. (1994) *Aroma: The Cultural History of Smell*, London: Routledge

40 https://www.businesswire.com/news/home/20180910005394/en/Global-Male-Grooming-Products-Market-2018-2023--

41 The ad can currently be seen at: https://www.youtube.com/watch?v=Tj3dh9i4zLs

42 Rayburn, W. (1969) *Flushed with Pride: The Story of Thomas Crapper*, London: Macdonald and Co.

43 Smyth, R. (2012) *Bum Fodder: An Absorbing History of Toilet Paper*, London: Souvenir Press

44 Greed, C. (2019) 'Join the queue: Including women's toilet needs in public space', *Sociological Review*, 67, 4, pp. 908–926

Parking

1 Dennis, K. & Urry, J. (2009) *After the Car*, Cambridge: Polity Press

2 Garfield, S. (2005) *Our Hidden Lives: The Everyday Diaries of a Forgotten Britain 1945–48*, London: Ebury Press

3 https://www.gov.uk/government/news/public-health-england-publishes-air-pollution-evidence-review

4 Bates, J. & Liebling, J. (2012) *Spaced Out: Perspectives on parking policy*, RAC Foundation

5 Marsden, G. (2014) 'Parking policy', in Ison, C. & Mulley, S. (eds) *Parking: Issues and Policies,* Bingley: Emerald

6 Chen, F.-C. (2013) *Cab Cultures in Victorian London,* PhD thesis, University of York

7 Spurling, N. (2019) 'Making space for the car at home: planning, priorities and practices', in Shove, E. & Trentmann, F. (eds) *Infrastructures in Practice: The Dynamics of Demand in Networked Societies,* London: Routledge

8 https://assets.publishing.service.gov.uk/government/uploads/system/uploads/attachment_data/file/800502/vehicle-licensing-statistics-2018.pdf

9 Gunn, S. (2013) 'People and the car: The expansion of automobility in urban Britain, 1955–70', *Social History,* 38, 2, pp. 220–237

10 Transport Statistics Great Britain, 2020, Office for National Statistics

11 Moran, J. (2006) 'Crossing the road in Britain, 1931–1976', *The Historical Journal,* 49, 2

12 Moran (2006)

13 Department for Transport (2019) *Reported Road Casualties in Great Britain: 2018 Annual Report,* Department for Transport

14 'Black day for inventor of yellow line', *Independent,* 24 April 1997

15 Quoted in Merriman, P. (2019) 'Relational governance, distributed agency and the unfolding of movements, habits and environments: Parking practices and regulations in England', *Environment and Planning C: Politics and Space,* 37, 8

16 Young, M. & Willmott, P. (1962) *Family and Kinship in East London,* Harmondsworth: Pelican, at p. 159

17 Spurling (2019)

18 Gunn (2013)

19 Balcombe, R .J. & York, I. O. (1993) *The Future of Residential Parking,* TRL Project Report 22, Transport Research Laboratory, Crowthorne: Berkshire

20 *The Times,* 18 November 1954

21 *The Times,* 30 January 1958

22 *The Times,* 25 October 1958

23 *The Times,* 27 November 1959

24 'Unlovely Rita', *The Economist,* 15 January 2004

25 Gunn (2013)

26 Royal Commission on the Police (1962) *Final Report,* Cmnd. 1728

27 'Mr Marples plea on parking', *The Times,* 27 September 1960

28 Quoted in Merriman (2019)

29 Richman, J. (1973) 'Police auxiliaries – Traffic wardens: Some socio-logical aspects', *The Police Journal: Theory, Practice and Principles*, pp. 46–60

30 May, A. D. & Turvey, I. G. (1984) 'The effects of wheel clamps in central London: Comparison of before and after studies', *Working Paper. Institute of Transport Studies*, University of Leeds

31 Cullinane, K. & Polak, J. (1992) 'Illegal parking and the enforcement of parking regulations: Causes, effects and interactions', *Transport Reviews*, 12:1, pp. 49–75

32 Jones, P. M. (1991) 'UK public attitudes to urban traffic problems and possible countermeasures: A poll of polls', *Environment and Planning*, 9, pp. 245–256

33 Elliott, J. & Wright, C. (1982) 'The collapse of parking enforcement in large towns: Some causes and solutions', *Traffic Engineering and Control*, 23; Cullinane & Polak, op. cit.

34 https://trid.trb.org/view/210753

35 *Hansard* HL Deb 14 November 1989, vol. 512, col. 1218

36 Smith, J. (1994) 'Controlling parking: Experience in the United Kingdom', *Crime Prevention Studies*

37 https://www.mirror.co.uk/news/uk-news/cowboy-clampers-who-bullied-drivers-98449

38 Rye, T. & Coglin, T. (2014) 'Parking management', in Ison, C. & Mulley, S. (eds) *Parking: Issues and Policies*, Bingley: Emerald

39 RAC Foundation figures

40 'In Praise of Aberystwyth', *Guardian*, 4 June 2012

41 https://www.rbkc.gov.uk/PDF/Blue%20Badge20booklet%20April11-16664.pdf

42 Jacobs, J. (1961) *The Death and Life of Great American Cities*, New York: Vintage

43 Merriman, P. (2019) 'Relational governance, distributed agency and the unfolding of movements, habits and environments: Parking practices and regulations in England', *Environment and Planning C: Politics and Space*, 37, 8

44 Source: https://publications.parliament.uk/pa/cm201314/cmselect/cmtran/118/118.pdf

Order, order . . .

1 Janowitz, M. (1975) 'Sociological theory and social control', *American Journal of Sociology*, 81, 1, pp. 82–108

2 Famously, Stanley Cohen in *Visions of Social Control* (Cambridge: Polity Press, 1985: 3) described the term 'social control' as having 'become something of a Mickey Mouse concept'.

3 Pearson, C. (2021) *Dogopolis: How Dogs and Humans Made Modern New York, London, and Paris*, Chicago: University of Chicago Press

4 Trotter, S. (2019) 'Birds behaving badly: The regulation of seagulls and the construction of public space', *Journal of Law and Society*, 46, 1, pp. 1–28

5 Hermer, J. & Hunt, A. (1996) 'Official graffiti of the everyday', *Law and Society Review*, 30, 3, at p. 47

6 Marenin, O. (1982) 'Parking tickets and class repression', *Contemporary Crises*, 6, pp. 241–266

7 Hume, D. (2007) *An Enquiry Concerning Human Understanding*, Oxford: Oxford University Press

8 Bauman, Z. (2000) *Liquid Modernity*, Cambridge: Polity, pp. 7–8

9 https://www.ofcom.org.uk/tv-radio-and-on-demand/advice-for-consumers/television/what-is-the-watershed#:~:text=There%20are%20strict%20rules%20about,TV%20before%20the%209pm%20watershed.&text=The%20watershed%20means%20the%20time,for%20children%20can%20be%20broadcast.

10 https://www.channel4.com/producers-handbook/ofcom-broadcasting-code/protecting-under-18s-and-harm-and-offence/offensive-language

Postscript: the pandemic and orderliness

1 https://www.the-tls.co.uk/articles/everyday-life-in-lockdown-essay-joe-moran/

2 A range of sources have been used here, the most important of which were: the *Guardian* and *Independent* newspapers, the Health Foundation, the BBC, and the government's COVID-19 website

3 https://www.gov.uk/government/speeches/pm-statement-in-the-house-of-commons-11-may-2020

4 https://www.gov.uk/government/news/prime-minister-announces-new-local-covid-alert-levels

5 https://www.ucl.ac.uk/news/2020/oct/significant-rise-no-confidence-governments-handling-covid-19

6 Harari, D. & Keep, M. (2021) *Coronavirus: Economic Impact*, House of Commons Library Briefing Paper, no. 8866, April

7 Nice, A. (2020) 'Extraordinary coronavirus restrictions on personal freedom require proper parliamentary scrutiny', https://www.institute-forgovernment.org.uk/blog/coronavirus-restrictions-parliamentary-scrutiny

8 Taylor, S. (2021) Understanding and managing pandemic-related panic buying, *Journal of Anxiety Disorders*, 78

9 https://www.businessinsider.com/coronavirus-panic-buying-toilet-paper-stockpiling-photos-2020-3?r=US&IR=T#panic-buying-could-also-be-seen-in-the-uk-where-the-owner-of-an-amusement-arcade-swapped-the-toys-in-his-grabber-machine-for-toilet-paper-and-hand-sanitizer-instead-11

10 https://www.times-series.co.uk/news/18306569.supermarkets-release-feed-nation-statement-tackle-coronavirus-panic-buying/

11 https://www.kantarworldpanel.com/global/News/Record-grocery-sales-as-shoppers-prepare-for-lockdown

12 https://www.theguardian.com/news/2020/apr/03/off-our-trolleys-what-stockpiling-in-the-coronavirus-crisis-reveals-about-us

13 https://www.ons.gov.uk/peoplepopulationandcommunity/healthandsocialcare/healthandwellbeing/bulletins/coronavirusandthesocialimpactsongreatbritain/29may2020#concerns-about-the-coronavirus

14 Bentall R. P., Lloyd, A., Bennett, K., McKay, R., Mason, L., Murphy, J., et al. (2021) 'Pandemic buying: Testing a psychological model of overpurchasing and panic buying using data from the United Kingdom and the Republic of Ireland during the early phase of the COVID-19 pandemic', *PLoS ONE*, 16(1)

15 Brown, J., Barber, S. & Ferguson, D. (2021) *Coronavirus: Lockdown Laws*, House of Commons Library, Briefing Paper 8875, 9 April

16 https://www.bbc.co.uk/news/uk-england-derbyshire-52095857

17 https://www.bbc.co.uk/news/uk-england-derbyshire-52055201

18 https://www.derbyshiretimes.co.uk/health/coronavirus/police-dye-water-buxton-blue-lagoon-deter-swimmers-during-coronavirus-lockdown-2521350

19 https://www.derbytelegraph.co.uk/news/local-news/derbyshire-police-criticism-george-osborne-4002920

20 https://www.bbc.co.uk/news/uk-52245937

21 https://www.crestadvisory.com/post/policing-the-covid-19-lockdown-what-the-public-thinks

22 https://metro.co.uk/2020/04/08/police-launch-online-form-snitch-people-flouting-lockdown-12528765/?ico=pushly-notifcation-small&utm_source=pushly?ito=cbshare

23 HMICFRS (2021) *Policing in the Pandemic: The Police Response to the Coronavirus Pandemic During 2020*, London: HMICFRS

24 NPCC (2021) 'Fixed penalty notices issued under COVID-19 emergency health regulations by police forces in England and Wales', 25 February

25 https://www.theguardian.com/law/2020/jul/08/one-in-10-of-londons-young-black-males-stopped-by-police-in-may

26 Quoted in, Harris, S., Joseph-Salisbury, R., Williams, P. and White, L. (2021) *A Threat to Public Safety: Policing, racism and the Covid-19 pandemic*, London: Institute of Race Relations

27 HMICFRS (2021) *The Sarah Everard Vigil – An Inspection of the Metropolitan Police Service's Policing of a Vigil Held in Commemoration of Sarah Everard on Clapham Common on Saturday 13 March 2021*, HMICFRS, 18 May

28 Shaw, D. (2021) 'Policing at Clapham and policing the pandemic: the public are supportive, but clear warning signs too', Crest Advisory https://www.crestadvisory.com/post/policing-at-clapham-and-policing-the-pandemic

29 https://blogs.lse.ac.uk/politicsandpolicy/lockdown-social-norms/#Author

30 https://www.bbc.co.uk/news/uk-52228169

31 Jackson, J., Bradford, B., Yesberg, J., Hobson, Z., Kyprianides, A., Posch, K. & Solymosi, R. (2020) 'Public compliance and COVID-19: Did Cummings damage the fight against the virus, or become a useful anti-role model?' *British Politics and Policy Blog*, London School of Economics, 15 June

32 https://blogs.lse.ac.uk/politicsandpolicy/public-compliance-covid19-june/

33 https://www.bbc.co.uk/news/uk-52228169

34 https://www.bbc.co.uk/news/magazine-19834975

35 https://www.imperial.ac.uk/media/imperial-college/medicine/sph/ide/gida-fellowships/Imperial-College-COVID19-Population-Survey-20-03-2020.pdf

36 Anderson, C. & Hobolt, S. (2020) 'No partisan divide in willingness to wear masks in the UK', https://blogs.lse.ac.uk/covid19/2020/11/18/no-partisan-divide-in-willingness-to-wear-masks-in-the-uk/

37 Wright, L., Steptoe, A. & Fancourt, D. (2021) 'Trajectories of compliance with COVID-19 related guidelines: Longitudinal analyses of 50,000 UK adults', unpublished paper, University College London

38 Jackson, J., Posch, K., Bradford, B., Hobson, Z., Kyprianides, A., & Yesberg, J. (2020) 'The lockdown and social norms: Why the UK is complying by consent rather than compulsion', *British Politics and Policy*, London School of Economics, 27 April

39 Sturgis, P., Jackson, J. & Kuha, J. (2020) 'Lockdown scepticism is part of the Brexit divide', LSE Policy and Politics, 8th June: https://blogs.lse.ac.uk/brexit/2020/06/08/20111/

Acknowledgements

My academic career has been punctuated by research on matters like riots and crowd disorder, and yet I have long harboured a desire to write about public *orderliness*, and to do so without most of the baggage that goes along with scholarly publishing. Early ideas for this book were primarily focused on my fascination with signage – that proliferating jumble of instructions found on walls, lampposts, fences, doors and, indeed, seemingly every nook and cranny of the modern world. The burgeoning of such signage, with its commandments instructing us what to do and not to do, felt like a significant indicator of the changing nature of modern society. Perhaps this was a jumping off point for a study of British social order? Although, in the end, they didn't make it into this book, I give my thanks to everyone who spotted weird and wonderful signage and who took the trouble to photograph it and send it to me. Please don't stop! Intriguing though signs were, it was really dog shit – or, more accurately, the lack of it – that started me going. Just how did we become a nation of bag-wielding poop scoopers? And what did this transformation of our streets and our behaviour say about our daily lives and the nature of modern Britain? From these small deposits the larger project grew. It was then simply a question of finding other, similar questions one could ask that would illuminate some of the ways in which the everyday has changed in the past half-century or so.

This book has had a long and complex history. For a significant period of time I worked on it with my friend Andy Ward. We had first worked together in the mid-nineties on a book with Rogan Taylor on the Hillsborough tragedy (*The Day of the Hillsborough Disaster: A narrative account*, Liverpool University Press, 1995) and I was delighted when he came to collaborate with me on *Orderly*, as we came to refer to it. An author of decades standing, with dozens of books behind him and a keen eye for unusual and humorous stories, Andy contributed in numerous ways to the development of this book. In the last few years, however, his involvement became increasingly limited, as his health declined. The final version reflects considerably less of his vision than might otherwise have been the case. Publication is a bittersweet moment as Andy is not able to share in the achievement. I offer my sincere thanks to Andy for all he contributed, and to Margaret Lear for all that she has done in very sad circumstances.

There are many others to whom a debt is owed. A great number of people have had to listen to me bang on about the 'dog-shit book': my family first and foremost, of course. My gratitude to them all for their love, kindness and patience. I hope they'll find something in it they enjoy. In addition to typically generous support, my wife, Mary, also took time to read, comment and offer helpful counsel on the first chapter (and the acknowledgements, it should be noted!). Friends have not been spared either. My thanks to all, and in particular to Andrew Dillon, Alison Goodbrand, and Chris and Liz Kenn for their forbearance while the spectacular beauty of walks in various of parts of England, most usually the Lake District, was sullied by talk of . . . well, I'll not mention it again. Jill Peay was a source of kindness, solicitude and advice to both Andy and me over many an afternoon cuppa, sometimes with cake, as the book idea developed. Paul Rock, in typically speedy and insightful form, was kind enough to read an initial rough draft of the whole book, offered some sage advice, and released me from at least an element of worry that it had absolutely nothing of interest to say. I'm also hugely grateful to Lucy Bryant who provided very helpful research assistance in the final stages of several of the chapters. Along the way, Joe Moran's work on a number of subjects in this book, and much besides, has been a source of enlightenment and inspiration. Thanks are due to him also for permission to quote from his work, as it is also to Louis Barfe, Steve Woolgar, Daniel Neyland and *The Economist*. For other advice and guidance, my thanks go to Sarah Trotter, the British Society of Criminology, Kate Herrity and David Wilson.

On the publishing front, a debt is due to both Daniel Crewe and to Duncan Proudfoot. Daniel was one of the earliest in the publishing world to show interest in the book. Although, in the event, he changed jobs and the book didn't travel with him, we were hugely grateful for his interest and support, and for his early thoughts on what we were doing. Duncan was our initial editor at Robinson and, again, although he moved on before the book came to fruition, we were enormously grateful for his support and ongoing encouragement. For helping see the book through to its final form, I would like to extend grateful thanks to all at Robinson who have been involved, including Ben McConnell, Rebecca Sheppard, Zoe Bohm, Zoe Carroll, Una McGovern, Aimee Kitson, Henry Lord and Nico Taylor.

Tim Newburn, April 2022

Index

Note: page numbers in **bold** refer to illustrations.

on-trade sales 104
'safe' 119–21, 146
sensible 118–21
and smoking 99–100, 106
social attitudes towards 100, 129
and Sunday closing 116
taxation 110–12, 119, 120
teetotallers 104, 146, 148
and the workplace 101–2, 136–44, 147, 276
drones 308–9, 311
drug-taking 211
drugs testing 143
du Gay, Paul 171–3
Durham prison 224
Durkheim, Émile 318

Eastbourne 18
Edinburgh 38
Edward VII 166
elderly
    and COVID-19 294, 319
    and smoking 54
electronic call forward (ECF) systems 183, 185
electronic cigarettes 89–90, 93, 94
Elias, Norbert 46–7, 197, 226–7, 281–2
Elizabeth II 296
Elliott, Denholm 139
Elliott, Rosemary 55
ENCAMS (Keep Britain Tidy) 34
England, Colin 20
Ennis, Mrs Sarah 21
Entwistle, John 19
Environmental Protection Act (EPA) 1990, Section 87 33
Eperon, Ian 40
Equalities Act 2010 214
Europe, and drinking 128, 146–7
Evans, Keith 263
Everard, Sarah 313
Exposition Universelle, Paris 1899 230
Exxon Valdez disaster 141

Fabians 112
facial recognition technology 223
Falkirk 37
Federation of Tour Operators 79–80
fines 283, 310
First World War 103, 111–13, 116, 291
fixed penalty notices (FPNs) 34, 258, 282–3, 312

flight 78–80
Floyd, George 313
folk devils 131
folkways 6
football 139–40
Foreign Office 140
Forty, Adrian 227
Foster, Arlene 300
Foucault, Michel 281–2
Fox, Kate 149, 151–2, 154
France 320
Freeth, Stephanie 86
Freud, Sigmund 227
Friends of the Earth 257
Froggatt, Sir Peter 70–1

Gallagher, Mo 211
Gascoigne, Paul 139–40
gastropubs 108
Gauke, David 309
gay marriage 2
Gayetty, Joseph 230
Geertz, Clifford 7
George V 50–1, 167
George VI 167
GetMeIn 191
Gilbert-Scott, George 199
Gin Act 110–11
gin craze 102
Glade 228–9
Godber, George 61
Goffman, Erving 158, 321
Gorringe, Chris 186–7
governance, failure of 292
Great Depression 103
Great Exhibition 1851 202–3
Greaves, Jimmy 139–40
greed 4
Greed, Clara 204, 206–7, 213
greetings, non-contact 321–2
Grocer, The (trade magazine) 170, 174
Guardian (newspaper) 62, 262–3, 315
gulls 277
Gunn, Simon 247
Gusfield, Joseph 8

Hamilton, Alan 210
Hancock, Matt 296, 304
handwashing 323
Hart, Carol 38
Hartley, Chief Superintendent 213
Harvester 108